AN ILLUSTRATED ENCYCLOPEDIA OF
MILITARY UNIFORMS
OF THE 19TH CENTURY

AN ILLUSTRATED ENCYCLOPEDIA OF
MILITARY UNIFORMS OF THE 19TH CENTURY

An expert guide to the Crimean War, American Civil War, Boer War,
wars of German and Italian unification and colonial wars

KEVIN F. KILEY • DIGBY SMITH • CONSULTANT: JEREMY BLACK MBE

LORENZ BOOKS

This edition is published by Lorenz Books, an imprint of
Anness Publishing Ltd, Hermes House, 88–89 Blackfriars Road,
London SE1 8HA; tel. 020 7401 2077; fax 020 7633 9499
www.lorenzbooks.com; www.annesspublishing.com

If you like the images in this book and would like to investigate using
them for publishing, promotions or advertising, please visit our website
www.practicalpictures.com for more information.

UK agent: The Manning Partnership Ltd; tel. 01225 478444;
fax 01225 478440; sales@manning-partnership.co.uk
UK distributor: Book Trade Services; tel. 0116 2759086; fax 0116 2759090;
uksales@booktradeservices.com; exportsales@booktradeservices.com
North American agent/distributor: National Book Network;
tel. 301 459 3366; fax 301 429 5746; www.nbnbooks.com
Australian agent/distributor: Pan Macmillan Australia; tel.1300 135 113;
fax 1300 135 103; customer.service@macmillan.com.au
New Zealand agent/distributor: David Bateman Ltd;
tel. (09) 415 7664; fax (09) 415 8892

Publisher: Joanna Lorenz, Editorial Director: Helen Sudell
Executive Editor: Joanne Rippin, Copy Editor: Jonathan North
Designer: Nigel Partridge, Artists: Simon Smith, Carlo Molinari, Matthew
Vince, Jim Mitchell, Tom Croft, Sailesh Thakrar, Nick Spender, Rob Craig
Proofreading Manager: Lindsay Zamponi, Editorial Reader: Jay
Thundercliffe, Production Controller: Mai Ling Collyer

ETHICAL TRADING POLICY
Because of our ongoing ecological investment programme, you, as our
customer, can have the pleasure and reassurance of knowing that a tree is
being cultivated on your behalf to naturally replace the materials used to
make the book you are holding. For further information about this
scheme, go to www.annesspublishing.com/trees.

PUBLISHER'S NOTE
Although the advice and information in this book are believed to be
accurate and true at the time of going to press, neither the authors nor the
publisher can accept any legal responsibility or liability for any errors or
omissions that may be made.

CONTENTS

WARFARE IN THE 19TH CENTURY

The 19th century was an age of imperial, revolutionary and civil conflict, culminating in the fall of the old order and the rise of the new. It was also a century of great progress in weapons technology, on land and at sea, with the mass-development of German Mauser rifles, smokeless gunpowder, the Gatling gun, and the shell guns that caused the demise of wooden-walled men-of-war ships. This rapid change in weaponry drastically changed fighting tactics and uniforms. The initial advantage one side had with the introduction of a new weapon was quickly dispelled once the enemy obtained the same, and hand-to-hand fighting gradually gave way to artillery bombardments and entrenchment. Once designed for maximum impact, intimidation and long-range identification, by the end of the century uniforms were being used for camouflage, anonymity and to disguise rank.

▲ *At the close of the century uniforms had been adapted to blend in with the terrain. Here, after the Battle of Tientsin in 1900, the international expedition force is dressed in practical items of uniform in muted colours.*

◄ *The 4th Dragoon Guards muster in London for departure to the Crimea in 1854. Uniforms in the middle of the 19th century were as flamboyant and colourful as they had been in the Napoleonic era, designed for high visibility on smoke-filled battlefields.*

WAR IN THE CRIMEA

From the conclusion of the Napoleonic Wars in 1815 until the beginning of the Crimean War in 1854 there were no major European conflicts to disturb the general peace. That is not to say that there were not enough small conflicts and revolutions to keep the armed forces of Europe's major powers occupied. Indeed, there were two major revolutions in Europe. In 1830 a revolution in France removed the Bourbons for good and made Louis-Philippe king of the French.

The revolutions of 1848 were widespread and much more dangerous for the established order. France and Prussia were shaken, with the monarchy in France again being overthrown and a republic replacing it. There was also unrest in the Austro-Hungarian empire. Italy was rocked by revolt in the south against the Neapolitan Bourbons and against the Austrians in the north.

▲ *Czar Nicholas I of Russia was a repressive, conservative and totalitarian ruler. On the eve of his death, the Russian empire had reached its historical and geographical zenith.*

▼ *Napoleon III. A nephew of Napoleon I, his reign culminated in a monumental military debacle, which would have had his uncle spinning in his grave like a top.*

▼ *Lieutenant General Sir George Brown and staff, 28 March 1854. The bicorns seem out of place, particularly when seen with the undress caps. General Brown saw action in the Napoleonic Wars, and commanded the Light Division in the Crimea.*

European Power Struggles

Following 1848, the year of revolution, all of Europe's powers sought to reassert their strengths. Russia was continuously interested in expanding her influence and her possessions, and a new spate of international aggressiveness brought her into conflict with her old enemy the Ottoman empire once again. However, the main cause of the Crimean War was a continuing dispute between France and Russia which was mainly a matter of national prestige. France was now ruled by Napoleon III (the nephew of Napoleon I, the exiled emperor) a man who now re-established the French empire (and referred to it as the 'Second Empire' in deference to his famous uncle). The leaders of the French and Russian empires, Napoleon III and Nicholas I, were increasingly drawn into belligerent rhetoric.

Nicholas hoped to gain territory at the expense of the Ottomans, and both France and Great Britain came to the aid of the ailing Ottoman empire in an attempt to keep the balance of power and to curtail Russian ambitions in the

Balkans. There were diplomatic efforts to forestall armed conflict, including a conference called by the Austrians in Vienna, but when Russia moved troops into the principalities of Moldavia and Wallachia and the Ottomans, gauging that they had French and British support, prepared to react. In October 1853 the Ottoman empire declared war on Russia. Both British and French public opinion and national concerns were in sympathy with the Ottomans and in March 1854 France declared war on Russia, followed by Britain shortly thereafter. The allies were later joined by the Kingdom of Sardinia in January 1855.

Administrative and Military Failure

The conflict in the Crimea is particularly noted in military history for the scandalous way in which it was mishandled. Preparations for war were outmoded and inefficient, although the embarkation and transportation of troops, supplies and equipment to the Crimea went reasonably well. The war itself was a series of errors, bad management and general military ineptitude. The best-handled forces of all the belligerents were probably those under French command, but even there some woeful inadequacies were

▲ *The 23rd Royal Welch Fusiliers at the Battle of the Alma 20 September 1854. In this action, Sergeant Luke O'Connor of the regiment won the Victoria Cross for gallantry.*

apparent. The organization of the armies of all the combatants were in need of reform.

The troops lived and fought in miserable conditions, disease was rampant and, since major European campaigns had not been conducted for almost 40 years, the necessary expertise was just not at hand. As it was, the

allies defeated the Russians, presenting the new czar, Alexander II, with a military disaster as a coronation present (Nicholas I had died in March 1855). The best remembered military action of the war was the famously doomed charge of the Light Brigade, as it came to be known, at the Battle of Balaclava; an action that was itself the result of an error in orders from the British commander.

▼ *The return of the survivors of the charge of the Light Brigade, 25 October 1854.*

ITALIAN AND GERMAN UNIFICATION

In the late 18th century both Italy and Germany were divided into fragmented states and kingdoms; in Germany there over 300 separate political kingdoms, principalities, duchies, bishoprics and free cities. Napoleon I did much to rationalize the situation, fusing territories together to create larger states, but this created tensions within Italian and German lands.

Consolidation of German States

Although the people shared a common culture and language, the different political entities did not share common goals and objectives, and through Europe's numerous wars and conflicts, Germans would inevitably end up fighting other Germans. The allied leaders who met at Vienna in 1814–15 to settle the issues of colonies and territorial 'restoration' (in actuality

▼ *Prince Otto von Bismarck, Paris, September 1870. Bismark wanted to shell the city into a speedy surrender, but was overruled.*

to divide the plundered goods taken from Napoleon's empire) attempted, in part, to restore the map of Europe to what it had been in 1789. However, too much had taken place in the intervening decades to accomplish that conservative task.

The myriad small German states had been consolidated, although Prussia took the opportunity to grab as much of western Germany, as well as half of Saxony, at the Congress of Vienna. Prussia and Austria, both of which gained from the defeat of the French, vied, as they had for decades, for control over the German lands. Prussia, it seemed, had gained the most and was now finally gaining the upper hand. A series of wars consolidated Prussian hold over her neighbours and further diminished the influence of rival German states and, inevitably, of Austro-Hungary. This empire had fared so badly in the revolutions of 1848 that Prussia was increasingly free to assert her

▲ *Joachim Murat, King of Naples 1805–15. Murat succeeded Joseph Bonaparte, Napoleon's elder brother, to this throne.*

dominance. The appointment of Otto von Bismarck as Chancellor in 1862 gave Prussia a further advantage. A second war with Denmark (the first had been in 1848) gave Prussia victory, and she went on to humiliate Austro-Hungary and her few allies in 1866 and France in 1870.

German unification was Bismark's aim and he achieved it through war and careful diplomacy. The Chancellor 'engineered' three wars with weaker opponents, Denmark, Austria, and finally France, and was victorious in all. These victories brought Germany under the leadership of Prussia and a German empire was finally established (and in the concluding phase of the Franco-Prussian War the German emperor was declared to be such at

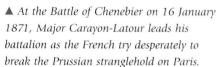
▲ *At the Battle of Chenebier on 16 January 1871, Major Carayon-Latour leads his battalion as the French try desperately to break the Prussian stranglehold on Paris.*

▲ *Giuseppe Mazzini was another Italian patriot, but a democrat, who fought hard to prevent the establishment of a monarchy.*

Versailles, in 1871). All of Germany, save Austria, was brought under Prussian domination and would henceforth be known as the German empire (or the Second Reich).

Italian Unity

Italy had not known unity since the fall of the Roman empire. The states of Renaissance Italy had squabbled among themselves or fallen under foreign hegemony. Napoleon split the peninsula into north (the kingdom of Italy ruled by a viceroy) and south (Naples) but failed to give what many

modern Italians yearned for: a united, independent state. His fall led to the Austro-Hungarians re-exerting their suzerainty in the north in 1814 and only secret societies and plots kept alive any hope of Italian independence. The House of Savoy (ruling the Kingdom of Sardinia), which had been exiled to Sardinia during the Napoleonic Wars, took control over Piedmont and Genoa while the Bourbons returned to Naples. Nevertheless, the aspiration for independence continued and, fuelled by revolutions in 1830 and 1848, the desire to establish an Italian state transformed into a political movement. This was partially hijacked by the House of Savoy (which saw itself as the natural head of a united Italy) which

went to war against Austria in 1859 with French help and acquired various states (Tuscany, Parma and Modena) as a result. Garibaldi was truer to the ideal, and landed 1,000 red-shirted volunteers in Sicily. His men defeated the forces of Naples and, allied with Sardinia, made possible the declaration of a united kingdom of Italy in 1861 (Venice and, controversially, Rome, were added later).

▼ *Austrian forces cross the River Mincio from Lombardy into Piedmont at Sesto Calende in March 1859, an act which allowed France to enter the war in support of Piedmont.*

THE AMERICAN CIVIL WAR

The causes of what became the American Civil War in April 1861 have been variously listed as states' rights, taxation, the economy, slavery and the meaning of the United States Constitution but it does seem that violent disagreement over slavery was the motor behind the conflict.

The expansion of the United States westward created problems of what to do with the Native American population and whether the new states being created from the new territories should be slave states or 'free' states. The Southern slave-holding states saw their 'way of life' threatened because if the new states were admitted to the Union as 'free' states, the free states would hold a majority in Congress and be able to pass laws abolishing slavery, ruining fortunes and the Southern plantation economy. Cotton was 'king' in the South's agrarian economy where 10 per cent of the population owned 90 per cent of the wealth.

Arguments raged in Congress whenever new states were to be admitted to the Union and compromise was only achieved when it was agreed that for every 'free' state admitted to the Union there would be one slave state. Meanwhile an 'abolitionist' movement, intent on abolishing slavery, arose in the North, to further intensify the issue.

▼ *John Brown was an ardent abolitionist whose choice to fight slavery with unauthorized and brutal violence helped create 'Bloody Kansas' in the 1850s.*

▲ *The Battle of Gettysburg, 1863, the largest battle ever waged on the North American continent, was one of the turning points of the war. After this decisive defeat, Robert E. Lee's Army of Northern Virginia was never able to launch a sustained offensive again.*

Abolitionist Uprising

This idea that violence could solve the slavery issue expressed itself in Kansas in the 1850s. Abolitionist John Brown and his followers had planned a slave uprising. They raided Harper's Ferry, where there was a federal arsenal, but were captured by a company of United States Marines, under the command of Colonel Robert E. Lee (accompanied by Lieutenant J.E.B. Stuart). Brown was put on trial for treason, found guilty, and hanged in 1859.

This small, armed rebellion was significant in that it brought the slavery issue to the forefront of politics and polarized the states. The stage was set for secession and now only a catalyst powerful enough to ignite the powder keg of rebellion was needed. The election of Abraham Lincoln in November 1860 provided the spark.

The Union

When the states of the American South (the Confederacy) seceded in early 1861, they did it because Abraham Lincoln was elected president of the United States and they believed (wrongly) that he was going to immediately abolish slavery. However, for all the trouble that slavery had caused in the United States, slavery was not the overwhelming reason why the majority of young men answered the call to arms in 1861.

Northern boys flocked to the colours to fight for 'the old flag' and to preserve the Union. The average Southerner joined the army in order to fight for their rights and to defend their land from invasion and Northern aggression. Some 90 per cent of the Southern white population did not own slaves and while they undoubtedly accepted the idea of slavery, they did not actively participate in it. Slavery as an issue in the war did not come to the fore until the issuance of the Emancipation Proclamation in early 1863, prompted by the defeat of Lee's first invasion of the North at Antietam in September 1862.

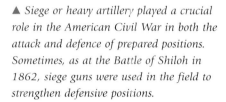

▲ *Siege or heavy artillery played a crucial role in the American Civil War in both the attack and defence of prepared positions. Sometimes, as at the Battle of Shiloh in 1862, siege guns were used in the field to strengthen defensive positions.*

▼ *A Union soldier of the 31st Pennsylvania Regiment, with his entire family and their belongings, in the basic conditions of Camp Slocum, near Washington DC, 1862.*

The Confederacy

The Confederate states faced another political issue in late 1862 and early 1863 with Lincoln's decision to raise regiments of black troops in the Union Army. Those that were raised in liberated (or conquered, depending on your point of view) areas of the South from freed slaves, such as Higginson's 1st South Carolina Volunteer Infantry Regiment, were one thing, but regiments raised on Northern soil from black freedmen were another (such as the regiments raised in Massachusetts where the famous 54th Regiment of Massachusetts Volunteer Infantry under young Colonel Robert Gould Shaw came into being). These regiments were officered by veteran white soldiers who volunteered to take a commission in a black unit. The Confederate Congress passed a law stating that any black man taken under arms would be returned to slavery even if he was a free man and that any white officer would be executed. Incensed, Lincoln responded that if any of his soldiers were executed, a like number of Confederate prisoners of equal rank would be executed in reprisal. The Confederate Congress quickly rescinded its decision.

The long and bitter controversy between the North and the South was finally decided in a long and bloody war, the nation's most costly crucible.

BRITISH WARS IN SOUTH AFRICA

The final transfer of the settlements on the Dutch Cape to British rule in 1814 created resentment in that part of the population which had supported Dutch rule. These Afrikaners (many of them of Dutch ancestry) or Boers found themselves squeezed out and marginalized by British immigration in the years after 1814. Many of the frustrated Boers migrated northward in what was later known as the Great Trek. They crossed the Orange River, met and defeated the dreaded Zulus in 1838 and went into Natal, establishing a Boer Republic.

By 1843, however, the perceived instability of the Boer Republic in Natal prompted the British to annex it and many of the Boer settlers migrated to the Transvaal. From 1845 to 1848 there were periodic hostilities between the British and Boers as the 'march of empire' moved northward into Boer-occupied territory.

▲ *Lieutenants Neville and Coghill of the 24th Foot attempt to save the regimental colours from the Zulus at the Battle of Isandlwana.*

▼ *The Battle of Isandlwana on 22 January 1879 was an overwhelming victory for the Zulu impis. The destruction of the British forces there shocked Victorian Britain.*

Zulu Defeat

In 1852 the British government recognized the independence of the Transvaal, followed two years later by the recognition of the Orange Free State. In 1868, however, Basutoland was annexed as a British Crown Colony and British incursions into Boer territory continued in 1871 with the annexation of Kimberly to Cape Colony and the discovery of diamonds. The next year Cape Colony was granted self-government by the British.

In 1876 the idea of forming a federation of all of the Boer Republics with the British colonies failed and the next year the Transvaal was annexed by the British because the state had become bankrupt and the Zulus were menacing the colony. Two years later the British, with help from the Boers, went to war with the Zulus and won a decisive victory, breaking the nation and taking their king captive.

▲ *Dr Leander Starr Jameson led a raid into the Transvaal in December 1895 to support an uprising that never materialized. This raid was a forerunner to the last Boer War.*

German Involvement

In 1880 war broke out between the British and the Boers over the Transvaal. The result was a limited victory for the Boers in 1881. Paul Kruger became the president of the Transvaal and the Boers were granted self-government. Great Britain, however, still retained responsibility for the foreign affairs of the Boer state. In 1884 the Transvaal was granted greater independence by Great Britain and a new colonial power came upon the scene – Imperial Germany.

German growth and friendship seemed to present the Boers with the support of an ally. In 1884 Germany annexed south-west Africa, and this was a direct threat to British interests in South Africa. The next year (1885) the British annexed Bechuanaland to stop the expansion of the Germans and the Boers, leading to international tensions in southern Africa. This was compounded by the discovery of gold in the Transvaal in 1886, which led the British and others to flock to the area, to the consternation of the Boers.

Further British annexations of Zululand (1887), St. Lucia Bay (1884), Pondoland (1893) and Tongaland (1895), and the linking of Cape Colony to Natal, prevented any future expansion by the Transvaal colonists and stopped their attempts to gain access to the Indian Ocean.

The Last Boer War

The new colony of Rhodesia was established by annexing Matabeleland and Mashonaland, and the probability of hostilities was further heightened by the Jameson raid into the Transvaal by the British in 1896. Although this was defeated by the Boers, tensions remained and in 1897 a military treaty between the Transvaal and the Orange Free State was signed, resulting in the arming of the Transvaal.

Negotiations between the Boers and the British government failed in 1899 and 10,000 imperial troops were sent to South Africa. Both the Transvaal and the Orange Free State mobilized for war and an ultimatum to the British government to cease and desist was issued by President Kruger. It was ignored. For the next three years a bitter conflict waged between Boer and Briton, ending finally in Boer defeat, but with many military embarrassments for the British.

▼ *Lord Roberts was an outstanding general officer of the late Victorian period with many battlefield successes. This stylized painting shows British regulation uniform of the time.*

COLONIAL WARS EAST AND WEST

Most of the European powers possessed colonies before the French Revolution of 1789. The period after the close of the wars that followed that watershed in European history saw the acceleration of the desire by European powers to grab what remained.

Most of Spain's American empire was diminishing, and its comparative decline was exploited, by the United States. The Philippines were to go the same way. Portugal's declining hold over its empire was also looked upon by other European powers (including tiny Belgium which had a colony along the Congo) as an opportunity in the making. In the end, Portugal's African empire did manage to shuffle into the 20th century, preserved, in part, because of Portugal's participation in the Great War.

By 1900 very little remained outside European hegemony. Just about all of Africa was under European rule, much of Asia was heading that way and even China seemed to be fragmenting and falling under the sway of France, Germany and Great Britain.

▲ *A stylized portrait of Lieutenant Frederick Aikman winning the Victoria Cross at the Siege of Lucknow during the Indian Mutiny.*

▼ *Queen Victoria, Queen of the United Kingdom of Great Britain and Ireland, and from May 1876 the first Empress of India.*

Britain
Great Britain was the foremost economic power in the world and her gains in the war against Napoleon were further increased by acquisitions in Africa and Asia. The 19th century saw the great expansion of the British empire, over which 'the sun never set'. It was a period which saw the gradual transfer of India to British rule, and led to friction with an expanding Russia and an Afghanistan and Persia caught between these two great powers. It also saw British rule extend in Africa, sometimes in direct rivalry with European competitors (the infamous scramble for Africa), sometimes over the heads of settlers or natives who might not want to be ruled from London. Britain's wars were fought with redcoats shipped out as and when necessary from the British Isles, by colonists formed into volunteer regiments, from locals drafted into native regiments or by troops from other British dominions (such as the Canadian and Australian volunteers who were to serve against the Boers in South Africa).

France
To compete with the British and forestall competitive nations from gaining more territory, France also looked overseas for new worlds to colonize. The French eventually established themselves in East Asia and Africa. The process began when an expeditionary force was sent against the pirate-infested coast of North Africa in 1830, an event which quickly transformed itself into out-and-out

conquest. The French later expanded in West Africa and Asia as well as gaining control of the islands in the Pacific. They also ventured into Mexico in the 1860s. The French Army gained valuable experience in these colonial wars and they proved a valuable school for French military reformers. French troops had to fight long and hard against the natives of North Africa, and had to adapt to new ways of fighting and harsh conditions. Whether using conscripted troops from metropolitan

▼ *The Spanish–American War gave the United States a small colonial empire in the Caribbean and won status for the country.*

▲ *The French attempt to form a colonial empire in the Western hemisphere led to vicious guerilla warfare in Mexico.*

France, foreign volunteers (the famous Foreign Legion) or local troops raised from natives, France managed to conquer Algeria, Senegal, Vietnam (Indochina) and various Pacific islands as well as furnish expeditions for various colonial enterprises (such as war with China in the 1860s and during the Boxer Rebellion).

▼ *French attempts to colonize Mexico ended in the execution of their imposed emperor, Maximilian, by rebel leader Benito Juárez.*

Germany and Italy
The third major European power to play the colonial game at this time was Germany, who entered the contest late, after becoming an empire in 1871, but quickly sought out a place in the sun in East Africa (which would see interesting campaigns during World War I) and the Pacific. The Germans used some European troops as military police but also raised units of local, native personnel.

Italy, believing that a colonial empire was a prerequisite for international respect, also went into Africa with mixed success in the latter half of the 19th century.

THE CRIMEAN WAR

The Crimean War was at first a military continuation of the historic quarrel between Russia and Turkey, with the ostensible motivation of the protection of Christians under Turkish rule. Britain, however, saw an opportunity to challenge Russia's sea power in the Black Sea and France was quick to join in with her. The Kingdom of Sardinia joined the allies later. Like most wars, the one that evolved in the Crimea was ill thought through and poorly planned, and the British force in particular suffered from hopelessly inadequate command and logistics, resulting in almost the entire force succumbing to injury or disease. The resultant public outcry at this squandering of men's lives resulted in bringing down the British government. It also led to the establishment of Florence Nightingale's nursing principles and a radical improvement in the proper medical care of Britain's forces fighting overseas.

▲ *The civilian dress of Lord Raglan (left) British Commander in the Crimea, is a telling contrast to the formal military appearance of Omar Pasha (centre) and General Pelissier (right). Raglan's command experience was inferior to that of his Turkish and French counterparts.*

◄ *The wounded French general Pierre-François-Joseph Bosquet is evacuated from the captured Russian Malakov redoubt at Sevastopol on 8 September 1855.*

THE THIN RED LINE

It was not until 1877 that the title of 'Crimean' was given to this conflict, so greatly mismanaged by all concerned. It was a war which pitted Russia against an alliance of the Ottomans, Britain, France and, later, Sardinia.

Imperial Rivalry

British politicians had long been obsessed with the fear that Russia's eastward expansion would threaten their Raj in India. This paranoia made them open to any plan to impede such growth. Although eventually known as the Crimean War, fighting actually took place not only in the Crimean peninsula, but also in the Baltic and on the Russian Pacific coast.

Russia butted up against the Ottoman empire in the Caucasus mountains and Persia on the east and on the northern rim of Bosnia, Serbia, Moldavia and Wallachia (modern Romania) to the west. Czar Nicholas I of Russia was keen to gain warm water ports for his fleet, and this would bring him into conflict with the Ottoman empire; but the causes of the war were – in part – of a religious nature. Russia

▼ The city of Sevastopol was repeatedly bombarded and reduced to ruins during its siege, and the destruction of the naval base was completed by the allies after it fell.

accused the Ottomans of oppressing Christians living within the empire. Nicholas demanded the right to act as protector to the 10 million Orthodox Christian subjects within the Ottoman empire; this was rejected by Sultan Abdul Medjid and, in July 1853, Russian troops entered Moldavia and Wallachia. On 5 October of that year, Turkey declared war on Russia and on 4 November, a Turkish army under General Omar Pasha defeated a smaller Russian force under General Prince Mikhail Dmitrievich Gorchakov at Oltenitsa, near Bucharest. To the east, on Turkey's Black Sea coast, a Russian

▲ The Battle of Sinope, 30 November 1853; the crushing victory of a Russian squadron over a weaker Turkish force spelled the end of the age of sail-powered, un-armoured men-of-war. The effects of explosive shells were

naval force attacked the Turkish naval base of Sinope on 30 November 1853, using explosive shells for the first time in naval warfare. Of the seven Turkish frigates, three corvettes and three steamers in Sinope, Russian Admiral Pavel Stepanovich Nakhimov's six ships of the line, two frigates and a brig destroyed or badly damaged all but one steamer, which escaped.

▲ *Extensive photographic records exist of this conflict. This scene of the allied encampment c.1855 is taken in mild weather, but the relaxed dress of the troops is still remarkable.*

Turkish casualties were 2,960 killed against 37 Russian dead. This action sounded the end of the era of the old, wooden-walled ships and the introduction of steam-powered, armour-plated vessels and explosive ammunition for naval artillery.

Britain sensed the emergence of a navy potentially fit to rival her own and resolved to enter the war on the Ottoman side, to neutralize the threat. On 28 March 1854, Britain and France also declared war on Russia. The king of Sardinia (who ruled much of modern-day Italy) joined them in January 1855.

Expeditionary Forces

A British expeditionary force consisting of 27,000 men in a cavalry division, 5 infantry divisions and 60 guns, with staff and 'supporting services', was despatched. To the government's surprise, this effort stripped Britain bare of troops. Command of the expedition was given to Lord Raglan, who until this time had never even commanded a battalion.

The French contingent was commanded by Marshal Armand-Jacques Leroy de Saint Arnaud, until his death on 29 September 1854. At this point Lieutenant General François-Certain Canrobert (known as 'that bastard Canrobert' to his British colleagues) took over. Canrobert had a considerable and distinguished record in colonial warfare in North Africa, as had Saint Arnaud. The initial French expedition was 20,000 infantry, 72 guns, but no cavalry. The Turks

▼ *Officers on the staff of Lieutenant General Sir George Brown, 1854. Staff officers lived in relative comfort and were well supplied – a far cry from the deprivation of the men.*

contributed 7,000 infantry, some guns, but no cavalry. These forces were opposed by 33,000 Russian infantry, 3,400 cavalry and 120 field guns.

The allies first landed at Varna, on the Black Sea coast of modern-day Bulgaria on 31 May 1854, aiming to throw out a Russian force in the area; obligingly, the Russians promptly withdrew. The allies remained around Varna until 5 September, pondering what to do and eating the entire area bare. Eventually, they decided to take the Russian naval base of Sevastopol, on the western side of the Crimea. An unopposed landing was made on 24 September, in Kalamita Bay, 40km (25 miles) north of the target.

In the other theatres of the war, on 26 June 1854, a Franco-British fleet blockaded the Russian base of Kronstadt, near St Petersburg in the Baltic. On 21 August a Royal Navy squadron bombarded the Russian naval base at Kola (now Murmansk) in the White Sea. In late August 1854, another Franco-British flotilla attacked the Russian naval base at Petropavlovsk on the south-eastern side of the Kamchatka peninsula. The operation was an utter fiasco, 209 Allied lives being lost to 115 Russians. This ended the war in the Pacific.

DAILY LIFE IN THE CRIMEA

Conditions of life and service in all the armies of 1854 were extremely harsh when viewed from our modern perspective, but, for the working classes, they were often more attractive than many possibilities available in civilian life and industry.

The British Army

This was the age of spit and polish for British soldiers, with lots of buttons and badges to be polished, boots to be kept mirror-like, belts to be whitened, barrack rooms to be kept spotless on a daily basis, drill and fatigue parades alternating with guard duties and 'pokey drill' (musketry training) to keep the men busy from reveille to lights out, seven days a week.

Life on campaign was full of opportunities for being charged with petty 'offences' by any malicious lance corporal. Company commanders held daily 'courts' to deal with such offences and could award minor punishments, such as confinement to barracks, extra parades or fatigue duty. More serious offences were dealt with by the commanding officer, who could punish more severely if he thought fit. Really serious offences were sent to be

▼ *Men of the 60th Rifles (King's Royal Rifle Corps), c.1830 in barracks.*

▲ *Major General James Bucknall Estcourt with his staff in 1855. Apart from the staff officers in their coats, we see on the left an officer of a flank company, with wings.*

dealt with by a court martial. Punishments meted out at this level might include imprisonment for years in a military jail; in extreme cases, flogging or even the death penalty were applied.

British Conservatism

The revered Duke of Wellington died in 1852; his attitudes and doctrine still held firm sway in the British Army of 1854. The weaponry was no longer exactly the same as at Waterloo in 1815, but the introduction of breech-loading, rifled muskets would not occur until 1867, thus there was no apparent need to change the tactics of infantry and cavalry.

Apart from the old percussion-cap pattern musket, the Brown Bess (1842), two new smoothbore weapons were just coming into service. These were the 1851 model Minié rifle (invented by French Captain Claude-Etienne Minié in 1849) and the 1853 model, 0.577 inch calibre Enfield rifle; like the Brown Bess both were muzzle-loading weapons. A new drill manual

for these weapons was printed in 1854. All three weapons went to the Crimea, complicating the resupply of ammunition. As far as the soldier's personal equipment was concerned, very little had changed since Waterloo. The shako was of a different shape and now had peaks fore and aft, the ammunition pouch and sword and bayonet were still carried on crossed bandoliers and long, dark blue trousers had replaced the white breeches and long gaiters of the English and Lowland Scottish regiments. Each regiment still wore its own unique regimental lace loops to the front of the red jacket. The dress of the cavalry and Highland regiments had scarcely changed at all. But these gaudy uniforms were to be shown to be insufficient for the wear and tear of warfare and the harsh climatic conditions they were worn in.

▲ *General Pierre Bosquet (1810–61) and Captain Dampierre of the French forces, encamped outside Sevastopol.*

▲ *The Battle of Inkermann on 5 November 1854 and the gallant attack of Lieutenant General Sir George Cathcart on Russian lines.*

The totally inadequate supply and logistical system aggravated the misery of the troops. The press had eventually reported the appalling situation of the army to the British public. Everyone in Britain was enraged. An opposition member of Parliament, Henry Drummond, said during a debate on the government's conduct of the war:

'I impute it the gross incompetence of some men that a catastrophe has occurred, without a parallel in history, that an army three times victorious has been left to perish – to be utterly destroyed – by the incompetence of those whose duty it was to have supported it.'

On 23 January 1855, Lord Aberdeen's government fell as a direct result of the scandal.

Allied Troops

France, Britain's main ally in this conflict, had had experience in North Africa since 1815, and benefitted from recent combat experience, in a way that Britain's didn't. France sent Imperial Guards, Line Infantry, and Cavalry regiments to the Crimea; all fought well, especially the African regiments.

The Ottoman army had recently undergone a series of often unpopular reforms, as Sultan Mahmud tried to modernize his army into a more European-style force. By the time of the Crimean War these reforms had been largely accepted and the troops fought effectively and well in the harsh conditions of the Caucusus.

Sardinia entered the conflict at a late stage, and for various political reasons, but supplied a force of 10,000 men to fight with the allies. These troops arrived in January 1855 in time to aid in the siege of Sevastopol.

▼ *The tents and pack mules in the allied camp show that the picture was taken after the terrible winter of 1844, when soldiers starved and froze in mud huts and bivouacs.*

Russian Forces

The Crimean War was a contributing factor in the Russian abolition of serfdom in 1861: Alexander II saw the military defeat of the Russian serf army by free troops from Britain and France as proof of the need for emancipation. The Crimean War also led to reform of its military practices and weaponry. During the Crimean War, however, the Russian army was built on hurridly and poorly trained conscripts, and the tally of lives was extremely high.

BRITISH COMMANDERS AND STAFF

Although the French Army and Navy had a specific and well-defined system of badges of rank for all levels from private to general and field marshal, as early as 1805, the British lagged far behind in these uniform distinctions.

General Officers

Generals and field officers (majors and above) began to wear rank badges from 1810, but individual rank was still often shown only by the superior quality of the embroidery of the uniforms, the waist sashes and the sword-hilt knots.

Generals on parade and in court dress wore bicorns with black cockade, gold brooch, white over red feather plumes and gold cords. They had red coats with dark blue facings, gold buttons and lace and gold, fringed epaulettes. Ranks were initially shown by gold chevrons, point down, on the lower sleeve. A field marshal wore six chevrons, evenly spaced; a general wore four; a lieutenant general had six, but in two groups of three, a major general wore two groups of two, and a brigadier general wore one chevron on the cuff and two others farther up the forearm.

Staff Officers

Aides-de-camp to generals wore the same uniforms as generals, but with a gold aiguillette on the left shoulder instead of the epaulette.

Officers of the general staff wore red coats, dark blue facings and silver buttons, lace and epaulettes. They also had a silver aiguillette on the left shoulder. The badges initially introduced for generals consisted of the crossed sabre and baton, with stars and the crown as appropriate.

Rank Badges

Generals wore their badges of rank on their epaulettes and on the shabraques of their horses, as is shown by the mounted portrait of Prince

George, the Duke of Cambridge, who was promoted to lieutenant general in 1854; he wears the crown, crossed sabre and baton and the star of the Order of the Bath. Apart from the red tunics, all officers could also wear the much cheaper, dark blue, double-breasted undress uniform, with knee-length skirts. This had no facings and no badges of rank. With it was worn the jaunty undress, dark blue cap, with gold embroidered headband, peak and top button. General officers wore a gold and crimson waist sash,

▼ LIEUTENANT GENERAL HRH THE DUKE OF CAMBRIDGE, 1854 *The Duke was an army officer and served as commander-in-chief of the British Army from 1856 to 1895. At the time of the Crimean conflict he was in command of the 1st Division (Guards and Highland brigades) of the British Army in the East. The Duke fought at the Battle of the Alma. He wears full dress uniform and the decorations of a Knight of the Garter, Knight of the Order of the Thistle, Knight of St Patrick, and Knight Grand Cross of the Order of the Bath. His holster covers and shabraque bear his badges of rank.*

sword belt and Mameluke sabre (with gold and crimson cord and knot). For inclement weather, a dark blue boat cloak could be added. This costume was very popular with all officers during the Crimean War. Badges of rank for junior officers were first introduced in 1855 and consisted of silver crowns and stars, worn on the collar. The star chosen for general use was that of the Order of the Bath, but

▼ MAJOR GENERAL SIR R. DACRES, 1854

The general wears the very practical, rather relaxed, dark blue undress uniform, much favoured during this war. The sole indicators of rank were the gold headband of the cap, the telescope, the gold and crimson sash and waist belt, and the scimitar. The rectangular gilt belt plate bears the full royal arms and supporters. Note the cylindrical, brown leather telescope case.

there were exceptions. Officers of the Household troops wore the star of the Order of the Garter (except for the 3rd or Scots Guards, who wore the star of the Order of the Thistle). An ensign wore a star on the collar, a lieutenant had a crown, a captain a crown in front of a star. These officers had a single gold stripe to the top of the cuff and a single gold stripe to top and front of the collar.

Field officers had a double gold stripe to the top of the cuff, gold braid edging to top, back and bottom of the trident-shaped cuff flap and gold braid to top, front and bottom of the collar. The silver rank badges on the collar were repeated (star, crown, crown and star) for major, lieutenant colonel and colonel. The dark blue undress caps of majors and junior officers had no gold embroidery; that of colonels had a gold peak edging.

Changes

In 1856 the Austrian method of indicating officers' ranks around the top of the crown of the shako was introduced. Company officers wore no braid, majors wore one gold band, lieutenant colonels and colonels wore two. Officers' badges of rank were worn on the collar until 1880, when they were moved to the shoulders. From this point until 1902 a captain had two stars, a lieutenant one and the most junior officer had just the epaulette. In the Crimea, officers of the centre companies of infantry regiments wore two fringed gold epaulettes; officers of the grenadier and light companies also wore red shoulder wings, under these epaulettes, laced in gold and decorated with gilt chains. These wings were abandoned later in the war. The main reason for this simplification was that it was found to be very uncomfortable to try to sleep in them.

▲ MAJOR GENERAL JL PENNEFATHER, 1854

The general commanded a brigade in the 2nd Division and took command of that division at the Battle of Inkermann. This figure shows the understated undress uniform. He carries a boat cloak. The hilt of the scimitar was of ivory with gilt fittings, the scabbard was gilt. In full dress, generals were resplendent in cocked hats, white over red drooping feather plumes, scarlet, double-breasted tunics, gold fringed epaulettes, crimson and gold sashes and scimitar knots, and gold embroidered waist belt and slings.

BRITISH INFANTRY

The uniforms of the British Army in 1854 were very much the same as those worn on the field of Waterloo in 1815, and the Crimean winter was to show just how inappropriate they were.

The Redcoats

English and Irish line regiments wore the shako, the Guards wore bearskins and the Scottish regiments the Hummel bonnet. For the Crimean War the Albert shako was in use. This was introduced in 1844 and was of black felt, with two peaks, brass chinstrap rosettes, black leather chinstrap, leather top and bottom bands, crowned brass badge

and company pompon: centre companies white over red, grenadiers white, light company green. Regimental badges distinguished regiments. Flank companies had smaller central regimental badge numerals, with a grenade or hunting horn above it. Cords were not worn. Sergeant majors and officers had brass chinscales. In 1856 the shako was replaced by a smaller one, with no rear peak. A dark blue undress cap, with peak, could be worn. The headband was black for normal regiments, red for royal and diced red and white for Scottish. The regimental badge, or number, was worn on

▲ SERGEANT MAJOR, 33RD FOOT, 1854 *Here rank badges are worn on the forearms; a practice that was very short-lived. He wears an officer-style shako plate and chin chains.*

◄ SERGEANT, 4TH FOOT, 1854 *This sergeant is from the grenadier company, as shown by his white pompon, grenade cap badge and white-edged shoulder wings.*

► PRIVATE 57TH FOOT, 1854 *This man of the Middlesex Regiment is in full service marching order. The wooden water bottle shows regimental and company details.*

the band, surmounted by a grenade or horn for flank companies. For corporals and below, it had no peak.

Regimental Distinctions

Unless otherwise noted, all regiments wore cap badges that consisted of their number and the crowned royal cypher. This was VR (Victoria Regina) from 1837 to 1901. Officers wore the badges shown in the table; other ranks normally had just the number of the regiment. Most (but not all) badges incorporated the Arabic regimental number and the crown.

▼ OFFICER, COLDSTREAM GUARDS, 1854
This officer wears parade dress. As the 2nd Regiment of Foot Guards, his buttons are arranged in pairs. He wears the star of the Order of the Garter on his collar, epaulettes, a square, gilt belt plate and buttons.

British Regimental Cap Badges and Facings

Regiment	Badge	Facings
(Those regiments that fought in the Crimean War are marked with an asterisk)		
1st or Royal Regiment*	Order of the Thistle, sphinx	dark blue
2nd (Queen's Royal)	the lamb	dark blue
3rd (East Kent)*	a dragon	buff
4th (King's Own)*	the lion of England	dark blue
5th (Northumberland) Fusiliers	grenade	gosling green
6th (1st Warwickshire)	an antelope within the garter	blue
7th (Royal Fusiliers)*	grenade	dark blue
8th (The King's Regiment)	white horse of Hanover	dark blue
9th (East Norfolk)*	Britannia	yellow
10th (North Lincoln)	the sphinx	later white
11th (North Devon)		Lincoln green
12th (East Suffolk)	castle and key	pale yellow
13th (1st Somersetshire)*	bugle horn, coronet and 'JELLALABAD'	blue
14th (West Yorkshire)*	tiger and 'INDIA'	buff
15th (York, East Riding)		white
16th (Bedfordshire)		white
17th (Leicester)*	tiger and 'HINDOOSTAN'	pearl grey
18th (The Royal Irish)*	the sphinx	dark blue
19th (1st York North Riding)*		grass green
20th (East Devonshire)*		white
21st (Royal Scots Fusiliers)*	grenade	dark blue
22nd (Cheshire)		buff
23rd (Royal Welch Fusiliers)*	grenade	dark blue
24th (2nd Warwickshire)	the sphinx	willow green
25th (The King's Own Borderers)		dark blue
26th (Cameronians)	star and wreath	pale yellow
27th (Royal Inniskilling Fusiliers)	Enniskillen Castle	pale buff
28th (North Gloucestershire)*	the sphinx (also back of hat)	bright yellow
29th (Worcestershire)		bright yellow
30th (Cambridgeshire)*	the sphinx and 'XXX'	white
31st (Huntingdonshire)*		white
32nd (Cornwall)	French bugle horn	white
33rd (1st Yorkshire West Riding)*	Duke of Wellington's crest	red
34th (East Lancashire)*		yellow
35th (Royal Sussex)		orange
36th (Herefordshire)	'FIRM' over '36'	willow green
37th (North Hampshire)		yellow
38th (Staffordshire Volunteers)*	Staffordshire knot	yellow
39th (Dorsetshire)*	castle and key	willow green
40th (2nd Somersetshire)	the sphinx	buff
41st (The Welch Regiment)*	Prince of Wales's crest	white
42nd (Royal Highlanders/ Black Watch)*	the sphinx	dark blue
43rd (Monmouthshire Light)	bugle horn	white
44th (East Essex)*	the sphinx	purple
45th (Nottinghamshire)		Lincoln green
46th (South Devonshire)*		pale yellow
47th (Lancashire)*		white
48th (Northamptonshire)*		buff
49th (Hertfordshire)*	dragon and 'CHINA'	dark green

▶

Regiment	Badge	Facings
50th (West Kent)*	lion over crown over '50'	black
51st (2nd Yorks, West Riding L.I.)	French bugle horn	olive green
52nd (Oxfordshire)	bugle horn	buff
53rd (Shropshire)		red
54th (West Norfolk)	the sphinx and 'MARABOUT'	popinjay green
55th (Westmoreland)*	dragon and 'CHINA'	dark green
56th (West Essex)*	castle and key	purple facings
57th (West Middlesex)*		lemon yellow
58th (Rutlandshire)	castle and key	black
59th (2nd Nottinghamshire)		white
60th (King's Royal Rifle Corps)	Maltese cross	red
61st (South Gloucestershire)	the sphinx	buff
62nd (Wiltshire)*	Maltese cross	buff
63rd (West Suffolk)*		dark green
64th (North Staffordshire)	Staffordshire knot	black
65th (2nd Yorkshire, North Riding)	tiger and 'INDIA'	white
66th (Berkshire)		dark green
67th (South Hampshire)	tiger and 'INDIA'	pale yellow
68th (Durham)*	bugle horn	dark green
69th (South Lincolnshire)		willow green
70th (Surrey)		dark blue
71st (Highland)*	French bugle horn	buff
72nd (Highland)*	thistles	pale yellow
73rd		dark blue
74th (Highland)	star of St Andrew	yellow
75th (Highland)	Indian tiger	yellow
76th	elephant	red
77th (East Middlesex)*	Prince of Wales's crest	yellow
78th (Highland/Rosshire Buffs)	elephant	buff
79th (Cameron Highlanders)*		blue
80th (Staffordshire Volunteers)	Staffordshire knot	yellow
81st (Loyal Lincoln Volunteers)		buff facings
82nd (Prince of Wales's Vol)*	Prince of Wales's crest	yellow
83rd (County of Dublin)		bright yellow
84th (York and Lancaster)	coronet and rose	yellow
85th (Bucks Volunteers)	bugle horn	yellow
86th (Royal County Down)	the harp	bright yellow
87th (Royal Irish Fusiliers)	grenade	dark green
88th (Connaught Rangers)*	the harp	bright yellow
89th (Princess Victoria's)*		black
90th (Perthshire Volunteers)*	bugle horn	dark buff
91st (Argyllshire)	star of St Andrew	white
92nd (Gordon Highlanders)	the sphinx	yellow
93rd (Sutherland Highlanders)*	thistles	yellow
94th		dark green
95th (Derbyshire)*		black
96th (Queen's Royal Irish)		buff
97th (The Earl of Ulster's)*		black
98th	dragon and 'CHINA'	buff
99th (Lanarkshire)		yellow
100th (Prince of W Canadians)	Prince of Wales' crest	blue
101st (1st Bengal European F)	grenade	blue
102nd (1st Madras European F)	grenade	dark blue ▶

There were three regiments of Foot Guards and these had distinctive badges: 1st or Grenadier (a flaming grenade cap badge), 2nd or Coldstream (the star of the Order of the Garter) and the 3rd or Scots (the star of the Order of the Thistle). They were further distinguished by single, double or triple tunic buttons.

The line had the following regiments: where the badge of the sphinx is mentioned, it is always upon a plinth with the word 'EGYPT' on it. The castle and key, with the motto 'MONTIS INSIGNIA CALPE' was

▼ **PRIVATE, 42ND FOOT, 1854** *The British were poorly prepared for their first winter in the Crimea, as this ragged Highlander demonstrates.*

awarded for service in Gibraltar 1779–83. The tiger or elephant was usually awarded for service in India. The dragon showed service in China. Regiments that wore the bugle horn were light infantry.

The Tunic

For privates and corporals this was single-breasted; sergeants, sergeant majors and officers wore double-breasted tunics with gilt buttons; other ranks' buttons were pewter. Corporals and below wore regimental braid to

Regiment	Badge	Facings
103rd (1st Bombay European F)	grenade	white
104th (2nd Bengal European F)	grenade	dark blue
105th (2nd Madras European LI)	French bugle	buff
106th (2nd Bombay European LI)	French bugle	white
107th (3rd Bengal European Inf)		white
108th (3rd Madras European Inf)		pale yellow
109th (3rd Bombay European Inf)		white
Rifle Brigade (wore dark green)	Maltese cross, bugle horn	black

▼ ENSIGN, SCOTS FUSILIER GUARDS, 1854
Note the silver thistles on the collar and the buttons on the coat arranged in groups of three, reflecting the seniority of the regiment. This officer is in marching order.

buttonholes (ten in pairs on the chest, three on each cuff flap, two at the rear of the waist); facings were worn on collar, shoulder straps and cuffs. The centre companies wore shoulder straps edged in lace and with a half-moon end edged in white tufting. The grenadiers and light companies wore red wings, edged and striped in regimental lace, with a wide, tufted roll along the outer edge. Sergeant majors wore unfringed silver epaulettes; officers had fringed golden epaulettes and those of the flank companies had wings and shoulder straps heavily decorated with gold chains. Turnbacks were white, with the company badge at the lower join. In 1856 a single-breasted tunic, with hip-length skirts was introduced for all ranks; all buttons were now brass or gilt and the officers' sash was now worn over the right shoulder, held by a crimson silk cord. Epaulettes were abandoned; officers' rank distinctions were silver crowns and stars worn on the collar, with gold lace to the cuffs according to rank. NCO badges of rank were worn on the upper right sleeve by staff sergeants and battalion company NCOs and on both upper sleeves by NCOs of the flank companies. A sergeant major wore four silver chevrons (point down) under a crown on the lower right sleeve. White linen trousers were worn

▶ GRENADIER SERGEANT, 33RD FOOT, WINTER FIELD DRESS, 1854 *The regimental number is worn under a brass grenade on the Kilmarnock cap. The musket barrel is plugged and the lock covered to keep it dry.*

in summer; dark blue, with a red side stripe were worn in winter. The equipment and rifle sling was of white leather, of the style worn in 1815, with the addition of a small, black percussion cap pouch on the front right of the waist belt. The rectangular packs were of black, waterproof canvas, with the regimental number in white. The light blue, wooden 'cask' waterbottle was carried.

BRITISH CAVALRY: HEAVY BRIGADE

British cavalry regiments were divided into heavy and light, mainly by the size of the horses that they used and the weapons that they carried. Heavy regiments rode horses of about 15–16 hands height at the shoulder and carried heavy, straight-bladed swords.

Heavy Dress

Much emphasis was also laid on the sartorial differences of the uniforms of the heavies and the lights, rather than any tactical considerations of the two arms. The heavy cavalry traditionally carried out the massed charges against the enemy lines; they were not used for scouting duties. Cavalry were usually formed into brigades, with a brigade consisting of two or more regiments. The heavy regiments included the Household cavalry, regiments of horse and dragoons.

Coats were single-breasted, with facings worn on collar, cuffs, turnbacks and piping. Dragoon regiments wore cuffs in the facing colour, with the top cut out in a 'V' shape. Breeches were dark blue with wide red side stripes. Boots were black and knee-high.

Household Cavalry

Britain's mounted Guards, or Household cavalry, wore a steel helmet with yellow metal fittings and the cross of the Order of the Garter, under a crown, on the front. The white bandolier had a red flask cord running along its centre. Single-breasted tunics were worn, closed with nine buttons, cuffs cut so that they rose diagonally to the rear and had a chevron on them. Gold lace was worn. Troopers wore shoulder straps, corporals and sergeants had aiguillettes on the left shoulder. White buckskin breeches and high, jacked boots completed the costume. Distinctions were as follows:

1ST LIFE GUARDS. Red coat, dark blue facings, white plume, blue shabraque
2ND LIFE GUARDS. Red coat, dark blue facings, white plume, blue shabraque
ROYAL HORSE GUARDS. Blue coat, red facings, red plume, red shabraque

The Household cavalry did not see service in the Crimea.

Dragoon Guards

All regiments had blue shabraques and yellow metal helmets with white fittings, often worn with a white cloth cover. Regimental distinctions were:
1ST (KING'S). Red coat, dark blue facings, red plume

◀ TROOPER, 5TH ROYAL INNISKILLING DRAGOON GUARDS, 1854 *The brass helmet worn by this trooper has brass edging and chinscales and a white 12-pointed star to the front, which encloses a yellow metal garter. Within the garter was displayed the regimental number in white. The regimental cap badge depicts the white horse of Hanover.*

2ND (THE QUEEN'S BAYS). Red coat, buff facings, black plume
3RD PRINCE OF WALES' (CARABINIERS). Red coat, yellow facings, black and red plume
4TH ROYAL IRISH. Red coat, dark blue facings, white plume

▼ CORPORAL, ROYAL SCOTS GREYS (NORTH BRITISH DRAGOONS), FIELD SERVICE MARCHING ORDER, 1854 *The brass eagle on the pouch lid commemorates the taking of the eagle of the 45th French Line Infantry Regiment at Waterloo. On the front of the busby is a brass 12-pointed star enclosing a white metal garter, within which is the regimental number in brass.*

5TH PRINCESS CHARLOTTE OF WALES'. Red coat, dark green facings, red and white plume
6TH DRAGOON GUARDS (CARABINIERS). Blue coat, white facings and plume
7TH PRINCESS ROYAL'S. Red coat, black facings, black/white plume.

Dragoons

The numbering system for the remaining cavalry regiments is complex; dragoons, hussars and lancers were numbered within one continuous sequence. Dragoons accounted for the 1st, 2nd and 6th regiments. The 5th Regiment had been disbanded in the 1790s and was not to be reformed until 1858. It was then converted to a lancer regiment in 1861. All dragoon regiments wore single-breasted red coats. Most dragoon regiments had white metal helmets with yellow fittings (could be worn with white cloth covers). Forage caps were often worn off-duty. The Greys were entitled to wear bearskins. Distinctions:
1ST ROYAL DRAGOONS. Dark blue facings, yellow braid and sash, black plume, blue shabraque. Sergeants wore the regimental badge of a lion on a crown above the three gold lace chevrons on their upper right arms.
2ND ROYAL SCOTS GREYS. Dark blue facings, yellow braid and sash, white plume, blue shabraque. Officers wore gold buttons and had facings on velvet cloth, the men wore pewter. Sergeants wore the regimental eagle in silver above the three gold chevrons on their upper right arms.
5TH VACANT.
6TH (INNISKILLING) DRAGOONS. Buff facings, yellow braid and sash, white plume. Sergeants wore the silver castle of Enniskillen over their three gold chevrons on the upper right arm. Officers' sabretache badge was the crowned royal cypher, behind the castle, all over a scroll bearing:

▶ 6TH INNISKILLING DRAGOONS, 1854 *From 1788, this regiment was also known as the Carabiniers. The buttons and belt plates bore the castle of Enniskillen. The dark blue, gold-edged holster covers bore the royal cypher 'VR'.*

'INNISKILLING DRAGOONS'. They also had facings shown on velvet cloth and their uniforms were of a much more superior cut.

In the late morning of the Battle of Balaclava, 25 October 1854, the heavy brigade – General Scarlett with 900 sabres of the 1st Royal Dragoons, 2nd Dragoons (The Greys), 4th and 5th Dragoon Guards and the 6th (Inniskilling Dragoon Guards) – were engaged in a successful clash with Russian cavalry as the Russians attempted to force their way toward the British base. This successful charge of the Heavy Brigade was later overshadowed by the notorious charge of the Light Brigade.

BRITISH CAVALRY: LIGHT BRIGADE

Light cavalry traditionally carried out the scouting and patrolling roles in an army; although, as seen in the Crimean War, they could charge the enemy in the same way as their counterparts in the heavy brigade could.

Hussars and Light Dragoons

Light cavalry were, however, mounted on smaller (and therefore more nimble) horses (about 14 hands height at the shoulder) and traditionally carried light sabres with curved blades (for cutting rather than stabbing). Light cavalry included the light dragoons, hussars and the lancer regiments. In France and Russia there were also regiments of mounted rifles (Chasseurs à cheval), which were also part of the light cavalry.

Light dragoons adopted a 'stove-pipe' shako in 1853; it had a top band in the button colour, a plume and a Maltese cross on the front, in the central disc of which was the regimental badge. It was usually worn covered in an oilskin cover. Hussar regiments wore black fur busbies with a bag to the right in the regimental colour and a short plume to the front. Instead of a tunic they wore dark blue dolmans and breeches with yellow braiding, cap lines and buttons, the breeches having two narrow yellow stripes. Collars and cuffs were dark blue unless otherwise noted. Regimental distinctions were as follows, the asterisks denoting which of the companies fought in the Crimean War:

3RD KING'S OWN LIGHT DRAGOONS*. Red collar, yellow buttons and braid, white plume

◀ TROOPER, 8TH HUSSARS (KING'S ROYAL IRISH), 1854 *This figure wears summer campaign dress, complete with haversack, he also carried a wooden water bottle. The Royal Warrant of 1751 gave their badges as 'VIII D' and in 1777 they were authorized to wear the harp and crown and the motto: 'PRISTINAE VIRTUTIS MEMORES' on their guidons. On their buttons was 'L' over 'VIII' over 'D'. On parades a red plume would be added to the shako. Troopers carried a carbine, slung over the left shoulder on a white leather bandolier, muzzle down. The small, ammunition pouch was worn on a narrower white bandolier over the right shoulder. The sabre belt was often worn over the waist sash. Cap lines prevented loss of the shako.*

▲ TRUMPETER, 4TH (QUEEN'S OWN) LIGHT DRAGOONS, 1854 *In action, trumpeters used bugles (worn here hanging from the figure's shoulder) to sound signals, instead of the longer trumpets. Trumpets (shown being blown here) were retained only for parade use. Trumpeters wore no bandoliers or cartridge pouches. This figure wears an oilskin cover to his shako, which obscures the badge of a crowned Maltese cross with the regimental crest (IV) in the centre.*

▼ **OFFICER, 11TH HUSSARS, 1854** *Officers of this regiment, in parade dress, wore dolmans and pelisses covered in the traditional, hussar-style gold lace. Elaborate gold embroidery edged the cuffs and other parts of the garments, including the small, false pockets at the sides of the waist. The red sabretache was edged in broad gold braid and bore the crowned, reversed royal cipher over the Irish harp and the regimental title on a scroll. The parade shabraque was dark blue, edged in gold according to rank, and bore the royal cipher and harp at the front and in the long, rear corners. A small leopard-skin saddle cloth was used. The elaborate harness included a horsehair tassel, in a gilt mount, hanging from the throat lash. Officer's buttons bore the sphinx, with the inscription 'EGYPT' on the plinth, over 'XI', over 'LD', between the peripheral inscriptions 'PENINSULA' and 'WATERLOO'.*

4TH QUEEN'S OWN LIGHT DRAGOONS*. Yellow collar, white buttons and braid, scarlet plume

7TH QUEEN'S OWN LIGHT DRAGOONS*. Red collar, yellow buttons and braid, white plume

8TH KING'S ROYAL IRISH LIGHT DRAGOONS (1822: 'Hussars' added to the title)*. Red collar, yellow buttons, red/white plume

10TH PRINCE OF WALES'S OWN ROYAL REGIMENT OF (LIGHT) DRAGOONS (1861: Prince of Wales's Own Royal Hussars)*. Red collar, white buttons, black/white plume

11TH PRINCE ALBERT'S OWN REGIMENT OF HUSSARS. Crimson collar and busby bag, white buttons, crimson/white plume, crimson breeches

13TH LIGHT DRAGOONS. Buff collar and busby bag, yellow buttons, white plume, buff stripes on breeches

14TH THE KING'S LIGHT DRAGOONS*. Yellow collar, white buttons and white plume

15TH KING'S LIGHT DRAGOONS*. Red collar and plume

18TH KING'S IRISH LIGHT DRAGOONS (Hussars) (disbanded in 1821; raised in 1858 as the 18th Light Dragoons)*. Blue collar, red/white plume.

The 19th Light Dragoons, 20th and 21st Hussars were originally the 1st, 2nd and 3rd Bengal European Light Cavalry regiments of the army of the Honourable East India Company, which were taken on to the British establishment in 1861.

Lancers

Britain had been impressed by lancers during the Napoleonic Wars and during more recent experience in India. The British military experimented with the weapon and converted some regiments into lancers.

Polish Traditions

As with other lancer regiments across Europe, Britain's lancers were dressed in a costume inspired by traditional Polish dress. Lancers wore the internationally recognized Polish headgear, a square-topped czapka (with the top in the facing colour), a tunic known as the kurtka (with facings shown on collar, pointed cuffs, lapels, plastron, turnbacks and piping), dark blue breeches with twin narrow yellow stripes, a yellow waist sash with two crimson stripes. Boots with spurs were worn.

Forage caps and stable jackets with overalls were worn off-duty. Officers had gold edging to collar and cuffs and wore the crowned royal cipher on their pouches. The gold bandoliers had a central stripe in the facing colour and fittings were silver. Officers' cockades bore the royal cipher in gold on velvet in the regimental facing colour, plumes were of cock's feathers. Distinctions:

9TH OR QUEEN'S ROYAL LANCERS. Blue kurtka, red facings, black/white plume
12TH (PRINCE OF WALES' ROYAL) LANCERS. Dark blue kurtka, red facings, red plume
16TH QUEEN'S LIGHT DRAGOONS (LANCERS). Red kurtka, dark blue facings, black plume
17TH DUKE OF CAMBRIDGE'S OWN REGIMENT OF LIGHT DRAGOONS (LANCERS). Dark blue kurtka, white facings and plume. Twin white trouser stripes. Sergeants wore a silver skull-and-bones badge on the stripes on their right arms. The regimental badge also consisted of this macabre device.

The 5th Royal Irish Dragoons, raised in 1858, would also be converted to lancers wearing dark blue kurtka, red facings and a green plume. Sergeants wore a silver crowned harp on their gold stripes on their upper right arms.

Charge of the Light Brigade

On 25 October 1854, the Russians launched an assault against the British base in Balaclava. Part of their force attacked some Turkish troops, posted to the north-east of the Allied line and overran some Turkish guns. Lord Raglan saw this and despatched Captain Lewis Nolan of the 15th Hussars with this fateful note: *'Lord Raglan wishes the cavalry to advance rapidly to the front and try to prevent the enemy carrying away the guns. Troop of horse artillery may accompany. French cavalry is on your left. Immediate.'* Nolan duly delivered his note; Lord Lucan read it and was mystified. He had no idea of what was going on with the Turkish guns. He was aware only of the Russian

◀ OFFICER, 17TH LIGHT DRAGOONS (LANCERS), 1854 *Note how fashion reduced the skirt turnbacks to minute size, but the gold braid 'waterfall' in the small of the back is retained. The skull-and-bones cap badge was also worn on the shabraque and holster covers; the buttons bore 'XVII', over the skull, with the bones crossed behind it, over crossed lances, over 'OR', over 'GLORY'.*

▶ SERGEANT, 11TH HUSSARS, 1854 *The badge above the chevrons is the crest of Prince Albert of Saxe-Coburg-Gotha: a tower, topped by a coronet standing in another coronet, bearing the Saxon clover leaves. Peacock feathers sprouting from the top coronet, over a scroll bearing: 'TREU UND FEST' (faithful and firm).*

batteries at the end of the valley in which he stood. He asked Nolan which enemy and which guns were meant; the general could surely not intend to send his brigade to certain destruction against the Russian battery? Nolan flung out his arm in a general easterly direction and retorted: *'There is your enemy! There are your guns, My Lord!'* Stung into action by this insolence, Lord Lucan ordered Lord Cardigan (commanding the Light Brigade) to charge with the Light Brigade along the valley and capture the Russian battery at its end. It was a little past two o'clock when the brigade moved off. In the front line were the 13th Dragoons, the 17th Lancers were on the left, the 11th Hussars were behind the 17th; in the third line were the 8th Hussars and 4th Light Dragoons. It seems Captain

▲ *Survivors of the 13th Regiment of Light Dragoons after the Battle of Balaklava, 1854.*

Nolan realized the dreadful mistake, for he began to gallop across towards Lord Cardigan; but was struck down by a shell splinter before he could achieve anything. Suffering heavy losses, the cavalry pressed on through the Russian guns, cutting down those that had not fled. They drove off the Russian cavalry behind the gun lines, and chased them almost back to the Tchernaya River, before being pushed back in their turn.

From a starting strength of 673 that morning the Light Brigade now had a mounted strength of just 195 officers and men.

▶ TROOPER, 13TH LIGHT DRAGOONS, ON PICKET DUTY, 1854 *Winter picket duty was miserable for both horse and rider. Permission not to shave had been granted, in view of the harsh weather. The cap badge in the centre of the crowned Maltese cross on the shako was an eight-pointed star, having 'XIII' over 'LD'. The buttons also bore this crest, with the peripheral inscription: 'PENINSULA WATERLOO' on the upper half and 'VIRET IN AETERNUM' on the lower half.*

BRITISH ROYAL ARTILLERY AND ENGINEERS

British artillery would play an important role in the Crimea, especially when field operations gave way to the long siege of Sevastopol.

The Royal Regiment of Artillery.

Artillery have traditionally provided the long-range, highly destructive firepower of armies on battlefields. British artillery was split into field and fortress (garrison) artillery. The field artillery was again subdivided into foot and horse artillery, consisting of the gun crews, who manned the guns, and the drivers, who moved the guns on campaign. They were organized into tactical units, batteries, of six or so guns with associated ammunition and logistical vehicles. The crews of foot artillery batteries marched with their guns; horse artillery battery crews were mounted, either on their vehicles and guns or on their own horses. Horse artillery had much increased speed of movement on the battlefield over foot artillery pieces.

Foot artillery wore dark blue, infantry-style uniforms, with two rows of ten brass buttons and red facings. Their belts were white. The red cuffs had dark blue, three-button, trident shaped rectangular flaps, which were edged in yellow or gold braid according to rank. The red collars bore a flaming grenade and were edged in yellow/gold braid. They wore the 1843-pattern Albert shako with a white plume and a large, eight-pointed brass star badge, bearing the royal arms over a cannon. The plume holder was in the form of a brass flaming grenade. The shako had brass chin chains, held by round bosses, bearing a flaming grenade. For parades epaulettes were worn; they had red straps with yellow edging and tassels for junior ranks, gold for sergeants and officers. Sergeants and officers wore crimson waist sashes. Officers' collars and turnback junctions bore gold grenades; field officers also had gold, laurel leaf embroidery to collars and cuff flaps.

◀ OFFICER, ROYAL HORSE ARTILLERY, 1854
The regiment adopted hussar costume (in which they still perform on ceremonial occasions) in artillery colours, to emphasize their high-mobility role. The busby had a red bag; rank badges were yellow for corporals, gold for sergeants, who wore the cannon over their stripes. Officers' gold-edged, dark blue shabraques bore the crowned royal cipher, over a cannon, over a red scroll bearing 'UBIQUE' (everywhere) all in gold.

▶ STAFF SERGEANT, ROYAL HORSE ARTILLERY, 1856 *This figure is based on a Roger Fenton photograph, taken during conflict, and is of interest for its deviations from regulations, as the need to cover the body outstripped the clothing re-supply system. The busby has a red bag, without caplines. Instead of a hussar-style dolman with yellow frogging, he wears a foot artillery tunic and seems to have brass grenades on his shoulder straps.*

◄ STAFF SERGEANT, ROYAL ARTILLERY, 1854
*This shako plate shows the royal arms over a
cannon. Officers had dark blue forage caps
with black peak and chinstrap; sergeants wore
a peakless, dark blue cap with gold headband
and red piping to the crown; corporals and
below had dark blue peakless caps with red
headband and
piping to the
crown. They
wore brass chevrons
over the headband.*

► SERGEANT, ROYAL SAPPERS AND
MINERS, 1854 *This figure wears the
forage cap of his rank and the red shell
jacket for summer field duties. Note the gold
shoulder cords. He is armed with a carbine.
In parade dress, a white plume on a shako,
gold, fringed epaulettes and a crimson waist
sash to a tunic with dark blue collar and cuffs
and white skirt turnbacks would be worn.*

worn with the forage cap. It had a red
collar, a single row of 14 buttons,
yellow/gold shoulder cords and plain
cuffs with a single button.

The artillery were armed with
carbines, sergeants wore straight
swords in black sheaths with brass
fittings. Badges of rank were
yellow/gold chevrons on the upper
sleeves, although Roger Fenton
(1819–69), one of the first war
photographers, photographed a
staff sergeant with four chevrons,
point up, on the right forearm
only. Sergeants wore a brass
cannon over their chevrons. Officers
could also wear the dark blue, double-
breasted frock coat in undress (with
the forage cap); it had a dark blue
collar and plain, dark blue cuffs.

Horse artillery wore the same colour
scheme, but in a hussar-style uniform,
with black fur busbies, red bag and five
rows of brass, ball buttons. Officers'
sashes were crimson, with gold barrels.
A plain black everyday sabretache bore
the royal arms in gold. A Roger Fenton
photograph shows a staff sergeant of
horse artillery in a busby, wearing a
tunic with six buttons and yellow
Austrian knots on his cuffs. He carried
a sabre on a white bandolier.

The blue trousers had a wide red stripe.
In barracks a dark blue forage cap was
worn; for officers it had a black peak,
gold headband and gold pompon on
top. It also had a black chinstrap. That
of senior NCOs had no peak or
pompon, but did have a gold
headband and a red piping around the
rim of the crown; that of corporals and
below had a red headband and brass
chevrons were worn on the front above
the headband. For barrack duties the
dark blue, waist-length shell jacket was

Engineers

The engineers had the tasks of
destroying, removing or circumventing
obstacles which impeded the
movement of their army, building
fortifications and bridges, and were
also responsible for any mine warfare.

Britain's Royal Sappers and Miners
wore a red coat faced dark blue, yellow
buttons, dark blue trousers with wide
red stripe, white belts. The details of
rank badges, forage caps and red shell
jacket all follow the style of the foot
artillery, but in sapper colours. The
forage cap had a blue top with red
piping for sergeants.

RUSSIAN GENERAL OFFICERS

After the Napoleonic Wars Russia was engaged in a string of conflicts with the Ottoman empire, Persia and ethnic minorities in the Caucasus mountains. Field officers gained experience but not promotion, and elderly generals and poor staff plagued the military.

Experienced Officers

The czar made great efforts to place army officers at the top of the social tree, making it a virtue to serve to defend Holy Mother Russia. He

also made great efforts to attract suitable, talented, non-aristocratic members of Russian society into the officer corps and set up several officer cadet training units, but demand was always outstripping supply, so compromises had to be made. It was also possible for suitable enlisted men to be commissioned. Officers of the Imperial Guard were drawn from the richest classes, then came the cavalry, the infantry and, lastly, the artillery. But the artillery officers, although relatively poor, had by far the best academic qualifications of the entire army. The salaries of Russian officers were less than half of their western European counterparts. One officer recounted that when he was stationed in Lithuania, he could only afford to buy bread and eggs to live on. The solution was to become a regimental commander and squeeze the regimental funds for personal use. Efficiency and the men's pay suffered accordingly. There were able and energetic Russian generals in the

◄ GENERAL OF ARTILLERY, FULL DRESS, 1854 *By this point, the dark green uniforms of the armed forces were almost black. This general wears the crowned imperial Cyrillic cipher 'NI' (Nicholas I) on his epaulettes, showing that he is a 'Flügel-Adjutant' (aide-de-camp) to the Czar. His many decorations include the Orders of the White Eagle, St George, St Andrew and St Stanislaus.*

► FIELD MARSHAL, FULL DRESS, 1856 *It seems that even field marshals in the Russian Army had to wear the heavy helmet, here with white, black and orange feather plume and gilt fittings. This highly decorated officer wears the light blue sash of the Order of St Andrew. The huge epaulettes bear the crowned imperial cipher 'NI' (Nicholas I). Around his throat is a jewelled, enamelled portrait. On his left breast is the eight-pointed star of the Order of St Andrew, over the four-pointed star of the Order of St George. Note that the bottom button of his cuff flap is left undone.*

Crimean War, but the difficulties that they had to contend with in the logistics, training and reinforcement limited their achievements. Two such were Vice Admiral Pavel Stepanovich Nakhimov, victor of the naval Battle of Sinope, and involved in the defence of Sevastopol, after his ships had been scuttled, and Vice Admiral Vladimir Alexeievich Kornilov, who commanded the city's defence and was killed there.

Generals

The uniforms worn by generals largely followed the patterns as for field officers of infantry; generals would wear the dark green, double-breasted tunics (with two rows of six buttons on the breast) and breeches, with red facings and gold buttons, lace and fringed, bullion epaulettes. The buttons bore the crowned imperial double eagle. Those generals who were also aides-de-camp to the czar, wore the crowned imperial cipher (Cyrillic N and an I for Nicholas I) in silver, on the fields of their epaulettes and a heavy gold aiguillette on the right shoulder. The red three-button cuff flap, the cuffs and the collar were covered with heavy gold oakleaf embroidery. A narrow red piping ran down the front of the tunic.

Field marshals wore a similar uniform but with red trousers with double gold side stripes. They also carried black batons with golden ends, all heavily decorated with gold oakleaves, crowned imperial ciphers and double eagles. Their silver waist sashes had two lines of black and orange dots along their length, with heavy silver bullion tassels hanging to the left hand side. Generals of artillery would have black facings and gold buttons and lace.

For court and social occasions, generals wore the bicorn with gold brooch, black, white and orange cockade and drooping feather plume, court swords, white gloves and black shoes. The hilts of their swords wore heavy silver, black and orange straps with silver tassels. For parade and field duties, they wore the spiked helmet, with or without plumes respectively, and straight-topped, black boots to below the knee, with silver spurs.

◀ AIDE-DE-CAMP, HORSE LIFE GUARDS, 1847 *This officer is a colonel; his epaulettes bear the crowned imperial cipher 'NI' for Nicholas I. On his gilt helmet plate is the silver star of the Order of St Andrew; at his throat, the light blue Prussian Pour le Merite is worn, partially covering the red cross of the Order of St Anna. To the lower left breast is the white cross of the Order of St John, over the Prussian Iron Cross of 1813.*

▶ GENERAL OF MILITIA, 1855 *This grey costume is much more sober and modest than the dress of the regular army, and seems to have no buttons at all. His massive gold epaulettes show three silver stars of a lieutenant general. His cap badge is a gilt, Russian version of the Prussian Landwehr cross of 1813. He carries a St George's sword, awarded for bravery, with black and orange sword strap and silver tassel. He wears the sash of the Order of St Anna, 1st Class.*

Staff Officers

Officers of the staff wore a uniform which was very similar to that of the generals, but with black facings and silver buttons, epaulettes and lace.

Undress Uniforms

There was also a simple, single-breasted undress version of the uniform for Russian generals and general staff officers. This had nine buttons on the chest, a plain red collar and plain red cuffs, without flaps or buttons. It was worn without the waist sash. Breeches and riding boots completed the uniform.

RUSSIAN INFANTRY

The Russian Army filled its ranks with annual conscription levies from its large civilian population, and the majority of new recruits were sent to serve in the line infantry.

Conscription

The czar would approve the manpower estimates presented to him by the War Ministry and each serf-owning aristocrat would be told how many 'fit and able' young men, between 18 and 35 years of age, were to be supplied. The total number raised was usually about 80,000 per year. Terms of service were for 15 and 25 years. The families of these selected

peasant recruits regarded the call-up for the army to be equal to a death sentence (with good reason) and the unlucky ones would be given a tearful send-off to begin basic training.

Serf-owners would make their selection from local troublemakers and would also take the opportunity to empty the town prisons. Soldiers' sons were automatically selected for military service, but they usually enjoyed state education and training from a young age. In 1834 the czar decreed that men with 15 years' good service could be sent on long leave, having to come back to barracks for only six weeks' training a year. This was a direct copy of the Prussian Krumper system first used during the Napoleonic era.

Life for Russian conscripts was harsh. Food was prepared in large kettles and usually consisted of cabbage soup and porridge. Meat was supplied, but it was of very poor quality. Black bread, salt and tea completed the diet. There was also a daily ration of vodka. More and better fare was provided on feast days. Pay was meagre, but the soldiers often hired themselves out as casual labourers and made more.

Organization

Russia's elite infantry consisted of the Imperial Guard and the Grenadier Corps each of three infantry divisions of two brigades with two regiments. The six line infantry corps each had three such

◀ **DRUMMER, 29TH NAVAL EQUIPAGE, 1855**
Following their success against the Turkish Navy at Sinope on 30 November 1853, the Russian Black Sea fleet withdrew into Sevastopol, where the ships were scuttled to block access to the harbour. The seamen contributed greatly to the conduct of the defence of the city. The equipage number appears on shako plate and shoulder straps. The shako is very like the British 1812 pattern, worn at Waterloo.

divisions. There were 42 infantry and 42 light infantry (Jäger) regiments; these numbers were worn on helmet plates and buttons. Each regiment was also named after cities, provinces or prominent persons (usually royal patrons). Each regiment had four field battalions and two depot battalions, but this was increased to eight battalions for the Crimean War.

Because of Russia's huge landmass and high population, the supply of new recruits was practically limitless. This meant the military hierarchy could afford to be somewhat casual about the good husbandry of their manpower. High wastage of men's lives on, but also behind, the front line was prodigal, mainly due to the utter lack of proper care from the commanders in charge. Of over a million recruits raised, trained and sent from Russia to the Crimea, close to half that number seem to have perished without coming close to any action. That the survivors were still loyal to the czar and his government is amazing. The deaths of so many young conscripts was a tragedy about which the Russian high command seemed relatively unconcerned.

Helmet, Shako and Cap

Russian infantry uniforms had changed little since the Napoleonic era; in particular, the systems of denoting the wearer's company, battalion, regiment and division were maintained on the uniforms of 1854.

The famous 1812-pattern Kiwer shako remained in service until about 1820. It was then replaced by a much taller, slightly bell-topped model bearing the imperial double eagle; in 1846 the Prussian-style 'coal scuttle', black leather helmet with tall spike and double eagle badge replaced it until 1855, when it was replaced for the line by a shako. The helmet front plate was pierced to show the regimental number for other ranks;

officers had silver numerals. The black-white-orange national cockade was worn behind the right hand chinstrap boss. For parades the regiments of the line wore white horsehair plumes in helmet spikes, the Guard, artillery, engineers and dragoons wore black.

▼ CORPORAL BUGLER, FINLAND GUARDS REGIMENT, 1854 *This figure wears summer parade dress, with guards' lace buttonholes to collar and cuff flaps, red swallows' nests and yellow drummer/bugler braid chevrons to the sleeves. Rank is shown by gold braid edging to top and front of collar, top of cuff and cuff flap and by his black, silver and orange sword knot.*

All musicians wore red plumes on parades. The men could also wear a peakless, dark green forage cap, with headband and top piping. On the front of this cap was the company designation in yellow. The shako, in turn, gave way to a low-crowned, dark green cap in the French style in 1860, with a headband in the facing colour: red for infantry, black piped red for light infantry regiments (Jägers). On parade the cap had a black horsehair plume.

▲ SERGEANT, 33RD INFANTRY REGIMENT, 1854 *The greatcoat collar shows the gold braid edging of his rank, as do the three gold braid stripes on the shoulder boards. The extremely long skirts of the greatcoat have been hooked up inside by six hooks to aid his mobility in action.*

▶ CAPTAIN, 9TH INFANTRY REGIMENT, 1854 *Officers wore the regimental number in silver on their cap plates. Above the crowned eagles of the cap plate was a scroll bearing the award for distinguished action in the regiment's history. Individuals could be awarded special St George's weapons for acts of bravery.*

◀ DRUMMER, 19TH JÄGERS, 1854 *The shoulder straps and swallows' nests are light blue, with the divisional number on the latter in yellow. Note the yellow service stripe on the upper left sleeve, showing ten years' good conduct. Jägers and the navy had black drum hoops and cord-tighteners.*

gold. Waist sashes and sword hilt straps were silver silk with two lines of square, black and orange dots. The officers' light brown greatcoat had gold shoulder straps with a single central stripe for company officers (two such stripes for field officers), and edging in the regimental shoulder strap colour. Small, five-pointed silver stars showed the rank: one = ensign, two = second lieutenant, three (in a triangle) = first lieutenant, four (one above the triangle) = captain. Field officers had a similar system; two stars = major, three = lieutenant colonel. A colonel wore no stars. Non-commissioned officers wore yellow/gold embroidery to cuffs and collars and rank was shown by a system of yellow/gold stripes on the shoulder boards (one to three narrow, then one broad for the ranks from lance corporal to sergeant major).

In 1854 infantry units were identified by their shoulder straps as follows: 1st regiment, red; 2nd, white; 3rd, light blue; 4th, yellow. The top piping of the forage cap showed the battalion colour: 1st, red; 2nd, white; 3rd, light blue; 4th, yellow; 5th, dark green; 6th, light green; 7th, brown; 8th, turquoise.

In 1882 a 'national' uniform was introduced; it was dark green and had buttons only on the shoulder straps, being designed to close with hooks and eyes. The dark green trousers went into knee boots. For normal duties a dark green peaked cap was worn; for parades a low, black lambskin cap with the double eagle badge. The only coloured parts of this uniform were the collar patches and

piping, shoulder straps and headband and piping to the top of the crown of the hat. In the same year the 1st brigade in each division wore red shoulder straps, the 2nd had light blue; the divisional number was worn on the shoulder straps, yellow on red,

▼ CAPTAIN, 32ND JÄGERS, 1854 *The Jäger regimental number was worn on the shield of the cap plate, in silver for officers, pierced through for soldiers. His rank is shown by four five-pointed silver stars on the gold shoulder boards and by his silver, black and orange sword knot. The collar of the greatcoat is green, piped in red. The skirts of his greatcoat are worn extended.*

Infantry Distinctions

Russian infantry wore dark green, double-breasted tunics, with red facings, three-button cuff flaps and yellow buttons. Belts were white with brass fittings. Greatcoats were very common and often worn on active duty; they were of brown cloth. Officers could also wear a dark green, knee-length frock coat, with plain dark green cuffs, with a red piping along the top edge. This was in much better quality cloth than that issued to the rank and file. Officers had fringed epaulettes which were gold, with red fields, having the divisional number in blue and green straps, red on white straps. The four regiments in the line divisions were identified by the colour of the collar patches and cap piping: 1st, red; 2nd, light blue; 3rd, white; 4th, dark green. The regiments in the grenadier divisions all had yellow shoulder straps with piping as follows:

▼ PRIVATE, JÄGERS, 1854 *Jägers and line infantry wore dark green forage caps, the former with a black headband, piped in red; the infantry headband was red. The company designation appeared on the front of the headband in yellow characters, the numeral followed by 'P' ('ROTA' or company) or 'ГР' (grenadier company). The crown of the cap was piped in the battalion colour.*

1st Division, red; 2nd, light blue; 3rd, white; 4th, yellow. All wore black waistbelts. Badges of rank were worn on collars, cuffs and shoulder straps, very much in the same way as they are worn today.

The infantry wore white trousers in summer, green in winter. Short boots were generally worn, mostly in natural or, sometimes, blackened leather.

Jägers

These light infantrymen, often used as skirmishers, wore infantry uniforms with dark green collars, piped red and red cuffs. Unlike the infantry of the line they had black leather belts rather than white belts and straps.

Infantry of the Imperial Guard

The foot regiments of the Imperial Guard were Russia's elite infantry units. They wore line infantry style uniforms, with two lace loops (in the button colour) on the collar and three on the cuff flap. Facings for each regiment of the Life Guards were as follows: Preobrazhensky Regiment, red collars, cuffs and flaps; Siemenovsky Regiment, light blue collar piped red, red cuffs and flaps piped white; Ismailovsky Regiment, dark green collar piped red, red cuffs and flaps piped white; the Jäger Regiment, dark green collars and cuffs piped red, red cuff flaps piped white; Moscow Regiment, red; the Grenadier Regiment, collar light blue piped red, red cuffs and flaps; Paul Regiment, dark green collar piped red, red cuffs and flaps; Finland Regiment, dark green collar and cuffs piped red, red flaps; Lithuania Regiment, yellow collar cuffs and flaps, the former piped dark green; Kexholm Regiment, light blue collar piped yellow, yellow cuffs and flaps; the St Petersburg Grenadier Regiment, dark green collar piped yellow, yellow cuffs and flaps; Volhyinia Regiment, dark green collar and cuffs piped yellow, yellow cuff flaps. The last four regiments had white buttons and lace and yellow trouser stripes, the senior regiments had yellow buttons and red trouser stripes. Belts were white.

▲ DRUMMER, 33RD INFANTRY REGIMENT, 1854 *The greatcoat collar shows the infantry red, the shoulder straps give the division. His greatcoat skirts are hooked up to improve his mobility. The regimental number is pierced through the shield on the cap plate. Note the imperial eagle in the oval on the drum.*

Weaponry

The Russian infantry were armed with the M1845 smoothbore, muzzle-loading percussion musket. Just coming into service in 1854 was the rifled percussion musket, equipped with a back sight, usually given to the best shots. Officers carried swords.

RUSSIAN CAVALRY

Russian cavalry contained cuirassiers, dragoons, hussars, lancers, Cossacks and mounted rifles. There were few opportunities for the use of cavalry in this war.

Cuirassiers

Russian cuirassiers wore the black leather helmet with comb and black horsehair crests (red for trumpeters) and brass chinscales and front plate. Guards regiments wore the star of St Andrew on this plate, the line wore the eagle and the Military Order regiment wore the star of St George.

Russian Dragoon Distinctions

Regiment	Collar	Collar piping	Cuffs	Buttons
Life Guards	red*	—	red*	yellow
Borisoglebsk	green	crimson	crimson	yellow
Charkov	deep yellow	—	deep yellow	yellow
Finnland	white	red	white	yellow
Ingermanland	black	—	black	white
Irkutsk	white	—	white	yellow
Jamburg	green	red	red	white
Kargopol	orange	—	orange	white
Kazan	crimson	—	crimson	yellow
Kiev	crimson	—	crimson	white
Kinburn	yellow	—	yellow	white
Kurland	light blue	—	light blue	yellow
Mitau	white	red	white	white
Moscow	pink	—	pink	white
Narva	green	pink	pink	white
New Russia	light blue	—	light blue	white
Nizhegorod	green	white	white	white
Orenburg	black	—	black	yellow
Pskov	orange	—	orange	yellow
Riga	red	—	red	yellow
St Petersburg	pink	—	pink	yellow
Serpuchov	green	yellow	yellow	yellow
Siberian	white	—	white	white
Smolensk	yellow	—	yellow	yellow
Starodub	red	—	red	white
Taganrog	green	pink	pink	yellow
Tiraspol	green	red	red	yellow
Tver	blue	—	blue	yellow
Vladimir	green	white	white	yellow
Zhitomir	red	white	red	white

* with yellow laces.

◀ COLONEL, CAUCASIAN COSSACKS, 1854
This officer wears silver-topped cartridge cases on each breast and is holding a highly decorated, silver-hilted dagger. His decorations include the Orders of St George, St John and St Anne. His regiment has won an honour scroll, seen above the cockade on his fur cap.

Tunics and belts were white, the overalls were grey, with twin stripes in the facing colour. Cuirasses were brass for the guard, black for the line. In 1840 the most extreme form of the enlarged comb and crest was adopted; six years later, the Prussian-pattern steel helmet, with eagle on top, was introduced. The first ranks of all regiments were issued with lances. In 1882 all line cavalry regiments (except Cossacks) were converted to dragoons.

Dragoons

The dragoons wore shakos with red pompons, white plumes and cords, fittings in the button colour. The green tunic had nine buttons, the dark green overalls had wide stripes in the facing colour. In 1840 the dragoon uniform altered; collars had piping a patch in the facing colour and a button on the

Caucasian Cossacks		
Regiment	**Tunic**	**Beshmet**
Caucasus	blue	red
Kuban	blue	white
Coper	blue	yellow
Volga	blue	light blue
Stavropol	blue	grey-green
Gor	brown	red
Greben	brown	yellow
Mosdak	brown	white
Kislar	brown	light blue

▲ JUNIOR OFFICER, ATAMAN COSSACKS, 1855
The uniform of the Cossacks had changed little since the time of the Napoleonic Wars and was still based on the national costume of the regiment's homeland. Note the crowned, Cyrillic cipher 'HI' on his bandolier.

▲ TROOPER, 12TH (INGERMANLAND) HUSSARS, 1854 *He is shown in field service dress, with an oilskin cover (which bears the number of his squadron painted on) over his shako. Note the small, black pouch for percussion caps for his short-barrelled carbine.*

front ends; the old Swedish cuffs had rectangular flaps added, the epaulettes were of metal in the button colour and the green waist sash was piped in the facing colour. Belts were white.

Cossacks
These light, irregular horsemen were used as scouts, patrolling in advance of the army and to the flanks. They wore their national costume, usually dark

▶ TROOPER, TWER DRAGOONS, 1855
Dragoons wore the infantry-style helmet. The epaulettes are of brass scales on a backing of the regimental facing colour. Chevrons on the left arm are for 15 years' good conduct. Note the unusual method of hanging the sabre.

blue, with black fur caps and baggy blue trousers. Their belts were black. Officers wore silver epaulettes, badges of rank followed the rest of the army.

Mounted Rifles

In 1813 eight dragoon regiments were converted to mounted rifles and thus became part of the light cavalry arm. They wore the infantry Kiwer shako with cockade and green cords, green overalls with two wide stripes in the facing colour, green tunic with green collar and white buttons. Facings were worn on the collar piping, shoulder straps, cuffs and turnbacks. In 1817 green collars with patches in the facing colour were introduced as were white epaulettes. For the Crimean War the mounted rifles wore the infantry helmet. They then adopted the kepi when that was introduced. By 1870 there were 18 regiments of mounted rifles; in 1882 they were converted to dragoons. Russia had large numbers of light cavalry and these were, as was their wont, colourfully uniformed.

Hussars

The hussars wore the usual colourful, elaborate costumes that we know in western countries. By this point in history, hussars were just as likely to be used in massed cavalry charges as heavy cavalry regiments. Although the cavalry played an active role in the early stages of the Crimean War, once the allies began the siege of Sevastopol, the Russian cavalry had little or nothing to do in their mounted role. The men were used as infantry and the horses were eaten.

▶ SERGEANT, LIFE GUARD CUIRASSIERS, WINTER FIELD SERVICE, MARCHING ORDER, 1845 *Here we see the ridiculous size to which the helmet comb and crest had grown; it must have destabilized the riders when on the move. Note the dark blue patch and white button on the front of the collar and the silver tassel on the sword strap. On the light blue shoulder strap is a golden stripe.*

In 1840 the uniform colour scheme was as shown below and was valid at the time of the Crimean War. The table is after Knötel; a very reliable source. The regimental braid was also the colour of the trim to sabretache and shabraque. This trim was in wolf's tooth style until 1840, thence smooth. The barrel sashes were in the colour combination of the shako and the regimental braid. The capes worn by the hussars (known as pelisses) were edged in grey fur, belts were white. The grey overalls bore side-piping in the shako colour. They wore the shako with eagle plate, pierced with the regimental number until after the Crimean War, then the infantry kepi, with drooping black plume, was adopted, the upper part in the regimental colour. The Attila tunic eventually replaced the dolman. As with the mounted rifles, each regiment rode horses of a particular colour.

Lancers

The Russian Army introduced Lancer regiments in 1803. Imperial lancers were part of the light cavalry and wore the traditional Polish costume of square-topped cap (the czapka), slate-blue kurtka and grey overalls. The top half of the czapka was in the regimental colour. Regiments rode horses all of the same colour. All regiments wore white buttons, except the Guard Lancers, who had red facings and czapkas, yellow buttons and scale epaulettes. Only the front rank were equipped with lances and they carried no carbines. The second rank were armed with carbines, but no lances, it having been established that both ranks carrying lances resulted in chaos. Like the rest of the Russian cavalry, once the siege of Sevastopol had begun, the men were deployed in other city garrisons.

Russian Hussars

Regiment	Dolman	Pelisse	Braid	Shako	Shabraque and sabretache
1 Sumsk	grey	grey	white	red	grey
2 Klästitz	dark blue	dark blue	white	light blue	dark blue
3 Elizabethgrad	grey	grey	orange	grey	grey
4 Luben	dark blue	dark blue	white	yellow	dark blue
5 Wittgenstein	dark blue	dark blue	orange	yellow	dark blue
6 Oranien	light blue	red	white	light blue	light blue
7 Pavlograd	green	light blue	orange	light blue	green
8 Ferdinand	red	dark blue	white	red	dark blue
9 Achtirsk	brown	brown	orange	yellow	brown
10 Alexandria	dark blue	dark blue	white	red	dark blue
11 Kiev	green	green	orange	red	green
12 Ingermanland	light blue	light blue	orange	light blue	light blue
13 Pavlovitch	light blue	light blue	white	light blue	light blue
14 Württemberg	green	green	white	light blue	green

▼ TROOPER, 15TH (BELGOROD) ULANS, 1854
The three silver chevrons over three yellow on the upper left sleeve indicate that this veteran has served his original 20-year commitment and then re-enlisted. The regimental number is stamped through the shield on the czapka plate. His chin scales are in the regimental button colour. In later years, the top of the czapka (which was in the regimental facing colour) was much reduced in size, in line with international military fashion. This regiment was supposed to be mounted on light chestnuts.

▲ TROOPER, HUSSARS KIT *1 Cavalry carbine. 2 Grenadier's pouch. 3 Epaulette of a staff officer. 4 Epaulette of a major of the 20th Infantry Division. 5 The cap plate of an officer of the 22nd Infantry Regiment.*

◄ TROOPER, 6TH (PRINCE OF ORANGE) HUSSARS, PARADE DRESS, 1854 *The pelisse of this regiment was white, with black fur trim and white buttons and lace. The sabretache was in the shako colour, as it was for all regiments. This regiment rode greys.*

RUSSIAN ARTILLERY

The Russian artillery in the Crimean War were noted for their reliability and bravery under fire.

Artillery

The Russians recognized artillery as being a major component on the battlefield before many other European nations. They ensured that their artillery was more numerous than that of their enemies. Once the siege of Sevastopol began, the field artillery guns were distributed around the perimeter

◀ BOMBARDIER, 4TH HORSE ARTILLERY BRIGADE, 1854 *The rank of bombardier is shown by the gold braid to the top of the cuff and front of the cuff flaps. The helmet plate is pierced with the brigade number. The brass buttons bear the brigade number over crossed gun barrels. The dark green forage cap had a black headband showing the battery number in yellow. Red shoulder straps bore the divisional number in yellow.*

of the city and functioned as part of the static defences. Russian gunners defended their batteries in Sevastopol with great courage and dedication, especially at the Malakoff.

Foot Artillery

Uniforms of the foot artillery generally followed the developments of those of the infantry. The dark green coats had black collars, cuffs and turnbacks, all piped in red. The red, rectangular cuff flaps had three brass buttons, there were nine buttons on the front of the coat. The red shoulder straps bore the brigade number in yellow; for junior officers ('Junkers') the shoulder straps were edged in thin gold braid. The helmet bore a brass eagle plate, with the brigade number pierced through for soldiers, in silver for officers, over

▲ *The Battle of Malakoff, during the Crimean War, was fought between the French and Russian armies on 7 September 1855 as a part of the siege of Sevastopol.*

crossed cannon barrels. Black, drooping horsehair plumes were worn for parades. Belts were white with brass fittings and infantry sabres were carried. The soldiers wore peakless, dark green forage caps, which had a black headband that had red piping around the crown and to top and bottom edges. On the front of the headband was the designation of the battery in yellow. Drummers wore the same distinctions as those of the infantry.

Officers' forage caps were of the same colours with small, black leather peaks and they had the imperial cockade, in black, orange and silver, at the front centre of the headband. Badges of rank for soldiers were shown by wide gold braid to top and front of the collar and to the top of the cuff. Officers wore gold-edged epaulettes, having red fields bearing the artillery brigade numerals in gold. They also had infantry pattern sashes, swords and sword straps. Trumpeters wore the same distinctions as the cavalry.

▼ GUIDON BEARER, 16TH FOOT ARTILLERY
BRIGADE, 1855 *The helmet plate is
worn with an honour scroll above
the eagle; the brigade
number appears on
helmet and buttons. This
officer cadet wears the
initials of his battery
(1st) on the band of his
forage cap, together
with the Cyrillic 'B'.*

▼ LIEUTENANT, 17TH ARTILLERY BRIGADE,
1855 *The gilt buttons would bear '17' over
crossed cannon barrels, as would the helmet
shield. Junior officers were allowed to wear
white mohair sashes in the field, instead of
the more expensive yellow silk versions. The
gold divisional
number is worn
on the red field
of the gold
epaulette.*

▼ PRIVATE, 2ND SAPPERS, 1853 *Sappers
wore silver buttons, belt plates and helmet
plates. The number '2' appeared on the
shield of the helmet plate and over crossed
axes on the buttons. The yellow divisional
number
appears on
red shoulder
straps.*

Horse Artillery

The horse artillery wore dragoon-style
uniforms in foot artillery colours. The
collars of their dun-coloured greatcoats
were black, piped red to top, front and
bottom with a red, rectangular patch
on each side, with a button at the rear
end. Horse artillery wore blue-grey
cavalry overalls with red side piping.
They wore white belts with brass
fittings, and their sabres ('shashkas')
were slung from their waist belts in the
Russian style, from the convex sides of
their sheaths.

Sappers (Engineers)

During the siege of Sevastopol, Russia's
engineers were used to build and
repair the defensive works around the
city. It was hard, dangerous, repetitive
work, much of it carried out under fire.
Due to their involvement in mining
and counter-mining operations,
the engineers are generally referred to
as 'sappers'. They wore line infantry
uniforms with black collars and cuffs
piped red, red rectangular, three-button
cuff flaps and white metal buttons.
Helmet plates were of white metal and
their regimental number was worn
over crossed axes. Black plumes were
worn for parades. Belts were white.
They were armed as the infantry.

FRENCH INFANTRY

France was once again ruled by an emperor, this time the nephew of Napoleon I. Napoleon III was approved as emperor shortly before the war with Russia and he used the opportunity to strut the international stage, sending an expeditionary force to the Crimea.

▼ OFFICER, 1ST ZOUAVES, 1854 *The twin gold Hungarian sleeve knots denote a lieutenant. He is in field service dress (without the gold parade epaulettes). The regimental number appeared on the front of the low-crowned kepi.*

Imperial Guards

Many French Army units had been in action in North Africa since 1815, so many commanders, officers and men had recent combat experience; this gave them a distinct advantage over their British colleagues. The French contingent in the Crimea performed very well, in particular their African regiments. The Imperial Guard (only raised in 1854) wore blue coats with white plastrons, red epaulettes, collar, cuffs and piping, white cuff flaps, yellow buttons. Flaming grenades on the collar. Trousers were blue until 1856, thence red. They had bearskin bonnets with brass plates bearing a grenade, red plumes. White belt with oblong brass plate bearing a flaming grenade. Voltigeurs of the Guard wore the shako with cockade, eagle badge, yellow side chevrons, red plume with yellow tip, blue tunic with pointed blue cuffs, with one button on the cuff and one above it, yellow collar and piping. Red epaulettes with yellow crescents, red trousers, white belt as before, white spats. The Chasseurs à pied of the Guard wore the same costume, but with yellow piping and green epaulettes, white buttons, pointed cuffs.

The Chasseurs were distinguished by yellow braid across the chest and yellow grenades on the collars. Zouaves of the Guard were dressed as for those of the line, with orange braid and the turban for full dress was white. This dress was supposed to be an imitation of native North African dress; it was not a reliable imitation but it was popular with the troops and became fashionable across the world.

Line Infantry

In 1822, the French line infantry wore a dark blue, single-breasted Spencer tunic, all regiments having brass buttons, all with red collars, contre-epaulettes, cuff flaps, turnbacks and piping. Grenadiers wore red epaulettes,

▲ TROOPER, 7TH DRAGOONS, 1854–68 *Regiment identity was shown by various colour combinations of the collars, lapels, cuff flaps and cuffs. On mounted duties in the field, the short dragoon musket was carried, butt forward, slung from the bandolier, across the right thigh. The baggy red trousers had been adopted in 1858.*

voltigeurs had green with yellow half moons. Centre companies wore blue contre-epaulettes with red half moons. In 1829 all regiments were issued red trousers. The collar had become open at the front in 1832. In 1852 the centre companies of infantry battalions received red epaulettes with green fringes. Two years later, the single-breasted frock coat replaced the Spencer. In 1855 the collar changed to yellow with a blue piping; in 1866 the piping was abandoned and yellow piping was added to the coat as were yellow cuff flaps. In 1867 the former elite companies lost their status and all now wore red epaulettes. In 1860 the coat skirts became short and the trousers wide and baggy.

▲ *In one of the Crimean War's defining moments, the French zouave Eugène Libaut installed the French flag on the top of the Russian redoubt in the Battle of Malakoff.*

The shako had progressively altered its shape; in 1835 it became taller and cylindrical; further alterations took place in 1837 and 1843; it was now blue with a red top band. In 1853 it was reduced in height and was smaller at the top than the headband.

Light Infantry

Generally the light infantryman's uniform followed the changes of that of the line, but with white buttons and pointed cuffs, yellow collar and piping, green epaulettes with yellow half moons. In 1840 they wore iron grey trousers, black belts, blue shakos with yellow trim. The regiments of light infantry were incorporated in to the line as the junior regiments numbered 75–102 in 1854.

◄ NATIVE OFFICER OF SAPHIS, 1854 *The first of such regiments was raised in Algeria in 1834. They fought in the Great War in similar costumes.*

► CORPORAL OF VOLTIGEURS, LINE INFANTRY, 1854 *The two orange bars on the forearm are his badges of rank, the two red chevrons on the upper arm are long service badges. The red and green epaulettes show that he is in the Voltigeurs.*

Zouaves

French zouaves wore a dark blue tunic of Arab cut, edged in red 12mm (½in) wide braid; the front bore two red arabesques, the top ends of which formed trefoils on the upper chest. The base of the arabesque formed a false pocket, lined in the regimental facing colour: 1st, red; 2nd, white; 3rd, yellow. A dark blue waistcoat was worn under the tunic. The fez (*chéchia*) was red with a sky blue cord and tassel. A green turban could also be worn. A sky blue waist sash was worn under the tunic. The baggy red breeches (*seroual*) were decorated with dark blue braid. Gaiters and their buttons were white, leatherwork was black.

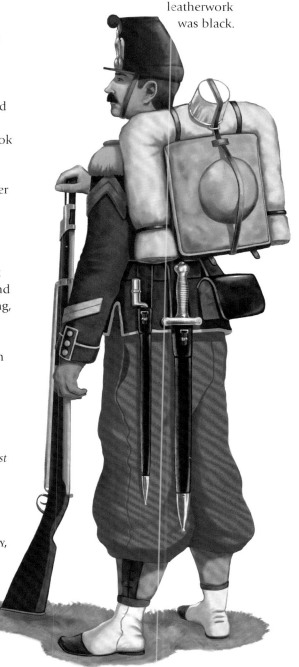

CHASSEURS D'AFRIQUE, FRENCH ARTILLERY AND ENGINEERS

The North African troops of France's Army were efficient, combat-hardened troops, while French artillery and engineers played an important role in the siege of Sevastopol.

Chasseurs d'Afrique

This North African cavalry was mainly French-officered and included many recruits of French origin resident in North Africa. The 4th Chasseurs d'Afrique took part in the Battle of Balaclava, on the western flank, helping the remnants of the Light Brigade to safety after their disastrous

charge. The uniform of this cavalry regiment was a red-topped kepi with sky blue band; above the band, the regimental number, white/silver braid, black peak. Sky blue dolman, silver buttons, black braid, light blue collar and cuffs. Black braid to collar and pointed cuffs. Officers had black bandoliers with silver picker equipment and black sabre slings, the men had white belts. The back seams of officers' sleeves were closed with 22 tiny silver ball buttons, along a black-edged slit, from cuff to elbow. They wore baggy red breeches with twin light blue side stripes. Arms were brass-hilted, light cavalry sabres in

◄ **PRIVATE, 1ST ENGINEER REGIMENT, 1854** *The cap badge retains the trophies of arms worn during the First Empire by these troops, as do their black facings. On the pouch was a flaming grenade badge. The method of carrying the brass-hilted sabre and ammunition pouch, on crossed bandoliers, was also a throwback to those days.*

▶ **JUNIOR OFFICER, FRENCH HORSE ARTILLERY, 1854** *This figure wears the traditional uniform, reminiscent of light cavalry, which was adopted by many horse artillery units throughout European armies. The grenade badge on the black bandolier and the crossed cannon barrels on the kepi show his regiment.*

◄ *An officer of the Chasseurs d'Afrique (right), in a low-crowned, red kepi and black bandolier, amid members of his regiment with white belts and the higher kepis.*

steel sheaths. Officers' rank badges were in the form of silver braid Austrian knots, which extended from cuff to shoulder.

The facings of the regiments prior to 1853 were: 1st – yellow piped light blue; 2nd – light blue collar and cuffs, yellow cuff flap; 3rd – yellow collar with light blue patches. After this date all regiments wore yellow collars, as did the newly raised 4th Regiment.

Squadron pompons on the front of the shako were: 1st – dark blue; 2nd – crimson; 3rd – dark green; 4th – sky blue; 5th – orange; 6th – tricolour.

Trumpeters, following a tradition current in many European armies, rode white horses.

Guard Artillery

Napoleon III's Imperial Guard (only recently raised in 1854) foot artillery wore the busby with red bag and cords and white over red plume, blue dolmans and breeches, red braid and pointed cuffs, three rows of yellow buttons, blue trousers with red side stripes. The horse artillery of the Guard wore the same, but with five rows of buttons, light cavalry equipment with blue sabretache, edged red, with a yellow eagle. There was black booting to the breeches. The blue breeches had a red stripe. Belts were white. The engineers wore blue uniforms with black facings and yellow buttons. The details of cut, shako and style followed the infantry pattern. Belts were white. Engineer officers played a key role in the siege, directing operations and supervising the digging of trenches and placing of mines, among other tasks.

Horse Artillery

France's mounted artillery had uniforms which followed the cavalry in style: blue with red facings and yellow buttons. The blue shako had brass crossed cannon barrels under the cockade at the front, with red top band, red pompon, side chevrons and cords. A drooping red plume was worn. The blue, double-breasted tunic had red piping to the blue collar and cuffs, to the lapels and bottom of the

► **OFFICER, HORSE ARTILLERY OF THE IMPERIAL GUARD, 1854** *The retention of the black braid hussar frogging on the chest of the dolman and the busby all point to the speed of movement of this highly mobile regiment and relate to that of the hussars. The two gold sleeve knots show he is a lieutenant.*

tunic, and red epaulettes were worn. There were blue grenades on the red turnbacks. Breeches were blue with twin, wide red side stripes and black leather booting up the insides of the legs. Belts were white and brass-hilted, light cavalry sabres in steel sheaths were carried. The black cartouche bore brass crossed cannon barrels under a flaming grenade.

Foot Artillery

Line foot artillery wore the same colours, but with dark blue infantry trousers with twin red stripes over white gaiters. They carried carbines.

Engineers

The engineers wore infantry shako with red trim and pompon and the engineers' brass badge (helmet, cuirass, crossed swords and a grenade pierced with the battalion number). The blue coats had black velvet collars, lapels, cuffs and cuff flaps, all piped red, yellow buttons with red epaulettes. Blue trousers with twin red stripes, white belts. In 1854 officers were given single-breasted tunics with black collars and cuffs and nine buttons on the chest.

SARDINIAN TROOPS

Sardinia entered the Crimean War on 1 January 1855 and sent a force of 10,000 men to fight with the allies against Russia. Although they missed the initial campaign, they fought well in the siege of Sevastopol.

Italian Politics

In 1854, the various states of the Italian peninsula were feeling their way toward unification, but Austria, which held a leading role in northern Italy, was very much opposed to this movement, known as

Sardinian Cavalry Distinctions		
Regiment	**Collar and cuffs**	**Trouser stripes**
Nizza	crimson	crimson
Savoy	black*	red*
Royal Piedmont	red	red
Genova	buff	buff
Novara	white	white
Aosta	red	red
Light	light blue	light blue
Cavalry (light blue shako with drooping, black horsehair plume. Officers wore a dark blue pelisse)		
* piped red		

the Risorgimento. In order to gain European support for this unification, King Victor Emmanuel II of Sardinia (the potential ruler of the united states of Italy), decided to send a contingent to the Crimea. He also traded his provinces of Nice and Savoy to France in order to gain French quiescence when he engaged the Austrians for control of northern Italy. His readiness to engage in international give-and-take was suitably rewarded.

Guard and Infantry

The cockade and officers' waist sashes were cornflower blue; in 1844 the infantry wore double-breasted frock coats, all regiments having white buttons. They had black leather

equipment on the Prussian model. On the shoulders were wings, blue for fusiliers, red for grenadiers, green for voltigeurs. The shako bore a heart-shaped badge with the regimental number, grenade or hunting horn, according to company. The Grenadier Guards wore black bearskins with brass grenade badge, red plume and cords and white lace loops to collar and cuffs. The Guards Rifles wore the shako with drooping plume, red over white; white loops to collar and cuffs, green shoulder wings.

◄ TROOPER, SAVOY DRAGOONS, 1854 *Here we see the full details of the rear of the trooper's coat, the piping on the pockets and all the equipment. The front of the helmet bears the silver cross of Savoy.*

► JUNIOR OFFICER OF BERSAGLIERI, 1854 *Officers in this regiment wore their sashes en bandoulier, like the cavalry, to emphasize the speed and dash with which they moved. The large cock's feather plumes are worn by the Bersaglieri even today. Officers wore brass scale epaulettes.*

This scheme was retained until 1860. The Bersaglieri wore a round hat with feathers. Apart from the palace troops, the infantry had 18 regiments, organized into 9 regional brigades, each brigade with its own facings.

Cavalry Regiments

From 1822 the brass helmet replaced the red shako. The helmet had a comb and drooping black horsehair crest; in 1843 this was changed for a steel helmet with black turban bearing the white cross of Savoy on the front, brass comb and chinscales. In 1843 the dark blue, double-breasted skirted tunic replaced the Napoleonic, waist-length style. All regiments wore white buttons. The grey-blue breeches had twin sidestripes; white belts were worn, and steel-hilted sabres were carried.

Artillery and Engineers

The foot artillery uniform followed that of the infantry; dark blue, double-breasted tunic, yellow buttons, black facings, yellow epaulettes with short yellow fringes. The shako had a yellow pompon, drooping black plume. Prior to 1845 the badge was a yellow eagle over crossed cannon barrels; it then changed to a white cross. The shako had brass chinscales. Belts were buff.

The horse artillery wore the same colour scheme, but with cavalry breeches, sabres and spurs. The sappers wore infantry uniform, faced crimson, crimson shoulder wings with crossed white axes on them, black shako plumes, black belts. In 1848 the shako gave way to a hat, like that of the Bersaglieri, with yellow pompon and drooping black plume.

▲ SAPPER, 1ST INFANTRY REGIMENT, THE SAVOY BRIGADE, 1853 *Sappers wore the grenadier company grenade on their shakos, instead of the usual shield with the regimental number. They also had the red shoulder wings. Note the pistol on his bandolier.*

▶ JUNIOR OFFICER OF THE HORSE ARTILLERY, 1854 *This lively figure conveys the dashing effect the horse artillery had on the move. The whole uniform is very French in style, including the wide band of gold braid around the top of the shako. The light blue silk waist sash is Savoy's national colour. His horse harness is of light cavalry style.*

OTTOMAN TROOPS

The Ottoman empire and Russia had fought for centuries, and the Crimean War was just one in a series of Russo-Turkish conflicts. The Ottoman empire provided troops for operations in the Crimea, and also fought in very harsh conditions in the Caucasus.

Organization

The Army had made repeated attempts since the 1790s to establish itself on a more European model. It was organized into corps (*ordu*) on the French model, each consisting of two divisions and an artillery brigade.

In 1820 Sultan Mahmud had given orders to increase the size of the Army; the Janissaries, by now a highly privileged corps, were ordered to send cadres to all the newly raised regiments. They regarded this as an insult and revolted. The rebellion was put down with customary severity and the 20,000-strong corps was killed. To emphasize this break with tradition, the sultan appeared in European dress, with a red fez. The infantry of the new army were ordered to wear dark blue jackets and trousers and skull caps. Artillery had light blue tunics and dark blue trousers; cavalry had green jackets, with red and white braid on the chest, red waist sash and blue trousers. Simpler uniforms were introduced by the time of the Crimean War.

Uniform Distinctions

Rank badges in the Ottoman Army make for a very complicated subject. Officers' rank badges were shown by a special ornament worn on both breasts (lieutenant general – two silver crescents, each with three silver stars; brigadier general – the same but with only two stars; lieutenant colonel – a golden crescent and golden stars; captain – gold crescent and silver stars; subalterns – just silver crescents) and by a special style of sabre, different for each rank. Generals' tunics were also liberally covered with gold lace embroidery and they also wore gold epaulettes, generals with bullion fringes, field officers with silk fringes. Belts were white except rifle regiments,

◄ **PRIVATE, INFANTRY RIFLE UNIT, 1854** *This man wears combat harness in black leather of German design and carries his rifle in the classic hunter's style. On his left hip he has a short spade.*

▲ **SERGEANT, FIRST ARTILLERY REGIMENT, 1854** *The uniform, with the hussar-style frogging on the tunic, points to a horse artillery unit, the blue tunic denoting that he belongs to the First Corps. His belt bears the almost ubiquitous flaming grenade of artillery units the world over.*

which had black leather equipment. NCOs also had black leather waist belts with silver rivet decoration.

At the time of the Crimean War, the Ottoman infantry wore a dark blue tunic and trousers (although overalls or grey linen trousers were also issued) with red stripes. The tunics had red facings, white piping. Rifle-armed troops wore black belts. The infantry wore shoes or even sandals (many went barefoot as supplies ran short), officers often had boots. A variety of greatcoats or hooded capes were worn in winter, as were civilian items. Most infantry wore the ubiquitous red fez, although, again, various local caps could be seen in the field. Cavalry sometimes had cloth wound around their turbans which could be worn under the chin. Cavalry and artillery wore camisoles, whose colour differed from

▲ GENERAL OFFICER, 1854 *Generals' uniforms in the Ottoman Army were richly embroidered in gold braid and tassels, and the equally elaborate trappings of his horse, together with his light scimitar-style blade, all indicate his high rank.*

◄ TROOPER, CAVALRY OF THE FIRST CORPS, 1854 *The dark blue tunic is of extremely simple design; he carries a sabre and carbine. Sergeants of cavalry and artillery wore large red chevrons, point up, on the upper left arm.*

corps to corps: 1, blue; 2, red; 3, purple; 4, brown; 5, buff; 6, light blue. Cavalry wore knee boots. All arms wore the red fez, with a brass button and dark blue tassel on top. For parades artillery wore a black velvet fez with a brass badge of the Koran.

Infantry and cavalry were armed with muskets of carbines, or with rifles. Leather equipment was rare and Ottoman troops had to make do with storing possessions in rolled blankets or haversacks and breadbags.

WARS OF GERMAN AND ITALIAN UNIFICATION

The wars that achieved the formation of the unified German and Italian nation states saw Austria's power and influence in Europe diminish, as it was sucked up by Prussia and the various Italian states. Austria's embarrassing defeat in the Austro-Prussian War of 1866 caused Italian patriots to take heart and to work (with France's implicit approval) to unify and expand their influence to the north-east, which was then under Austrian domination. Count Otto von Bismarck in Germany provided the political skill to forge a nation in arms, while Giuseppe Garibaldi campaigned for Italy's unification and freedom from Austrian rule. Italian unification was achieved in 1870; Germany's came a year later with the proclamation of the German empire at the Versailles Palace's Hall of Mirrors on 18 January 1871.

▲ *Giuseppe Garibaldi, a driving force in the unification of Italy.*

◄ *At the Battle of Artenay, south of Paris, on 10 October 1870, the I Bavarian Infantry Corps, under General von der Tann, overcame the Zouaves of the advanced guard of the Armée de la Loire, as the German armies closed on the French capital city.*

THE PRUSSO-DANISH WARS AND AUSTRO-PRUSSIAN ALLIANCE

Prussia and Denmark went to war in 1848, and the Danes fought the German states again in 1864. These wars revolved around the issue of who should own the disputed provinces of Schleswig and Holstein.

The Empty Peace

These provinces had revolted against Danish rule in 1848, and German support was forthcoming. An armistice in August 1848 did not entirely halt the revolt and on 6 July 1849, Danish forces attacked the small army of dissident Schleswig-Holstein, who were holding Fredericia. In a combined operation the Danes won a complete victory. Four days later a new ceasefire was agreed. A peace treaty was signed on 2 July 1850, with Prussia signing for the German Confederation. Within weeks, war broke out again, with the Danes winning a convincing victory at Isted on 25 July. On 1 January 1851 the First Schleswig War came to an end; the terms called for the Danes to administer Schleswig-Holstein, which Prussia rejected; the resultant peace became known as 'The Empty Peace'.

▼ *The Prussian Army crossing the frozen River Schlei at Arnis, 1 February 1864.*

The War of 1864

On 13 November 1863 the Danish government disclosed a new constitution in which Schleswig should be annexed again. Two days later, the childless King Frederick VII of Denmark died, without having signed the constitution. His successor, Prince Christian von Glücksburg (who ruled as Christian IX), signed it. The German states began to mobilize and send troops northward in early 1864. After a bloody campaign a ceasefire was agreed and a fruitless conference was held in London, where Danish intransigence led to a renewed bout of fighting on 26 June. In the next four days, the Germans overran all of Jutland and took Alsen. By 30 October 1864, the Danish king signed a treaty, revoking Danish claims to Schleswig-Holstein and Lauenburg. Schleswig and Lauenburg fell under Prussian control, Austria took Holstein.

Prussian victories were delivered by a very professional and efficient army organized along lines first established at the end of the Napoleonic Wars. In the 1860s Prussian troops fought the Danes then the Austrians; and went on to fight the French in 1870. They were victorious in all such conflicts.

▲ *The Austrian troops in the field wore sprigs of fir in their hats in the winter; in summer they wore oak leaves.*

Danish Infantry

Until 1842 Danish generals wore red coats, thence dark blue, of infantry cut with red piping, gold buttons and gold embroidery to the red collar and pointed cuffs. Badges of rank were golden epaulettes, thence shoulder cords, with from one to three large, six-pointed stars.

From 1842 the line infantry wore red, double-breasted tunics, with white buttons, light blue collar and pointed cuffs, all piped white. Trousers were light blue. The shako had a white loop and button, a red-white-red cockade and white chinscales. In 1848 the tunic was replaced by a dark blue, double-breasted coat, with dark blue collar and pointed dark blue cuffs piped red. Regimental numbers were worn on the shoulder straps in red. Belts were white; the trousers remained light blue. A dark blue kepi, with button, loop and cockade as before and red piping was introduced, later replaced with a light blue model, without piping.

Jägers wore dark green uniforms with red facings and yellow buttons; the battalion number on the shoulder straps in red. Their belts were black and they were armed with rifles and sword-bayonets. The Jägers were disbanded after the war of 1864. Non-commissioned officers wore from one

to three chevrons, in the button colour, on the lower sleeves. Officers wore fringeless epaulettes in the button colour, junior officers with one to three gold rosettes; field officers wore fringes and one to three stars; generals had bullion fringes and stars. The elite Life Guards Regiment retained the red,

single-breasted tunic, with light blue collar, shoulder straps and pointed cuffs, all piped white; Guards lace loops to collar and cuffs. Light blue trousers with a white side stripe; white belts. They wore bearskins with white chinscales and rayed star badge with a gilt crest.

▼ LIEUTENANT OF DANISH INFANTRY, 2ND BATTALION, 1848 *In this year, the Danish War Ministry ordered that the infantry should change from red coats to dark blue. As officers now stood out so starkly from their men, they made easy prey for enemy marksmen and were quickly ordered to revert to their old, red tunics. Rank was shown by the gold rosettes on their silver shoulder cords.*

▼ GUNNER, DANISH FOOT ARTILLERY, 1864 *Dark blue facings and brass buttons had long been the hallmark uniform of the artillery. He carries a short, straight sword, known in German armies as the* Faschinenmesser, *which could be used for cutting trees for building artillery positions or improving tracks on soft ground. In about 1870, the artillery uniform became dark blue with crimson collar patches and piping, brass buttons and black belts.*

▼ RIFLEMAN, DANISH 1ST JÄGER CORPS, 1864 *The unit designation appeared in red on the dark green shoulder straps of the 'Litewka', a tunic-like garment that was popular in the Prussian Army of the Wars of Liberation of 1813 to 1815. This figure wears the traditional black leatherwork of the rifleman. The rifle corps were disbanded after this campaign, when all infantry were issued with rifled firearms.*

Light Dragoon Regiments 1864		
Regiment	Collar, lapels and cuffs	Piping
Leib-Regiment Light Dragoons	black	yellow
Jutland Dragoons	green	none
Finnish Dragoons	light blue	yellow

◄ **DANISH JUNIOR OFFICER OF THE HUSSAR REGIMENT, 1864** *The light blue dolman was introduced in 1854; prior to that, collar and cuffs were crimson. Officers still wore crimson pelisses with black Astrakhan fur trimming, but the men now wore red, with black lambskin trim. The cypher 'C9' (Christian IX) is on the shield on the officer's bandolier.*

There was also a regiment of hussars, which wore a busby, light blue dolman with crimson collar and cuffs, white braid and buttons, crimson and white barrel sash, crimson pelisse with black fur. The shabraque was crimson, with light blue wolf's tooth edging, the sabretache crimson with the royal cipher in white. In 1845 the dolman became all light blue with white braid; the men wore red pelisses, the officers wore crimson. In 1870 the dolman was replaced by the light blue Attila with five rows of lace on the chest and a low-crowned, black kepi with short white plume and cords.

Danish Technical Troops
The Danish artillery wore infantry dress: red coats, with blue collar, cuffs and turnbacks, then yellow piping and buttons, dark blue trousers, black belts. The headgear followed that of the infantry. Engineers were dressed as for the artillery, but with black collar patches, red piping and yellow buttons.

► **TROOPER, JUTLAND DRAGOONS, 1864** *By this time, the Danish heavy cavalry regiments had been converted to light dragoons, using smaller, cheaper horses than before. This uniform is of fairly international cut, but in the Danish colours of red tunics. The metal shoulder scales are Bavarian style.*

Danish Cavalry
The cavalry wore white coats with white buttons, belts and yellow turnbacks; with distinctive facings being shown on collars, lapels and cuffs. In 1830 they wore a crested helmet of the Bavarian style, with yellow metal fittings but in 1848 this *Raupenhelm* was replaced by a closer-fitting, black leather helmet with a white metal comb, front plate, chinscales and trim to the peak. Light blue breeches with black leather boots were worn. Shabraques were red with white trim and crowned royal cipher ('F6' until 1839, thence 'C8'; ' F7' from 1848 until 1863, when it became 'C9')

▲ **DANISH CAVALRY SADDLE AND HARNESS, 1864** *Most armies used the double rein combination for their cavalry mounts. The saddle was the conventional 'English' style. Under the front of the shabraque was a pair of pistol holsters, usually with a blanket folded across the top. The square portmanteau held the rider's small kit.*

Prussian Guards Infantry pre-1866

Until 1897 there were four Foot Guards regiments and five Grenadier Guards regiments as well as the Guards Fusilier Regiment, each of two grenadier and a fusilier battalion. They wore line infantry uniforms but with two white lace loops to collars and Swedish cuffs. There was also the Guards Jäger Battalion and the Guards Schützen Battalion.

The grenadiers wore white belts and plumes (for parades), the fusiliers, Jägers and Schützen wore black; musicians wore red plumes and swallows' nests on the shoulders, in the facing colour, edged and decorated in the button colour. Drums were brass, with

hoops decorated in red and white triangles. NCOs wore lace in the button colour to collars and cuffs, white sabre straps with four black stripes and black and white tassels. From 1846, sergeants and above wore a large button at the rear of the collar patch, with the Prussian eagle upon it. Feldwebels (equivalent to warrant officer) wore sergeant's distinctions, carried no muskets and had officer-pattern swords and sword knots.

Officers' sashes were silver with two black lines along them; the silver tassels had a central core of black threads. Infantry officers of units wearing white belts carried straight swords in black sheaths with gilt firings, those with units wearing black belts carried curved sabres. The silver sabre strap had three black stripes on it and a silver tassel.

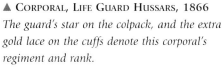

▲ **CORPORAL, LIFE GUARD HUSSARS, 1866** *The guard's star on the colpack, and the extra gold lace on the cuffs denote this corporal's regiment and rank.*

◄ **NON-COMMISSIONED OFFICER, PRUSSIAN INFANTRY REGIMENT NO 20, 1848** *This regiment was part of the III Army Corps in this campaign and thus wore red shoulder straps and white piping to the red cuff flap. The Waffenrock (service dress tunic) was dark blue with red patches on the front. The regimental number was worn on the shoulder strap, in gold for officers and in yellow wool for soldiers.*

▶ **SUTLERESS (MARKETTENDERIN) LIFE GUARD HUSSARS, 1866** *As in other armies, a licensed sutler or sutleress – a civilian with official licence to sell food and drink to troops – wore regimental uniform.*

From 1860 to 1866 all Prussian line infantry wore dark blue coats with dark blue collars, red collar patches, cuffs and cuff flaps; they were distinguished according to which corps they served in. In March 1867 this scheme was slightly altered; collars, cuffs and cuff flaps were now all red, and corps were distinguished by the colour of the shoulder straps and cuff flap piping.

Prussian Line Infantry pre-1866

Grenadier regiments had two grenadier battalions and a fusilier battalion (all with black plumes), the fusilier regiments had three fusilier battalions, the other regiments

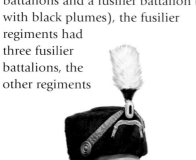

had two musketeer battalions and a fusilier battalion. The colours of belts and plumes were as for the Guard.

By 1848 the infantry wore a dark blue, single-breasted, hip-length tunic with eight buttons on the front, two on the cuffs (or three on the cuff flaps) and three on each hip-pocket flap. Certain regiments wore initials or numbers on their shoulder straps. The standing collar had patches in the regimental colour on each side. Those troops who wore black collar patches (artillery, engineers, Schützen and the 1st Kürassiers), had red or white piping to front and top of the collar and to the rear end of the patch.

Trousers were dark grey with a red side piping. In 1870 they became dark blue. It was common to wear the trousers in the boots in the field. In 1843 the high-crowned, coal-scuttle, black leather helmet was introduced; chinscales were of pinchbeck (an alloy of zinc and copper); all other metal parts were in the button colour. The Guards had a silver star on the chest of the eagle. Later, the minor German states had eagles with their own scrolls and inscriptions. The height of the helmet was reduced in 1857 and 1860.

For the line, the helmets were the same except as

from 4 July 1860 regiments 1–12 were grenadier regiments. On the breast of their eagles was a round plate bearing 'FWR' entwined. They wore black plumes for parades. Other regiments bore 'FR' on the eagles' breasts.

The following regiments received a battle honour for their part in the storming of the Düppel redoubts on 19 April 1864: the 3rd and 4th Foot Guards, 3rd, 4th and 8th Grenadiers, 13th, 15th, 18th, 24th, 35th, 53rd, 55th, 60th and 64th infantry regiments, 3rd and 7th Jäger battalions, 3rd Dragoons, 3rd Hussars, 11th Ulans and several artillery regiments. Prussian infantry

▶ Colour Bearer, Infantry Regiment No 78, Field Service Dress, 1870
This regiment was also part of X Corps, hence the white shoulder straps and light blue cuff piping. Note the heraldic button on the collar. He wears his blanket roll over his left shoulder and the black oilskin cover of the painted flag as a bandolier over his right. The brass cap is visible in front of his left hand.

◀ Sergeant, 2nd Westphalian Hussar Regiment No 11, 1864 *This was the old Lancers of Berg; he wears the Prussian cockade and silver and black sabre strap of his rank.*

and their allies wore a white armband in the campaign of 1870 to distinguish themselves from the French troops.

Prussian Jägers and Schützen post-1866

Apart from the Guards Jäger Battalion (with the usual lace decoration to collar and cuffs) there were also eight line battalions up to 1866. Battalions 5–8 were raised in 1845 from the Schützen battalions. These were later joined by the 9th, 10th and 11th battalions. In 1870, the 12th and 13th Reserve Jäger Battalions were added, then disbanded and the numbers remained vacant.

The Mecklenburg Jäger Battalion became the 14th in 1873, wearing dark blue coats, green facings, piped red and white buttons. The number 14 was worn in red on the green shoulder strap. Other Jäger battalions were uniformed as the line, but with dark green tunics, red collar and Swedish cuffs, dark green turnbacks piped red, yellow buttons. From 1845 they all wore red shoulder straps with the battalion number on them in yellow.

▼ CORPORAL, 1ST LANDWEHR HUSSAR REGIMENT, 1866 *The Landwehr cross on the mirliton, and the silver lace on the cuffs, identify this cavalryman. The use of the mirliton at this date was very rare.*

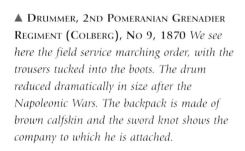

▲ DRUMMER, 2ND POMERANIAN GRENADIER REGIMENT (COLBERG), NO 9, 1870 *We see here the field service marching order, with the trousers tucked into the boots. The drum reduced dramatically in size after the Napoleonic Wars. The backpack is made of brown calfskin and the sword knot shows the company to which he is attached.*

▶ SENIOR NCO, LANDWEHR INFANTRY REGIMENT OF THE ARMY OF THE MAIN, FIELD SERVICE DRESS, 1870 *The red shoulder straps and no piping to the cuff flaps indicate that this figure is from the IV Corps. He has a green glass water bottle in a leather case and his notebook is stuffed into the front of his tunic. He wears the old Prussian shako of 1860. Note the officer-pattern sword knot.*

Prussian Landwehr post-1866

Landwehr was composed of older recruits, or those exempted from the front line. They performed garrison duties, or were used as escorts. They wore uniforms which resembled those of their parent arm of service. On their helmets they wore plates with the Landwehr cross on the eagle's chest.

Prussian Cavalry post-1866

Prussian cavalry was divided into light and heavy. Light cavalry officers wore curved sabres in steel sheaths. Their sabre fist straps were of black leather with three silver stripes, the tassel was silver. Apart from the hussars, cavalry officers wore a bandolier in the button colour, fittings the same, and a small black pouch. Guards officers wore the silver and enamel Guards star on the pouch (the Neumark Dragoons in gold), other regiments wore the crowned golden cypher 'FWR'.

By 1832 officers wore epaulettes in the button colour, field officers with thin gold/silver fringes. Colonels and captains wore two gold stars, lieutenant colonels and first lieutenants wore one. By 1867 the fields of the epaulettes were the same colour as the men's shoulder straps; the crowns, numbers and initials were of gold. Epaulette backing was red for most units, pink for those with pink facings, crimson for those with crimson. Cavalry wore dark grey overalls in the field with red side piping.

Prussian Kürassiers post-1866

By 1866 there were the Garde du Corps, Guard Kürassiers and eight line regiments; all had five squadrons, except the Garde du Corps, which had ten. From 1843 the armoured regiments wore single-breasted white tunics, with white collar, facings on the collar patches, Swedish cuffs, piping to the white shoulder straps, pocket flap, sleeve rear seam and hooks and eyes to close. The front of the coat, collars and cuffs were edged to top and front/back respectively, with white braid edged in the colour of the collar patch.

In 1866 the Kürassier Regiment Nr 1 was elevated to the Guard, becoming the Leib-Kürassier-Garde. The old black leather helmet with brass fittings, black comb and crest, was replaced in 1843

◀ TROOPER, GARDE DU CORPS, 1870
The high leather boots cover grey breeches with a narrow red side stripe. The steel spurs were of the buckle-on style. The brass helmet bears the eight-pointed silver star with an eagle in the circular centre. The cuirass is of steel, with brass plates overlaid front and back. The cuirass shoulder straps are covered with brass chains. His white bandolier has brass buckle, tip and slide. Note the piping in the facing colour to the back pocket flap.

with metal helmets, with two peaks, chinscales and a spike. Guards regiments and Regiment Nr 6 had them in yellow metal, the others in steel. Fittings were steel on the yellow helmets, brass on the steel helmets. For parades the two Guards regiments wore a crowned Prussian eagle. On their helmets they wore the star of the Order of the Black Eagle. Kürassier officers' epaulettes had backing in the colour of their collar patches.

Prussian Dragoons post-1866

Until October 1866 there were eight regiments of dragoons. They were then increased to 16 regiments. In 1867 the Mecklenburg cavalry became the 17th and 18th regiments and the Oldenburg cavalry became the 19th. The dragoons wore the helmet with a special, white metal eagle badge, the wings extending high to each side. Their coats were cornflower blue, the facings varied from regiment to regiment. The two Guards regiments wore white plumes, the line wore black. Belts were white.

Prussian Lancers post-1870

From October 1866 there were the 3 Guards and 16 line regiments, wearing the dark blue Polish costume, with tight-fitting tunic (kurtka) and the epaulettes in brass (silver for the 15th) on facing-coloured backing. From 1844 the sides of the square top of the czapka were in the colour of the epaulette fields, the top, head band and peak were black, chinscales were brass. A Prussian eagle (in the button colour) was worn on the front of the upper part. Cap lines and piping to the czapka sides were white (black and white/silver for

Prussian Dragoon Distinctions

Regiment	Facings	Buttons
1st Guards	poppy red	yellow
2nd Guards	poppy red	white
1st	poppy red	yellow
2nd	black	yellow
3rd	pink	white
4th	purple	yellow
5th	poppy red	white
6th	black	white
7th	pink	yellow
8th	lemon yellow	yellow
9th	white	yellow
10th	white	white
11th	crimson	yellow
12th	crimson	white
13th	poppy red	yellow
14th	black	yellow
15th	pink	white
16th	yellow	white
17th	poppy red	yellow
18th	poppy red	yellow
19th	black	white

NCOs and officers). From 1842 the czapka top half was reduced in size and in 1867 the tops were black leather.

▶ **NCO, NEUMÄRKISCHEN DRAGOON REGIMENT NO 3, FIELD SERVICE DRESS, 1870** *The dragoons adopted the helmet in 1842, but retained the old style when other regiments adopted the new models in 1857 and 1860. They also wore a special pattern of eagle plate on the helmet, dating back to the Wars of Liberation (1813–15). Helmet fittings were in the regimental button colour, but all regiments had brass chinscales. His status as sergeant is shown by the silver lace to collar and cuffs and to the black and silver tassel to his sabre strap. Dragoons used German, or heavy cavalry, style saddlery with a light blue shabraque with rounded corners, a wide edging and an outer piping in the facing colour.*

Prussian Hussars post-1866

From 1866 there were 16 regiments of Prussian hussars as well as a regiment of Life Guards. Dress followed the traditional style imitating that of Hungarian cavalry. From 1833 the collars and cuffs of the dolman were in the dolman colour. The dolman had three rows of ball buttons on the chest and piping to rear seams. NCOs wore five rows of buttons and gold/silver lace to collar and cuffs. Officers had gold/silver shoulder cords (plain for junior officers, plaited for field officers); colonels and captains wore

▼ **NCO, GUARDS PIONEER BATTALION, 1870**
This figure is in field service dress. Guards status is indicated by the white buttonhole loops to collar and cuffs. Were he to have been a private, he would have worn two such laces on the collar; as he wears rank lace to the collar, he wears only one such lace. Guards units wore white metal helmet fittings, but brass chinscales. He carries the rifled, rear-loading needle gun.

Hussars in 1866

Regiment	Dolman or attila	Collars and cuffs	Buttons and lace	Busby bag
Life Guards	poppy red	poppy red*	yellow	poppy red
1st Leib **	black	poppy red	white	poppy red
2nd Leib ***	black	black	white	white
3rd	poppy red	poppy red	white	poppy red
4th	brown	yellow	yellow	yellow
5th	blood red	dark blue	white	madder red
6th	green	poppy red	yellow	poppy red
7th	light blue	poppy red	yellow	poppy red
8th	dark blue	light blue	white	light blue
9th	light blue	light blue	yellow	light blue
10th	green	light blue	yellow	purple
11th	green	poppy red	white	poppy red
12th	light blue	light blue	white	white
13th	light blue	light blue	white	poppy red
14th	dark blue	dark blue	white	poppy red
15th	dark blue	dark blue	white	yellow
16th	light blue	light blue	white	yellow

* piped yellow. ** white shoulder straps, skull badge to busby.
*** red shoulder straps, white skull badge to busby.

Lancers

Regiment	Collar, cuffs and piping	Epaulette fields	Buttons
1st Guards	poppy red*	white	white
2nd Guards	poppy red**	red	yellow
3rd Guards	yellow*	yellow	white
1st	poppy red	white	yellow
2nd	poppy red	poppy red	yellow
3rd	poppy red	yellow	yellow
4th	poppy red	light blue	yellow
5th	poppy red	white	white
6th	poppy red	poppy red	white
7th	poppy red	yellow	white
8th	poppy red	light blue	white
9th	white	white	yellow
10th	crimson	crimson	yellow
11th	yellow	yellow	yellow
12th	light blue	light blue	yellow
13th	white	white	white
14th	crimson	crimson	white
15th	yellow	yellow	white
16th	light blue	light blue	white

* with white lace loops. ** with yellow lace loops.

two stars, lieutenant colonels and first lieutenants one star; the second lieutenant wore no stars. The pelisse was in the dolman colour with white fur trim, although from 1832 this became black.

In 1853 the dolman and pelisse were replaced by the laced tunic known as the Attila. Dark blue breeches, white bandoliers and plumes and fur busbies (with coloured bags, cockades, plumes and, in some regiments, badges) were worn. Colours varied from regiment to regiment. The men had black sabretaches on black slings, with the crowned cipher 'FWR' (in the button colour). Officers' coloured sabretaches were: Guards, 1st, 3rd, 6th, 7th, 13th and 14th – poppy red; 2nd and 5th – black; 4th – brown; 8th – dark blue; 9th 10th and 12th – light blue; 11th – green; 15th and 16th – yellow. Sashes were black and white.

Prussian Technical Troops post-1866

The uniforms of the foot artillery followed the style of the infantry pattern, with black facings piped red, dark blue, rectangular cuff flaps and yellow buttons. Poppy-red shoulder straps with yellow brigade numbers, and poppy-red turnbacks were worn. Musicians of line batteries wore black swallows' nests with yellow braid decoration. The Guard artillery had yellow lace loops to collars and cuffs. Musicians of the Guard were black, with

yellow braid and short, yellow fringes. In 1870 both horse and foot artillery wore hussar-style costume, with a blue kepi with red piping, blue dolman, red collar and pointed cuffs, yellow buttons and black braid.

Horse artillery followed cavalry trends, but in artillery colours and with Swedish cuffs. Their turnbacks were dark blue with red piping. The helmets originally had brass spikes, but these were quickly replaced by balls. The Guard batteries had brass eagles with the Guard's star, the line just the eagle and scrolls. Belts were white. Engineers had black velvet facings piped red, white buttons and Swedish cuffs; belts were black. Guard engineers had white lace loops to collars and cuffs.

▼ DRIVER, FIELD ARTILLERY, FOOT BATTERY, FIELD SERVICE DRESS, 1864 *At this time the front badge worn on the helmet was still the heraldic Prussian eagle, with 'FR' on the breast. In 1867 the collar of the tunic became all black, with a red piping.*

THE AUSTRO-PRUSSIAN WAR OF 1866

Prussian domination of Germany was assured by victory over the Danes and then the Austrians (with some allied German states) in 1866. Austria's unhappy positioned was augmented by Italian pressure on Austrian troops from northern Italy. This furthered the cause of German unification, soon to be crowned following victory over France. Italy's painful route to unification was completed with the occupation of Rome in 1870.

The Prussian king, Wilhelm I, and his chancellor, Graf Otto von Bismarck, accused Austria of violating the Gastein Convention on their joint rule of the duchies of Schleswig and Holstein, thus provoking the war that he wanted. Baden, Bavaria, Hanover, Hessen-Darmstadt, Hessen-Cassel, Nassau, Saxony and Württemberg joined Austria against Prussia in this war. Italy and the minor German states of Brunswick Lippe-Detmold, Oldenburg, Saxony-Anhalt, the Ducal Saxon states, Mecklenburg and Schwarzburg, sided with Prussia. Napoleon III of France assured Bismarck of France's neutrality; Britain was disinterested.

The Prussians marched into Saxony unopposed, as the Saxon Army had moved south, into Bohemia, to join up with their Austrian allies. On 3 July the Prussians caught the Austro-Saxons in a cramped position, with their backs against the upper Elbe between Sadowa and Königgrätz, with only one bridge over that river, and defeated them convincingly. This was the most significant European battle for decades, as it led to dramatic regrouping of the German states under Prussian leadership and the relegation of Austria to a peripheral role in this power bloc. Bismarck at once turned his mind and his energy to welding the newly acquired German states firmly into place in the Prussian military machine and began to work on plans for the inevitable conflict with France, which was to come.

Prussia annexed Hanover, Hessen-Kassel, Holstein, Nassau and the city-state of Frankfurt. Bismarck demanded that Austria cede Venetia to Italy and withdraw from the German Federation, thus leaving it under firm Prussian domination. Napoleon III was a party to these negotiations; he insisted that Prussia's North German Confederation must be limited to the northern bank of the River Main, which bisects Germany. Bismarck complied – and then continued to plan his agenda for France's downfall.

▼ *Otto von Bismarck of Prussia and Emperor Napoleon III meet at the Chaussee von Donchery on 2 September 1870.*

AUSTRO-HUNGARIAN TROOPS

Austro-Hungarian troops fought the French in Italy in 1859, and the Prussians and Italians in 1866.

Infantry

In 1866 the Austrian infantry consisted of 80 regiments, each of 4 battalions. Their facings and buttons are shown in the table.

They were armed with the

Austro-Hungarian Infantry Distinctions

Facings	German Regiments		Hungarian Regiments	
	Yellow buttons	White buttons	Yellow buttons	White buttons
Dark red	1	18	52	53
Sky blue	4	3	32	19
Grass green	8	28	61	62
Apple green	9	54		79
Ash grey	11	24	51	33
Rose red	13		5	6
Black	14	58	26	38
Madder red	15	74	44	34
Sea green	21	87	70	25
Emperor yellow	27	22	2	31
Pike grey	30	49	76	69
Lobster red	35	20	71	67
Light blue	40	75	72	29
Scarlet	45	80	37	39
Red brown	55	17	68	78
Dark brown		7	12	
Steel green	56	47	48	60
Pale red	57	36	65	66
Parrot green		10	46	50
Orange yellow	59	42	64	63
Sulphur yellow		41	16	
Cherry red	73	77	43	23

Lorenz M 1854, muzzle-loading rifled musket, which was no match for the Prussian needle gun. The uniform consisted of white, single-breasted coats; the Hungarian regiments wore

◀ REGIMENTAL DRUM MAJOR, 2ND (HUNGARIAN) LINE INFANTRY REGIMENT, KAISER ALEXANDER VON RUSSLAND, 1849

There was much variety among regiments as to how they dressed their musicians, as can be seen by the hussar-style lacing on this infantryman's tunic and the elaborate gold decoration to the whole costume. The regiment's facing colour was emperor yellow. Note the gold tassels. Some regiments gave their bandsmen reversed lapels in the facing colour. His rank is shown by the two bands of gold lace around the top of his shako, which in 1860 was altered to the smaller model, with a narrowed top. In 1850, the tunic became the modern, service dress style, but double-breasted, without turnbacks.

white lace 'bears' claws' on their cuffs and light blue breeches, decorated with black and yellow braid in short boots. The coat was replaced by the double-breasted tunic in 1849, with facings shown on collar, cuffs, shoulder straps and piping. In 1868 a single-breasted, dark blue tunic came into service, which was retained until the early years of the 20th century. German regiments wore white breeches and black gaiters until the 1830s, when light blue trousers with a white side stripe replaced them. Grenadiers wore black bearskin bonnets with a peak and large brass front plate, which was replaced by a brass grenade in 1840. In about 1850 these bonnets were withdrawn and the only badge distinguishing the grenadiers was now the brass grenades on the white bandoliers. A stovepipe shako was introduced in 1840, with black and yellow cockade and pompon. In 1853 it was replaced by a lower model in the form of a truncated cone, having a brass double eagle badge under the black-within-yellow pompon. Badges of rank were worn in the form of yellow/gold braid bands on the top of the sides of the shako.

Officers had the same system, but with gold edging to the peak. Austrian generals wore white tunics often with a light dove-grey coat. Rank was shown by combinations of silver stars on the gold braid at the front of the collar. Twin red trouser stripes were also worn. On one side of the body of the tassel of the sword strap was the double eagle, on the other, the crowned cipher 'F1'.

After the Italian campaign of 1859 falling collars were brought in. Officers now wore their yellow and black sashes over the shoulder, until 1868, when it reverted to being worn around the waist. Badges of rank for officers and NCOs were in the form of six-pointed gold or silver stars and silver/gold braid worn on the collar,

as well as the sword strap, gold braid to the shako and the officers' black and yellow sashes.

Border Infantry Regiments

These units were recruited in the Balkan region and wore Hungarian regimental uniforms, but they were traditionally issued with dark brown tunics made of local cloth and black belts. Facings and buttons are shown in the table right. In 1871 the Grenz infantry regiments were incorporated into the line.

▼ FIELD OFFICER, GERMAN INFANTRY, REGIMENT NO 14, 1859 *The badges of rank worn include the wide and narrow gold bands at the top of the shako, the double gold bands on the collar and the gold cuff edging. The imperial cipher 'FI' was worn in the black centre of the pompon on the shako, on the side of the gold bullion tassel of the sword strap and in the rear corner of the red shabraque, which also had a gold braid edging.*

Border Regiments

Regiment	Facings	Buttons
1 Liccaner	violet	yellow
2 Ottocaner	violet	white
3 Oguliner	orange	yellow
4 Szluiner	orange	white
5 Warasdiner Kreutzer	lobster red	yellow
6 Warasdiner St Georger	lobster red	white
7 Brooder	pink	yellow
8 Gradiscaner	pink	white
9 Peterwardeiner	grey	yellow
10 1st Banal	crimson	yellow
11 2nd Banal	crimson	white
12 Deutsch-Banater	sky blue	white
13 Wallachisch-Illyrisch	light grey	white
14 1st Szeckler	rose red	yellow
15 2nd Szeckler	rose red	white
16 1st Wallachisch	poplar green	yellow
17 2nd Wallachisch	poplar green	white

Cavalry

Austro-Hungarian cavalry consisted of heavy and light regiments. The mid-19th century was a period of flux for cavalry, but they still continued to resemble the mounted troops of the Napoleonic era.

Jägers

The Tyrolean Jäger Regiment wore pike-grey tunics and breeches, grass-green collar, cuffs and turnbacks and yellow buttons with black belts. Instead of the shako worn by most of the Austro-Hungarian infantrymen, Jägers wore the Corsican hat, with the left-hand brim turned up and dark green, cock's feather plume. The hat gradually reduced in size over the years. Volunteer (or Freikorps) Jäger units also made use of this traditional pike-grey colour for their tunics.

▼ **AUSTRIAN GENERAL, UNDRESS UNIFORM, 1859** *This is the practical, everyday dress of Austrian generals. The Feldzeugmeister rank (general with technical responsibilities) is shown by a triangle of three six-pointed silver stars on the gold braid at the front of the collar. The pattern of this gold lace is still used by Austrian and Russian officers today. Austrian generals also still wear the twin red trouser stripes. On one side of the body of the sword strap tassel was a double eagle, on the other, a crowned cipher 'F1'.*

▼ **PRIVATE, HUNGARIAN INFANTRY, REGIMENT KÖNIG VON PREUSSEN NO 34, 1866** *Madder-red facings and white buttons were the hallmark of this regiment, as well as the pointed cuffs to the tunic and the traditional, light blue Hungarian breeches, with their black and yellow braid decoration, which was also worn on the fronts of the thighs. He is shown in winter full service marching order, with large mess-tins strapped to the backpack. The water bottle is the same pattern as used in the Napoleonic War.*

▼ **JUNIOR OFFICER, HUNGARIAN INFANTRY, REGIMENT GROSSHERZOG VON HESSEN NO 14, 1866** *This regiment had black facings and yellow buttons. The facings and a button were worn on the collar patches of the greatcoat. For comfort in winter conditions, the officer is wearing knee high boots. Status is shown by his sash, his gold and black sabre strap and by gold braid bands around the top of his shako and the six-pointed stars (in the button colour) on the collar patches of his jacket.*

Kürassier Distinctions

Kürassiers	Facings	Buttons
1 Kaiser	dark red	white
2 Herzog Franz	black	white
3 Herzog Albert	purple	yellow
4 Kronprinz Ferdinand	grass-green	white
5 Sommariva	light blue	white
6 Liechtenstein	black	yellow
7 Lothringen	dark blue	white
8 Hohenzollern-Hechingen	scarlet	yellow

◀ LIEUTENANT, STEYER ALPEN-JÄGERS, 1866
This uniform is a direct connection to the Tyrolean Jägers of the Napoleonic era. This unit was a Freikorps (volunteer corps) raised in the province of Steyermark in the centre of present-day Austria. The usual army badges of rank are worn on the collar and he wears the black silk cravat with gold fringes used by the Austrian corps in Mexico in 1864–67. Officers' hats were edged in gold, those of the NCOs in yellow silk. This unit used buglers to give signals.

▶ LIEUTENANT, KÜRASSIER REGIMENT
KRONPRINZ FERDINAND NO 4, 1859 *The regiment's identity is shown by the grass-green collar tabs (Paroli), with a regimental button in the rear corner, cuffs and piping to the tunic and the white buttons. The short gilt peak on the cuirass indicates that this man is a junior officer, as do the two silver stars on his collar fronts. The crouching lions on the gilt sides of his comb were the same pattern as had been used in 1813. The cuirass was worn for the last time in this campaign.*

Light Cavalry

Austro-Hungarian light cavalry had consisted of chevauxleger regiments, as well as hussars, but the former had been disbanded in 1851. Most were converted into Ulan regiments, although one regiment (the 4th Chevauxlegers) was converted into the 7th Dragoons.

Dragoons

The dragoon regiments also wore white coats, breeches, belts and buttons. They were converted into Kürassiers in 1860, as shown below, and then back to dragoons in 1867. In 1840 the white breeches were replaced by light blue trousers. In 1850 the double-breasted tunic was introduced and the helmet crest was abandoned. The coats became light blue in 1868 and the trousers became red. In 1868 the facings of the dragoon regiments were: 1st, black; 2nd, dark blue; 3rd, deep red; 4th, light red; 5th, dark green; 6th, light blue.

Hussars

Austro-Hungarian hussar regiments, consisting mostly of Hungarian personnel, based their uniforms on traditional styles (a style imitated across Europe). A distinctive laced tunic was worn, known as a

Kürassiers

These heavy cavalrymen wore the black leather helmet with comb, black over yellow crest and gilt front plates and chinscales, white tunics, with facings on the collar patches, white breeches and knee boots. Only the front plate of the black cuirass was worn. The cuirasses were withdrawn in 1860 and in 1868 the Kürassier regiments were converted to the 1st–8th Dragoons.

In 1840 the white breeches had been replaced by light blue trousers with a white side stripe. In 1850 the helmet crest was abandoned and the tunic with skirts was introduced.

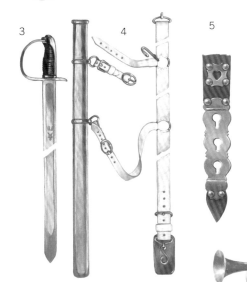

◄ Kürassier Officer's Kit, 1850 *1 Junior officer's cuirass. 2 Cuirass interior. 3 The straight-bladed sword. 4 Belt and steel sheath of cuirassier and dragoon regiments. 5 Gilt buckle of an officer's cuirass strap.*

In 1860 the 1st and 2nd Volunteer Hussars were raised; they became the 13th and 14th Hussars in 1862. In 1863 the headgear became the kutsma, with a brown fur headband and coloured cloth bag. Some regiments retained the older-style shako during the war against Prussia. All regiments now wore madder-red breeches.

In 1873 a low-crowned shako was introduced with black peak, head and top bands. The body was in regimental colours used for the kutsma bag.

dolman, as well as a fur-edged cape (pelisse). These were replaced by a simpler laced tunic, or Attila, in 1850, with rank being shown by gold or silver lace on the cuffs and insignia on the collar. Previously all regiments had worn black and yellow braid to dolman and pelisse. Belts were white, sashes black and yellow, the sabretache and shabraque were red with the crowned cipher 'F1' and a black-yellow-black edging. Grey overalls were often worn in the field. Steel-hilted sabres were worn in steel sheaths.

► Corporal Trumpeter, Dragoon Regiment Prinz Eugen von Savoyen, No 5 1859 *The light blue trousers replaced the white breeches in 1840; regimental facings were worn on collar, cuffs and piping to the rear of the jacket. In 1850 the black and yellow crest was removed from the comb of the helmet. In 1867 the regiment became the 13th Dragoons. Although the traditional red helmet crest of the trumpeters had been abandoned in 1850, the red swallows' nests, decorated with white tape, were retained. The white star on the collar and the black and yellow tassel on the fist strap indicate rank.*

Dragoon Facings and Buttons

Facings	Buttons	
	yellow	white
Dark red	3	1
Black	6	2
Scarlet	8	11
Grass green	9	4
Sulphur yellow	10	7
Emperor yellow	12	5
Madder red	14	13
White	15	

▼ Field Officer, Hussar Regiment Graf Radetzky No 5, 1865 *This officer is shown in winter dress. The fur cap, or kutsma, with eagle's feather replaced this regiment's old scarlet shako. Rank is shown by the broad silver lace over the cuffs.*

Ulan Distinctions

Regiment	Czapka top	Kurtka and breeches
1 Merveldt	emperor yellow	grass green
2 Schwarzenberg	grass green	grass green
3 Erzherzog Carl	scarlet	dark green
4 Kaiser	white	dark green

▼ TROOPER, 11TH HUSSARS, PRINZ ALEXANDER, 1859 *The shako had been grass green in 1854. The tight breeches were replaced by baggy, madder-red trousers in 1866. The crowned imperial cipher 'F1' appears on the shabraque and sabretache.*

▶ OFFICER, HUSSAR REGIMENT KÖNIG VON PREUSSEN NO 10, 1859 *Hussar regiments at this time were distinguished by the colour of the shako, their light or dark blue dolman (since 1850 an Attila), breeches and buttons. Shabraques and sabretaches were red with black and yellow edging and decoration.*

Ulans (Lancers)

Austro-Hungarian lancers were being expanded in the 19th century. These regiments wore the Polish costume; square-topped cap (or czapka), a green tunic (the kurtka) with red facings and piping, yellow buttons and 'waterfall' in the small of the back, black and yellow waist belt, green overalls with double red side stripe, white belts.

The czapka was worn with each regiment having a different coloured top half, black-within-yellow cockade under a black over yellow plume, black and yellow cap lines. Lances had black and yellow pennants.

In 1840 the plume was replaced by a drooping, black horsehair model. All regiments wore a dark green tunic, known as the *ulanka*, with red facings and yellow buttons. By 1854 there were 12 lancer regiments. They were distinguished by the colour of their czapka tops and by the colour of their buttons. In 1865 the czapka was replaced by the low-crowned, square-topped *tatarka* cap with brown fur headband, regimental top, black and yellow braid and eagle's feather. The kurtka was replaced by the light blue Atilla with red facings; regiments wore light blue trousers. In 1867 the czapka was reintroduced with a reduced square top half in the regimental colour and black horsehair plume. The lower front bore a brass double eagle badge and brass chinscales.

Artillery

In 1815 the foot artillery had been uniformed in a wolf-grey tunic and white trousers of infantry cut, red collar, cuffs and turnbacks, yellow buttons, black gaiters, white belts. The headgear was the Corsican hat with the left-hand brim extended and turned up. Black and yellow pompon and plume were worn at the front of the crown of the hat. In 1840 the grey tunic was replaced with a dark brown version with light blue trousers with a white side stripe. Ten years later, the tunic was replaced by the double-breasted, hip-length coat; in 1860, it became single-breasted, with fold-down collar. From 1851 the artillery had worn the shako, with a black drooping horsehair plume. Horse artillery wore the same as the foot, but were armed and equipped in dragoon style, jacket was as for the dragoons, with black knee boots and steel spurs.

Fortress artillery: as for the foot artillery, but with a broad red side stripe to the trousers.

Engineers, Miners and Pontoniers

Engineers wore a grey, foot artillery tunic and breeches, green facings, white buttons and belts; Corsican hat with plume and pompon. In 1840

the shako, with black plume replaced the hat, and belts became black. From 1868 they wore light blue tunics, faced red, grey-blue trousers.

Miners: dark blue tunics and trousers, dark red facings, yellow buttons, black belts. Pontoniers: dark blue, infantry-style tunic with red collar, Polish cuffs and turnbacks, Corsican hat with left brim turned up. White belts and buttons.

Train

Other ranks wore white coats of dragoon cut, yellow facings, white buttons and black belts, white breeches, knee boots, shakos with the black and yellow plume and pompon. Officers had brown coats, yellow facings and white buttons. In 1840 facings and trousers were light blue.

▼ MUSICIAN, FOOT ARTILLERY, 1859 *The musician's badges were swallows' nests in the facing colour, edged in the button colour, red plume and liberal decoration of the jacket with lace. The tunic was double-breasted in 1850.*

▶ ULAN REGIMENT KÖNIG BEIDER SIZILIEN, NO 12, 1866 *Ulan regiments were changing uniforms during this war. Officers received new, single-breasted light blue tunics and madder-red breeches. The men kept the old dark green kurtkas and overalls. The new tunics retained the 'waterfall' in the small of the back. The white 'Havelock' neck shields were a new innovation.*

TROOPS OF THE GERMAN STATES

Alliances between the German states were a common feature of the wars of German unification.

Hanoverian Infantry

By 1866 the Austrian and Prussian influences dominated the uniforms of this state. The infantry wore, dark blue, single-breasted tunics with red collars and cuffs, facings being worn on the shoulder straps. The Guard and the 1st (Leib-Regiment) wore white, the 2nd and 3rd had red, 4th and 5th yellow, 6th and 7th light blue. The regimental numbers were worn on the shoulder straps; in yellow on red straps, in red on the others. The Guard wore white buttons and buttonholes had plain Swedish cuffs. Their cap badge was star-shaped. The line wore yellow buttons and a white horse in a brass wreath on the shako; their red cuff flaps bore three yellow button holes. Grey trousers with a red side piping were worn.

In 1849 the Prussian spiked helmet was adopted, replaced by Austrian-style shakos in 1858. Badges of rank were shown by lace in the button colour to collar and cuffs and by yellow and white sashes and sword knots.

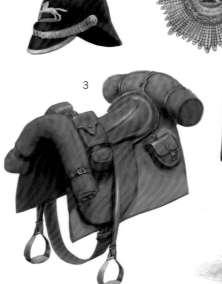

▲ HANOVERIAN INFANTRY KIT, 1866
1 Helmet of the Cambridge Dragoons.
2 Hanoverian Guards' star. 3 Artillery driver's saddlery. 4 Shako of a sergeant of the Hanoverian infantry.

◄ TROOPER, GUARDS KÜRASSIER REGIMENT, FIELD SERVICE DRESS, 1866 *The helmet and cuirass bear the brass, eight-pointed star of the Guelphen Order with the springing white horse of Lower Saxony. No holster covers were worn in the field.*

▲ CORPORAL 5TH INFANTRY REGIMENT, FIELD SERVICE DRESS, 1866 *The national cockade was black, yellow and white. Collars and cuffs were red for all infantry regiments. The Guards infantry wore white buttons and lace and their shako badge was an eight-pointed white star over a scroll. The line infantry regiments wore the white springing horse (head to the left as viewed) within a crowned brass wreath on the shako. The round, light blue water bottle is of the British pattern.*

Drummers wore swallows' nests in the facing colour with edging and decoration in the button colour. The brass drums had hoops painted in yellow and white. Belts were white with brass fittings. Sharpshooters were distinguished by yellow hunting horns on their collars. The infantry carried grey canvas packs with a brass plate on the top, right-hand side with the man's number stamped on it.

Hanoverian Cavalry

GARDE DU CORPS AND GUARDS KÜRASSIERS. White tunics, red facings, yellow buttons and button holes to the Swedish cuffs. The spiked steel helmet was of the same design as that of the Prussian Garde du Corps and had brass fittings but bore the gold star

of the Order of George over a scroll bearing 'PENINSULA-GARCIA-HERNANDEZ-WATERLOO'. White, drooping horsehair plumes were worn for parades. A steel cuirass, with brass fittings and trim and a red cuff was worn. The breast plate was decorated with the star of the Order of George. Grey breeches had a red side piping. The square shabraque was in the facing colour, edged in the button colour; harness was brown with steel fittings. GUARD CUIRASSIER REGIMENT. As for the Garde du Corps with cornflower blue facings, yellow buttons and a black cuirass with brass star, trim and red cuffs. Cuirasses were not worn in 1866. DRAGOONS. From 1849 the Hanoverian dragoons wore light blue tunics and the Prussian spiked helmet, the Pickelhaube, with the spike, chinscales and Hanoverian horse badge in brass, black plumes for parades. Trumpeters wore swallows' nests in the facing colour, edged and decorated in the button colour.
HUSSARS. Dark blue Attila for everyday, dolmans for parades. The dolman had yellow braid and buttons, the Attila yellow buttons but white braid. The winter Atilla had grey fur. A low-crowned, dark blue kepi for everyday

◀ CORPORAL TRUMPETER, CAMBRIDGE DRAGOONS, SERVICE DRESS, 1866 *Although a dragoon regiment, this unit rode the traditional wooden Hungarian Bock saddle, used by hussar regiments. There were 3 white laces to the cuffs and one on the collar. The old-fashioned helmet was decorated with the springing horse of Lower Saxony, in brass, over a scroll bearing 'PENINSULA WATERLOO GÖHRDE'. For parades the regiment wore drooping white horsehair plumes instead of the spike.*

▶ GUNNER, HORSE ARTILLERY REGIMENT, FIELD SERVICE DRESS, 1866 *The old British Tarleton helmet of the Napoleonic Wars is shown here, somewhat reduced in size. The dark blue turban, introduced in 1862, is held with narrow brass chains. The white over yellow plume is in the national colours. On the right side was a crowned yellow round disc with the royal cipher.*

Dragoons

Regiment	Facings	Buttons
King's Dragoons	red	yellow
Queen's Dragoons	white	yellow
Duke of Cambridge's Dragoons	crimson	white

use. In 1866 brown busbies were worn for parades; with white over yellow plumes, red bags, white cords and yellow crests on the front. Officers wore gold chevrons on the cuffs. The red sabretache was edged in yellow and bore the crowned royal cipher, also in yellow. Parade shabraques were richly decorated in red and gold. Grey breeches with red side piping. The steel-hilted sabres were carried in steel sheaths on white slings.

Hanoverian Artillery

Foot artillery wore dark blue infantry tunics with black facings, red piping and yellow buttons (buttonholes to the Swedish cuffs and collar). Red shoulder straps bore the battery number in yellow. Horse artillery wore the same colours as the foot. Up to 1862 they wore the Pickelhaube, from then they adopted black-crested Tarleton helmets, belts were white; light cavalry sabres were carried, and a peaked, dark blue cap with black headband was worn; those of officers had red piping to the crown and the top of the headband.

Hanoverian Train

Dark blue tunics, light blue collars and cuffs, red piping and shoulder straps, yellow buttons.

The shako bore the white horse

in brass wreath and was topped with the black-yellow-white cockade. NCOs had white/silver top bands to the shako. Black belts were worn as were the grey trousers with red side piping. They carried light cavalry sabres and carbines. Engineers wore foot artillery uniform with black facings and white buttons, black plumes for parades, black belts and the usual grey trousers.

Saxon Infantry

In 1862 the Saxon infantry received light blue trousers and light blue, single-breasted coats; all buttons were yellow. All coats were piped red, the light blue shoulder straps bore the battalion number in red. Those of the Leib-Brigade were surmounted by a red crown. The men of the Leib-Brigade wore sabres, the others had the short sword known as a *Faschinenmesser*. The pompon on the men's Austrian-style shako was in the collar colour and bore the company number in yellow; officers' golden pompons had centres in the brigade colour, with the battalion number in them. The shako badge was a white, eight-pointed star with the Saxon crest in the round centre. A light blue cloth cap, with cockade, peak, headband in the brigade colour and with a red piping to the bottom of the headband was worn in the 1866 campaign.

Officers initially wore stars of their rank on their epaulettes, but abandoned the gorget. They later adopted the Austrian-style rank badges in the form of stars on the collars. The NCOs wore rank laces

◀ SAXONY DRUMMER, LEIB-BRIGADE OF INFANTRY, 1866 *The drums had green and white hoops. Status is shown by red epaulettes with brass half-moons. The shako plate is a silver, eight-pointed star enclosing a green, black and yellow Saxon crest.*

▶ BOMBARDIER, SAXON HORSE ARTILLERY, 1862–67 *The Saxon artillery adopted the Bavarian-style crested helmet in 1843; the crest was red for trumpeters. The green and red uniform, with brass buttons was traditional for this service.*

to collar, shako top bands and the silver sword knots. In 1867 a Prussian-style helmet, with Saxon badge, was introduced, tunics became dark blue.

Saxon Jägers and Cavalry

Jägers wore green tunic with black facings, red piping and yellow buttons, dark grey trousers, piped red, and black belts. On dark green shoulder straps was a red horn and red battalion number. Saxony's cavalry (Reiter) regiments and the Guard regiment wore a black leather, Austrian dragoon-style helmet with brass fittings and front plate with the crowned royal cipher (JR), and black crest (the crest was abandoned in 1849). They wore light blue tunics, with brass buttons and light blue

◀ BAVARIAN TROOPER, 3RD CHEVAUXLEGERS REGIMENT, FIELD SERVICE DRESS, 1870
Although a light horse unit, heavy cavalry boots were worn. Pink facings and brass buttons were adopted in 1826. The saddle furniture was dark green, edged in pink, with rounded front corners and with the crowned 'L' monogram in the pointed rear corner. Brass shoulder scales were backed with pink.

white; 1st – poppy red; 2nd – purple; 3rd – black. Belts were black.

Saxon Artillery

The foot artillery retained the dark green uniforms with red facings and piping and brass buttons of infantry cut, with the shako. Belts were buff up to 1849 thence black with brass fittings. From 1867 they wore Prussian-style helmets with brass badge and ball top pieces, green tunics with red collar, cuffs and piping and yellow buttons.

The horse artillery had the same tunics as the foot, but with brass scale epaulettes and black leather booting to dark grey trousers. From 1843 they wore Bavarian-style crested black leather helmets, with brass star badge and fittings. They carried sabres. Horse furniture was dark green with red trim.

Engineers wore foot artillery uniform with green shoulder straps piped red. The train wore light blue tunics with black collar and cuffs, red piping and yellow buttons and shoulder scales. Light blue trousers with black booting; black belts.

Bavarian Infantry and Jägers

Infantry wore cornflower blue coats and trousers, with facings on collars and cuffs. The headgear was the high, black *Raupenhelm*. Jägers wore a green coat and trousers, with green facings and shoulder straps and white buttons.

Bavarian Cavalry

KÜRASSIERS. In 1866 they had light blue tunics, the 1st with red facings and piping and yellow buttons, the 2nd with red facings and white buttons, the 3rd with crimson and yellow, steel helmets with brass comb, chinscales and

black crests. Steel cuirasses with brass fittings and a red and white cuff. Light blue breeches with red piping.

CHEVAUXLEGERS. They wore the *Raupenhelm* with brass fittings, green tunics, with facings on collar and cuffs, green trousers with coloured side stripes and black boots, white belts.

ULANS. In 1863, a green chevauxleger-style tunic with crimson facings, yellow buttons for the 1st Regiment, white for the 2nd and the czapka.

▼ BAVARIAN DRUMMER, FUSILIER BATTALION, LINE INFANTRY, FIELD SERVICE DRESS, 1870
Bavarian helmets were reduced in height, but retained their distinctive characteristics. The drum hoops were striped in the national colours, repeated in the cockade on the helmet, above the lion's head chinstrap boss. The chinstrap has lost some brass scales.

facings on collar, Swedish cuffs and turnbacks. Brass shoulder scales and grey overalls with red side piping were worn. Belts were white.

In 1832 the tunics and trousers became light blue and buttons on the chest were replaced with hooks and eyes. In 1840 facing colours were abandoned; regiments were differentiated by the newly introduced cuff flaps: Guards – white, 1st – red, 2nd – light blue. In 1849 a 3rd Regiment was raised; it had yellow (later orange) cuff flaps. The collar and the edging to the rounded, light blue shabraque were in the cuff flap colour. In 1867 a new crested helmet was introduced. Facings were now: Guard –

Bavarian Artillery and Technical Troops

Foot artillery wore infantry uniform, in dark blue with black facings piped red, yellow buttons and brass shoulder scales. The *Raupenhelm* had brass side struts and a red plume. Horse artillery wore the same uniform as the foot, but in chevauxlegers cut, and their red plumes were of drooping horsehair.

Engineers were as for the foot artillery but with white buttons. Pontoniers had black facings, light blue plumes and white buttons; miners and sappers the same, but with yellow buttons; miners had a red plume with black base and crossed pickaxes on the coat tails. Sappers had a black plume with red base.

◀ BRUNSWICK SERGEANT OF INFANTRY, FIELD SERVICE DRESS, 1859 *The arm badge is a fencing qualification; his rank badges (silver stripes) are very British. He wears a waist sash in the national colours and in the fashion of the hussars.*

▶ BADEN PRIVATE, JÄGERS, FIELD SERVICE DRESS, 1860 *They still wore the tall, old Prussian helmet, here with the Baden griffin badge. The method of strapping on the backpack was different from that of the Prussian Army and was introduced in 1860.*

Duchy of Brunswick Infantry

From 1848 the infantry wore black uniforms with black braid and black glass buttons on the chest. Collar, shoulder straps and pointed cuffs were light blue. The trousers had a light blue side piping. NCOs' badges of rank were white/silver chevrons; sergeants wore silver and light blue hussar-style sashes. The shako bore a silver skull and bones and a black horsehair plume.

Duchy of Brunswick Cavalry

Hussars wore busbies with red bags, black dolman, pelisse and breeches (with red side piping), black braid and buttons, black belts and sabretache.

Duchy of Brunswick Artillery

Foot artillery wore the *Raupenhelm* with brass fittings and white plume, black infantry uniform with black collar and pointed cuffs, piped in yellow. There were two yellow laces to the sides on the collar, red side piping to the trousers. Horse artillery had black leather booting to the trousers. In 1867 the infantry shako replaced the *Raupenhelm*.

Baden's Infantry

Dark blue, single-breasted tunic and cuffs, facings shown on collar patches and shoulder straps. Black belts. The Leib-Grenadier-Garde wore red facings with yellow laces, white buttons; the line wore yellow buttons, the facings were: 1st Regiment – red; 2nd – white; 3rd – yellow; 4th – light blue. The Prussian-style Pickelhaube had a spike

and the Baden griffin with sword and shield; white plume for parades. Plain grey trousers. The Jäger battalion wore dark green tunics with yellow buttons, black collar and cuffs, red piping and shoulder straps, black plume for parades. In 1866, the men wore blue forage caps with red piping. Officers' sashes and sword knots were silver with red and yellow stripes.

Baden's Cavalry and Artillery

Dragoons wore the Pickelhaube with the brass griffin and spike, light blue single-breasted tunics with brass buttons, light blue overalls with white side piping and black booting. Facings were worn on collar, cuffs and

◄ **Württemberg Officer, Reiter-Regiment Konig Karl No 1, Field Service Dress, 1864** *It seems that the cavalry took the field in 1866 in the new uniforms shown here, with the regimental facings shown only on the collar. The cap badge was a brass shield with the regimental number in white. The saddle cloth was in royal blue, with a wide red edging and the crowned royal cipher 'KR' in red in the pointed rear corner. The portmanteau was royal blue, and piped in red.*

The new uniform from 1866 had a low-crowned, dark blue kepi with red band and top piping, crowned white metal shield with the regimental number, above this the red and black cockade, black chinstrap, white plume. For everyday use they wore a dark blue peaked cap with red band and cockade. Double-breasted dark blue tunic with white buttons, red collar, shoulder straps (with the company number), shoulder rolls and piping, dark blue round cuffs. Regimental identity was shown by the collar patches: 1st – white; 2nd – black; 3rd – orange; 4th – green; 5th – light blue; 6th – dark blue; 7th – deep red; 8th – yellow. Grey trousers with a red side piping, black belts in the Prussian style. Officers wore Austrian-style rank badges on their collars, black and red hussar-style sashes and sword knots.

Württemberg Jägers and Cavalry

Jägers wore the same as the line, but with green collar patches and facings and kepi with blue band, and a black plume on parades.

The cavalry consisted of four Reiter regiments. The uniform was as for the infantry, but the kepi had a red top, dark blue headband, brass crowned plate with white regimental number, white plume for parades. Dark blue, double-breasted tunic, dark blue collar and cuffs, red shoulder straps and

▶ **Württemberg, Private, 8th Infantry Regiment, Field Service Dress, 1864** *The programme for equipping the entire army in the clothing shown here began in 1864, but was so slow (due to reasons of economy), that the army took the field in 1866 in the old uniforms.*

shoulder rolls, red piping, grey trousers with wide red side stripe, white belts. Regimental facings were worn on the collar patches: 1st, light blue; 2nd, yellow; 3rd, red; 4th, white.

Württemberg Artillery

Foot artillery wore infantry style uniform in dark blue with black facings piped red and with red shoulder rolls, white buttons. The dark blue kepi had a black headband and red piping to the top; black plume. Black belts. Grey trousers with red side stripe. The horse artillery wore the same as the Reiter regiments, but in artillery colours. Engineers had brass buttons and fittings, yellow top band to the shako. Train troops had light blue facings.

shoulder straps: 1st – red, 2nd – yellow, 3rd – black piped red.

Artillery wore infantry uniform with black facings, piped red and yellow buttons. Engineers had white buttons.

Württemberg Infantry

For the 1866 campaign, they wore the old uniform. Tall, powder blue shako, with black leather headband, narrow white top band, large black and red cockade, white loop, royal blue double pompon (green for sharpshooters). A royal blue, single-breasted tunic, white buttons, red collars, pointed cuffs, shoulder straps and piping, royal blue trousers with red side piping, white crossed belts and a *Faschinenmesser*.

Nassau

In 1849 the six battalions of infantry wore yellow battalion numbers on the red shoulder straps on dark green, single-breasted tunics. Facings were black, piped red. In 1862 the Austrian artillery-style shako was introduced. Sharpshooters had yellow piping to their red shoulder straps. The leatherwork was buff with brass fittings up to the campaign of 1866, when it was blackened. Badges of rank were now on the Austrian model; officers wore eight-pointed stars on the fields of their gold epaulettes. Officers' sashes were orange, their sword knots were gold. The Jäger Battalion wore an all-black costume, with braid on the chest, and an Austrian-style shako. Jäger officers' orange sashes were in hussar style. The artillery had crimson facings and side stripe to grey trousers.

Saxe-Meiningen-Hildburghausen

This state's Jäger Battalion uniform in 1866 was Prussian: a Pickelhaube with brass spike, chinscales and fittings and silver, eight-pointed star with the ducal crest. Dark green coat with black leather equipment and facings piped red, black buttons and lace. Austrian-style shakos with black horsehair plumes for officers, who also wore their silver and green sashes over the right shoulder. In the campaign officers wore the old Pickelhaube.

Hessen-Cassel Infantry

The uniforms, rank badges and equipment followed the Prussian style, the Pickelhaube having brass fittings, with a silver star for the Guard and the brass, rampant Hessian lion with sword on the front for the line. Tunics were dark blue, with red collars, cuffs and piping. The Guard had white shoulder straps and Swedish cuffs, with two white laces to collar and cuffs and white buttons. Plumes were white. The 1st Line regiment had yellow, the 2nd crimson, the 3rd red. The line regiments all had red cuff flaps, piped in the facing colour. Trousers were grey with a red side piping. Belts were white. Officers' sashes and sword knots were silver and red. Jäger Battalion troops (in the Guards) had dark green tunics with red collar, cuffs, cuff flaps and piping, brass buttons, white shoulder straps with a yellow crown. The kepi had a yellow crowned cipher, and they wore black belts.

◀ SAXE-MEININGEN CORPORAL, INFANTRY REGIMENT, FIELD SERVICE DRESS, 1866
Despite the Prussian character of the uniforms of most of the minor German states, some preserved their own personalities, such as here with the black braid and buttons on the tunic. The helmet star bore the ducal badge. Officers wore silver and green silk sashes over the right shoulder and silver sabre straps and tassels to their dark green, black-laced dolmans. They also wore Austrian-style shakos, with drooping black horsehair plumes and gilt lion's heads to each side.

▶ NASSAU PRIVATE, 2ND INFANTRY REGIMENT, FIELD SERVICE DRESS, 1862 *The yellow '2' on the shoulder strap is the regimental number. Officers wore gilt, Russian-style epaulettes with the stars of their rank instead. The pattern of the spike of the helmet was unique. Shortly after this, Nassau uniforms were altered to the Austrian style; by 1866 the buff belts were black. The national cockade (orange, with a light blue rim) was worn around the right hand chinscale boss of the helmet. NCO ranks were shown by the yellow/gold edging to collar and cuffs and by the sabre tassels.*

◀ **REUSS CORPORAL OF FUSILIERS FIELD SERVICE DRESS, 1866** *The black leather system of linking the weight of the backpack to the front of the waistbelt was introduced in 1850. Reuss followed Prussian trends. NCOs also wore red sabre straps with yellow/gold tassels. The national cockade (black within red within yellow) was worn under the right-hand chinstrap boss.*

▶ **HESSEN-KASSEL TROOPER, LEIB-HUSSARS, PARADE DRESS, 1866** *Prussian influence is noticeable; in particular in the crests on the sabretache, but Hessen-Kassel's cipher was 'FWK' (Friedrich Wilhelm Kurfürst) instead of 'FWR' and the crowns are different. This man is shown in winter dress, with pelisse.*

1ST HUSSARS: brown colpack with red bag, brass chinscales, red-with-white pompon, white plume for parades. Light blue dolman and pelisse, white buttons and lace, red and white sash, grey overalls with black booting and red side stripe. Red sabretache edged white and bearing the white crowned cipher 'FWR', light blue shabraque with white edging and braid decoration. White belts, plain black pouch. Black harness with steel fittings. In the field they wore a peakless cap with red headband, white piping and top in the dolman colour.
2ND HUSSARS: same uniform and horse furniture but in dark blue, shabraque with red edging, and white braid.

The Schützen Battalion had dark green tunics, black collar and cuffs, red shoulder straps, yellow buttons fittings, kepi as for the Jägers, black belts.

Hessen-Kassel Cavalry

GARDE DU CORPS: brass helmet with the silver star of the Order of the Lion, white plume for parades, brass fittings. Brass cuirass with steel fittings. Buff tunic with red facings and piping, white gauntlets and belts, grey trousers with red side piping and black booting. Red pistol covers and square shabraque with the star of the Order of the Lion and black, red and white braid edging. Brass-hilted sword in steel sheath.

Hessen-Kassel Artillery

Dark blue, single-breasted tunics with black collar and cuffs, piped deep red, black turnbacks, yellow buttons, Swedish cuffs, grey trousers with red side piping, helmet with brass fittings, ball point, black plume for parades; white belts, Prussian-style equipment, black pouch with three-flamed grenade badge. Horse artillery wore the same, but with black booting to the trousers. Engineers had no Guards lace, but a helmet with white lion and fittings, black plume, white buttons. The artillery train had dark blue peaked cap with deep red headband and top piping, deep red collar and Swedish cuffs, yellow buttons, black belts.

Troops of Reuss

The younger line of the principality of Reuss had a battalion of infantry dressed in the Prussian fashion, with Pickelhaube with brass fittings and black plume, eight-pointed star with silver crest (quartered lions and cranes), black, single-breasted tunic with light blue collar, shoulder straps, piping and cuff flaps, yellow buttons. Grey breeches with light blue side stripe. Leatherwork was black with brass fittings. Officers' sashes were gold with red lines. NCOs had gold lace to collars and cuffs and red and yellow sabre straps.

THE FRENCH ARMY

In the war against Prussia, France's Second Empire paid homage to the uniforms of Napoleon I. Napoleon III even created an Imperial Guard, which imitated their Napoleonic counterpart.

Imperial Guard and Infantry

The Imperial Guard was recreated in 1854; the infantry had three regiments of grenadiers, four of voltigeurs and one of zouaves. They wore a modernized version of the uniforms worn in 1815; that of the zouaves is in the section on African troops.

Line Infantry

The uniform of the infantry early in the Second Empire of Napoleon III was revised a number of times. The light infantry had been incorporated into the line as the junior regiments numbered 75–102 in 1854. There were now also 20 battalions of Chasseurs à pied, raised in 1840.

In 1860 a new uniform was introduced; it was a dark blue, hip-length, single-breasted jacket, with very brief skirts. The collar and cuff flaps were yellow. Baggy red trousers were worn in white gaiters. The shako was 13cm (5in) tall and of black leather. It bore an eagle plate and the regimental number on a grenade, under the tricolour cockade and pompon; a short plume was worn for parades. Belts were black. Officers' coat skirts were almost knee-length. Officers of the elite companies wore gold grenades or horns on their collars. Rank was shown by gold lace knots which extended from cuff to upper arm, the number and width of the laces increasing with rank. Line infantry officers' belt plates were oblong, with chamfered corners. The Chasseurs wore a similar uniform, but with white

buttons, iron grey breeches and pointed cuffs. In 1868 they also received double-breasted tunics and narrow trousers. Officers of Chasseurs wore sword belts closing with a hook between two bosses decorated with hunting horns. The carried sabres in steel sheaths, as did the line.

The 1860 uniform was unpopular; the gaiters hurt the troops and the shako was too heavy. In December 1867 a new uniform

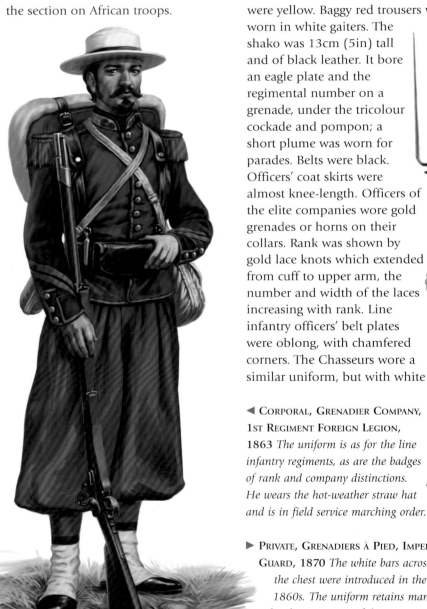

◀ CORPORAL, GRENADIER COMPANY, 1ST REGIMENT FOREIGN LEGION, 1863 *The uniform is as for the line infantry regiments, as are the badges of rank and company distinctions. He wears the hot-weather straw hat and is in field service marching order.*

▶ PRIVATE, GRENADIERS À PIED, IMPERIAL GUARD, 1870 *The white bars across the chest were introduced in the 1860s. The uniform retains many of the characteristics of those from the time of Napoleon I.*

The Foreign Legion

A Foreign regiment was raised for French service in January 1837; it was two regiments strong in 1840, but was reduced to one in December 1861. The red over dark blue kepi had yellow piping to the band and up the sides, front and back of the crown. The regimental number was on the front in red. The white kepi cover with neck shield (Havelock) was common to all units in Africa and other tropical spots from 30 August 1862.

They wore line infantry uniform, with nine large brass buttons on the front, bearing 'REGIMENT ÉTRANGER' within two concentric rings. The centre bore the regimental number (this was discontinued after the amalgamation of the two regiments). The collar was yellow, plain for the fusilier companies, embroidered with red

▶ GUNNER, HORSE ARTILLERY, 1870 *The elaborate cap lines looped across the chest are 'fashion accessories' with a dashing, light cavalry flavour. He is shown without sabre belt or slings.*

▼ INFANTRY AND CAVALRY ARTILLERY KIT, 1870 *1 Waist belt with brass loops for the backpack straps. 2 Officer's sabre. 3 Backpack. 4 Officer's field service sabre knot. 5 Cap badge, bearing the regimental number.*

▲ GUNNER, FIELD ARTILLERY, FIELD SERVICE DRESS, 1870 *They wore infantry-pattern uniforms, with their own facings and badges to pouches and skirt turnbacks. He carries a carbine slung on his back.*

was decreed. It was a double-breasted, thigh-length tunic, with two rows of seven buttons. The collar was yellow, cuffs plain blue, piped at the top in yellow. The red trousers were no longer baggy. The shako was 11cm (4in) high, of red cloth and lost the eagle plate. The dark blue head band bore the regimental number. Officers' rank was shown on epaulettes and in lace rings to cuffs and shakos. Grenadiers wore a red grenade on the collar, voltigeurs a red horn.

grenade or hunting horn for the elite companies. The tunic was piped with red to front and lower hem, to the top of the cuff, the cuff flaps and the belt loops. The vertical false tail pockets were also piped in red; the turnbacks bore red company emblems: grenades, horns or five-pointed stars. Junior rank stripes and long service chevrons were of red wool, sergeants' of gold.

Fusilier companies in the foreign legion wore green fringed epaulettes with green straps and red crescents; grenadiers' epaulettes were red, those of the Voltigeurs were yellow. The white shirt had a royal blue collar and front trim. A wide waist sash (grey or royal blue) was worn under the tunic.

◄ **ZOUAVE, 1ST REGIMENT, 1870** *The uniform was modelled on the local dress of the Arab population, adapted for military use. A white turban was often wound around the red fez for parades. They used standard, line infantry weapons and equipment.*

► **COLONEL OF ENGINEERS, SERVICE DRESS, 1870** *This officer is from the 1st Regiment, as shown by his collar badges. His rank is shown by the five gold laces to kepi crown and to the cuffs, as well as by his heavy gold epaulettes. He wears the medal of the Legion d'Honneur.*

Artillery and Engineers

French artillery and technical troops played a key role in the war against Prussia, as did troops brought over from the colonies in North Africa.

The foot artillery uniform retained the dark blue, red-faced and yellow-buttoned traditional colour scheme and followed the developments of the infantry. They wore red epaulettes. The trousers were dark blue with twin red side stripes. Belts were white. The horse artillery followed suit, but with black booting on the trousers; the gunners carried light cavalry sabres, with brass hilts in steel sheaths.

Engineers wore uniforms of infantry style with black facings piped red and red epaulettes, dark blue trousers with twin red side stripes. Their shako badge was the Grecian helmet and cuirass within trophies of arms.

Zouaves

The first Algerian units raised in 1830 became a regiment of three battalions in 1842, which was expanded into the 1st, 2nd and 3rd regiments of Zouaves in 1852. Each regiment was associated with a province, either Algeria, Oran or Constantine. In March 1855 another regiment, the Zouaves of the Imperial Guard, was formed; this became the 4th Regiment in 1870. The Zouaves wore dark blue tunics of Arab cut, edged in red braid, 12mm (½in) wide; the front was decorated with two red arabesques, the top ends of which formed trefoils on the upper chest. The base of the arabesque formed a false pocket, lined in the regimental facing

All infantry regiments of the Foreign Legion received baggy, red breeches, and tan leather gaiters trimmed in black were worn, as were lighter, white garments in summer, together with short white spats. Belts were black with brass fittings.

After the end of the Second Empire in 1870, French army uniforms remained basically the same, but the red regimental number was added to the dark blue collar patches as well as the kepi. The yellow piping was removed from the cuff flap.

colour: 1st – red, 2nd – white, 3rd – yellow. A dark blue waistcoat was worn under the tunic. The fez (*chéchia*) was red with a sky blue cord and tassel. A green cotton turban could also be worn. A sky blue waist sash was worn under the tunic. The baggy red breeches (*seroual*) were decorated with dark blue braid. Gaiters and their buttons were white, leatherwork was black. The Zouaves of the Imperial Guard wore the same uniforms, but with yellow braid decoration and pointed red cuffs.

Officers wore dark blue, single-breasted tunics, of the same cut as for the Chasseurs à pied, with nine buttons on the chest and three small ones on each dark blue cuff. Gold epaulettes were worn in full dress.

Tirailleurs Algeriens

There were three regiments of these Turcos in light blue tunics as for the Zouaves, facings were: 1st – red, 2nd – white, 3rd – yellow. The fez was red with a sky blue cord and tassel. A white cotton turban could also be worn. A red waist sash was worn under the tunic. The baggy light blue breeches were decorated with yellow piping. Gaiters

 ▶ SERGEANT, 2ND TIRAILLEURS ALGERIEN, *1870 These troops were also known as 'Turcos' and they dressed in an adaptation of the local custom. This figure's rank is shown by the two gold chevrons over his cuffs, which were pointed to emphasize the speedy, light infantry nature of his role. The regimental facing colour is shown in the lining to the pockets of his jacket.*

and their buttons were white, leatherwork was black. Officers wore light blue, single-breasted tunics, of the same cut as for the Chasseurs à pied, with nine buttons on the chest and three small ones on each dark blue cuff. The collar was yellow with light blue front tabs. These were plain up to 1872. The red-topped, light blue kepi had gold lace according to rank and the gold regimental number on the front.

Saphis

Facing colours for these three regiments were as for the Zouaves. Arab soldiers wore a red felt fez without tassel, red turban, red tunics of Arab cut, with sky blue cuffs and braid decoration, sky blue waistcoats with black braid, closed to the waist, sky blue Arab breeches, crimson waist sash. A red burnous was worn over a white cotton burnous. French soldiers in the Saphis wore the red felt fez with sky blue cord and tassel, or a white turban, edged blue. The French officers wore royal blue kepis, red tunic with black braid, royal blue breeches of Arab cut with red decoration. Undress was a dark blue, single-breasted tunic with nine buttons, sky blue breeches with red side stripes. Native officers wore light blue cuffs to their red tunics.

◀ TROOPER, 1ST CHASSEURS D'AFRIQUE, *1870 This figure wears the light cavalry uniform, equipment and dolman that were introduced in 1862. The kepi later became shorter than shown here. The horse harness for the Chasseurs was also of light cavalry style.*

Chasseurs d'Afrique

There were three regiments dressed in a sky blue tunic with yellow collar and pointed cuffs, red breeches. The red fez had a cord and tassel in the squadron colour: 1st – dark blue, 2nd – crimson, 3rd – dark green, 4th – sky blue, 5th – orange, 6th – tricolour. The wide red breeches had black leather booting to the knee, with hussar-style cutout. Kepi with red top, sky blue band and silver lace, sky blue dolman with yellow collar and cuffs for all regiments with six white buttons, black braid, red breeches with two sky blue side stripes and a sky blue piping between them.

Cavalry

The French cavalry consisted of an Imperial Guard, line cuirassiers (heavy cavalry), dragoons and light cavalry (hussars, chasseurs and lancers). CUIRASSIERS. Trousers were red with black leather booting, the steel helmet had brass comb and fittings and a black horsehair crest. Red over white over blue plumes were worn for parades. The steel cuirass had brass fittings. After 1870 the regimental numbers were worn on the collar.

There was also a cuirassier regiment in the Imperial Guard; it wore a dark blue tunic with red collar, cuffs

Dragoon Distinctions		
Regiment	Collar, Lapels, Cuff flaps and piping	Cuffs & Epaulettes
1 & 2	deep pink	green
3 & 4	green	deep pink
5 & 6	yellow	green
7 & 8	green	yellow
9 & 10	crimson	green

and turnbacks, white epaulettes, aiguillette and breeches. The helmet had a brass turban with the crowned 'N'. A regiment of carabiniers was also raised in the Imperial Guard. DRAGOONS. In 1870 there were ten regiments of dragoons; their tunics were green, with rectangular cuff flaps. Trousers were red with black booting, belts white. They wore the brass helmet with leopard skin turban, comb and black horsehair crest. Buttons and belt fittings were brass, pouches black. After 1868 they wore a single-breasted dark blue tunic with brass buttons, white collar, piping and cuff flaps, red epaulettes and trousers.

The dragoons of the Imperial Guard wore light green tunics, white lapels, epaulettes and cap lines, red collars, light green cuffs and turnbacks piped in red, red grenades on the turnbacks. LANCERS. The traditional Polish uniform was worn but by this time, the czapka top had become lower and smaller. The kurtka was dark blue, the trousers red, with a wide blue side stripe; white epaulettes were worn by

all regiments. The front of the czapka bore a semi-circular sunburst plate; cap cords, buttons and metal were white.

In 1855 a lancer regiment was raised in the Imperial Guard; it had a sky blue czapka with white trim and a yellow plate. They wore a white kurtka with sky blue collar, lapels, cuffs, piping and turnbacks. The plume, cap cords, epaulettes and trousers were red. The buttons were apparently white. The lance pennant was white over red, the shabraque and portmanteau were sky blue, edged in a wide white band, outer edge piped red.

◀ JUNIOR OFFICER, 4TH CUIRASSIERS, 1870
The basic uniform of 1815 can still be seen here. The colouring of the collar and cuffs identify the 4th Regiment. The baggy trousers were worn by most of the army at this point.

▶ LIEUTENANT, 4TH LANCERS, 1870 *The eight lancer regiments were differentiated by combinations of red, yellow and blue lapels, collars, cuffs, turnbacks, piping and czapka tops. From the Polish headgear of the Napoleonic lancers, there had been a continuous trend toward the smaller czapka top seen here.*

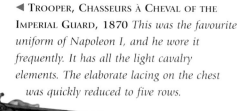

◀ TROOPER, CHASSEURS À CHEVAL OF THE
IMPERIAL GUARD, 1870 *This was the favourite
uniform of Napoleon I, and he wore it
frequently. It has all the light cavalry
elements. The elaborate lacing on the chest
was quickly reduced to five rows.*

CHASSEURS À CHEVAL. In 1831 they wore
the traditional green, single-breasted
coat with red epaulettes having green
fields. The tall shakos had drooping
black plumes. Red trousers were worn.
Shortly afterward, fur caps were
introduced, but in 1848 these were
replaced by red shakos. In 1856 the
tunic had 18 rows of black lace and
3 rows of white buttons. They now
wore small busbies and had black
sabretaches with copper eagle badge.
This was supposed to be the uniform
worn in 1870, but photographs exist of
officers of the 4th Regiment in Metz
that year in the Attila with six rows of
lace. The 1st, 6th and 9th regiments
wore sky blue Attilas with white
buttons and black braid; light blue
collars and cuffs piped red.

There was a regiment of Guides and
one of Chasseurs à cheval in the
Imperial Guard in 1870; Guides wore a
busby with white over black plume,
dark green dolman with madder-
red cuffs, five rows of buttons and
yellow braid, green pelisse, red
trousers with orange side stripe.
Chasseurs à cheval of the Guard
wore the same, with white braid.
HUSSARS. The eight regiments in 1870
wore a busby with red bag and
pompon. Collars and trousers were
red. Black sabretaches bore a copper
eagle. The pelisse and barrel sash were
abolished in 1862. In 1869 the 1st and
8th regiments received the Attila.

▶ TROOPER, 5TH HUSSARS, 1870 *French
hussar uniforms still retained the elaborately
laced dolman, but the barrel sash and the
traditional pelisse had been abandoned,
the latter replaced by an Attila, with six rows
of lace. The lid of the sabretache bore a
crowned imperial eagle in copper, looking to
its left. The dolman was also abandoned
after the war of 1870.*

Hussar Distinctions

Regt.	Dolman & Pelisse	Shako	Braid
1	sky blue	madder red	white
2	brown	sky blue	white
3	light grey	madder red	white
4	light grey	sky blue	white
5	dark blue	madder red	white
6	light green	madder red	white
7	light green	madder red	yellow
8	sky blue	sky blue	yellow

Chasseur Distinctions

Regiment	Collar	Cuffs
1 & 2	red	green
3 & 4	green	red
5 & 6	yellow	green
7 & 8	green	yellow
9 & 10	crimson	green
11 & 12	green	crimson
13 & 14	blue	green
15 & 16	green	blue
17 & 18	deep pink	green
19 & 20	green	deep pink
21 & 22	orange	green
23 & 24	green	orange

THE WARS OF ITALIAN UNIFICATION

Italian unification was a long, painful process. It was only completed in 1870 with the annexation of Rome, a city elevated to the capital of united Italy.

Wars of Independence

There were to be a succession of revolts and wars before most of Italy was united. The most significant were in 1848, 1859 and 1860 but the long-awaited goal was not to be achieved until Prussia crushed Austria in the war of 1866 and the Papal States were annexed in 1870.

The wars of 1848 and 1859 were largely without result. In the conflict of 1860, Giuseppe Garibaldi and his 'Thousand' volunteers sailed from Genoa on 5 May 1860 to Marsala, on the western tip of Sicily, landing in the Kingdom of Naples to tumultuous public welcome and floods of further volunteers. On 1 October, Garibaldi and his volunteers defeated the army of the Bourbon ruler of Naples. He then moved eastward across the island, through Palermo to Messina, gathering republican supporters. On 20 August he landed in Reggio, just across the straits of Messina, then moved north to Naples. On 1 October he defeated the army of the Bourbon king, Francesco II of Naples, at the Battle of Volturno. Control of southern Italy fell into his hands, but the republican Garibaldi then surrendered his realm to Victor Emanuel II, the king of Piedmont-Sardinia.

On 17 March 1861, Victor Emanuel was declared constitutional king of Italy. This left Venetia, in the north-east of the peninsula, still under Austrian control (the Austrians were expelled in 1866) and the Papal States still independent. Garibaldi unsuccessfully marched on Rome (defended by Papal troops and the French). The Italians annexed Rome in 1870, after the French had evacuated the city.

Up until Italian unification in 1860, the country was divided into the states

▲ *Garibaldi leads his Red Shirts to victory over the Neapolitan Army, 15 May 1860.*

of Modena, Naples, the Papal States, Parma, Sardinia and Tuscany. The uniforms of the armies of these mini-states were varied and complex.

Troops of the Papal States

The pope had a Swiss Guard in their red, yellow and blue slashed doublets, much as they still wear today.

The line infantry wore white, single-breasted uniforms of Austrian cut from 1830, with shakos. From 1848 the French style was adopted, the 1st Regiment having dark blue collar and plain round cuffs, the 2nd with orange; both with brass buttons. Belts and breeches were white. The grenadier companies wore red epaulettes, the voltigeurs had yellow and green. Officers wore white and gold silk waist sashes and sword knots. For

▶ REPUBLIC OF ROME, LANCER OF THE LEGIONE ITALIANA, 1849 *This unit was part of the troops of the Papal States. Fatigues were a red fez together with the famous red shirt.*

parades, the grenadiers wore black bearskins with red cords and plume and a brass grenade badge on the front. Carabiniers wore bearskins with white cords and a red plume. Tunics were dark green with crimson piping, buttons and lace were white. They had red epaulettes.

There was also a cavalry regiment with black, Austrian-style helmets with brass comb – bearing a black caterpillar crest – front plate and chinscales. The single-breasted tunic was green with red facings, the breeches grey with a red side stripe, white belts, steel sabre sheath.

Troops of Modena

All troops wore the cockade of sky blue within white. All badges of rank were Austrian-pattern. From 1850 onward, soldiers wore a dark blue, hip-length double-breasted tunic with yellow buttons and dark grey trousers with a white side piping. Equipment consisted of white belts, and musket slings were also white. Officers' tunics were black. Infantry wore an Austrian-style shako with cockade and sky blue rosette at the front centre, and a black chinstrap. Officers had gold braid ranking to the shako crown. The Jäger battalion wore pike-grey tunics and trousers of Austrian style, with grass-green collars and pointed cuffs, white buttons. They wore a wide-brimmed black Corsican hat, with cock's feather plume, black belts and rifle sling.

Generals had dark blue coats with red facings and gold buttons, bicorns with dark green plumes, gold silk waist sashes and sword knots.

The state's dragoon regiment wore medium blue tunics and trousers with white buttons and belts, yellow facings and side piping, a black leather helmet of Austrian pattern, with brass front plate, comb and chinscales and a blue over white crest for parades

The artillery wore dark blue tunics with black facings piped red, yellow buttons, white belts and Corsican hats. Engineers had dark blue tunics, yellow buttons, cherry-red facings and pike-grey trousers with a cherry-red piping. Their belts were black; they wore infantry shakos with a black plume.

Troops of Naples

This kingdom's troops wore red cockades, officers' sashes and sword knots were red with narrow silver stripes. The 12 line infantry regiments wore dark blue tunics, facings differed for each regiment: 1st – sky blue; 2nd – light red; 3rd – black; 4th – amaranth; 5th – green; 6th – orange; 7th – yellow; 8th – pink; 9th – light blue; 10th – blue; 11th – amaranth; 12th – green. Grenadiers had bearskins with red plumes and cords for parades, the others wore kepis. Jägers wore dark green coats with black, hussar-style braiding on the chest, three rows of white ball buttons, yellow collar and plain cuffs, white belts and trousers. They wore Austrian-style shakos with a white horn front badge. The four Swiss infantry regiments wore red tunics and cuff flaps, yellow buttons, white epaulettes and belts, light blue

trousers. Facings: 1st – light blue; 2nd – yellow; 3rd – dark blue; 4th – black.

The cavalry wore helmets of Sardinian style, black turban, steel headpiece and brass comb with black crest, green tunics, yellow collar, shoulder straps, rectangular cuff flaps and piping, brass buttons, white belts and trousers. Lancers had czapkas, with red top half, brass fittings and a black plume, blue tunics and collar patches, red collars, pointed cuffs, lapels, white breeches and belts. The artillery wore a black kepi with red band and red double pompons and brass fittings, dark blue, single-breasted tunics with yellow buttons, red collar, plain round cuffs, epaulettes, turnbacks and piping, dark blue breeches and white belts. The artillery train wore a uniform similar to the French horse artillery, with blue pointed cuffs, edged in red.

◀ MODENA, TROOPER OF DRAGOONS, 1859
The helmet shows some Austrian influence, as does the uniform's simplicity. The crest was worn only for parades and is in the colours of the national cockade.

▶ PARMA, CAPTAIN, GRENADIERS OF THE GUARD, PARADE DRESS, 1850 *When Charles III became Duke of Parma in 1849, he reclothed his army in the Prussian-style regulations of 1842, replacing the eagles with three fleurs-de-lis.*

Troops of Parma

All troops wore the state's cockade of red, within blue, within gold. The household troops consisted of Grenadier Guards and Musketeer Guards. The Grenadiers were dressed as for the line, but with gold laces to their red collars and cuffs, and with red plumes. The Musketeers of the Guard wore the same but with black plumes and belts, white buttons and lace. From 1842 the infantry wore Prussian-style Pickelhauben with brass fittings. The Prussian-style single-breasted, hip-length tunic was dark blue with brass buttons. Facings to the low, standing collar, the round cuffs and rectangular cuff flaps varied with the battalion. The 1st wore light blue; the 2nd

wore white; the 3rd wore yellow. The crossed bandoliers were white. In 1859 the cuff flaps were abolished. The Jägers wore dark green tunics with back facings piped red (the latter abolished in 1859), black plumes, light blue trousers. Generals wore the Pickelhaube with gilt fittings and white, drooping feather plumes; single-breasted, dark blue tunics with red collars and cuffs, having gold embroidery, buttons and shoulder cords; light blue trousers. Their gold silk waist sashes had thin red and blue stripes along the length, as did their sword knots. Until 1859 company officers' rank badges were gold stripes along the top of the cuffs, and lilies on the epaulette straps. Field officers wore fringed golden epaulettes.

From 1850, the cavalry (Guides) wore the Pickelhaube and dark blue tunics with red collar and plain round cuffs, white belts and plumes and a dark blue and white belt. In 1859 the helmet was replaced with the Sardinian cavalry kepi. Their lance pennants were red, yellow and blue.

Foot artillery wore infantry-style uniforms with black belts, black facings piped red with brass buttons and yellow lace loops to collar and cuffs until 1859. Horse artillery wore the same, but double-breasted, with buff bandolier and waistbelt. Engineers; as foot artillery but with white buttons.

Troops of Sardinia

Grenadier companies wore red shoulder rolls and grenade badges on the shako, the light companies wore green rolls and hunting horn shako badges, the centre (fusilier) companies

◀ SARDINIA, OFFICER, 16TH INFANTRY REGIMENT, CAMPAIGN DRESS, 1849 *The shako, which is of the new pattern, was adopted in this year. The cross of Savoy appears on his belt buckle.*

▶ SARDINIA, BERSAGLIERE, 1848 *In the mid-1850s the tunic was altered to single-breasted. The strap system for the pack was of the Prussian model.*

wore dark blue shoulder rolls and crowned shields on their shakos, pierced with the regimental number. Belts were black for line troops, white for the Guard.

Officers wore epaulettes in the button colour, with thin fringes for junior officers, bullion for senior officers. Their sashes and sword straps were sky blue. The kepi followed the French development. The rifle-armed light infantry, or Bersaglieri, wore the billowing, cock's feather plumes to their hats. The cavalry wore dark blue tunics and sky blue helmet crests. The artillery wore the classic dark blue with black facings and brass buttons, facings edged in yellow piping. Shakos bore the white metal cross, belts were buff. Engineers wore artillery uniform with white buttons and yellow collar and cuffs and black belts.

Troops of Tuscany

From 1848 the infantry wore white, single-breasted tunics, with standing collar and plain round cuffs. In 1849 the bell-topped shako was replaced by that in the Austrian style, with cockade, loop and button and black leather chinstrap. The white coat was replaced by a double-breasted, dark blue, hip-length tunic, with white buttons and belts. Facings and piping were red, trousers were light blue with a red side piping. The Guard Battalion (Velites) wore the same uniform, but with red trousers and a red plume. Rank badges were of Austrian style. The Jägers wore pike-grey tunics with grass-green facings and yellow buttons, black belts and Corsican hats. These items, and the overall appearance, were all of Austrian style. Cavalry

wore infantry-style tunics, red facings, brass buttons and a black leather, Austrian-style helmet, with brass comb and fittings. Their light blue trousers had twin wide red stripes, with a narrow red piping in the middle. Belts were white with brass fittings. Foot artillery wore infantry uniform, but with yellow piping to collar and cuffs, light grey trousers (piped yellow) and buff belts. Generals wore infantry-style tunics and trousers, the latter with twin wide red stripes, having a narrow red piping between them. They had gold, fringed epaulettes and gold silk sashes and sword knots with narrow red stripes along them.

Garibaldi's Troops

Giuseppe Garibaldi's famous Red Shirts wore loose-fitting smocks dyed red along with varied headgear (from the round pillbox-style cap, to Corsican hats or a simple fez).

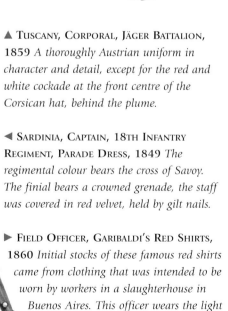

▲ TUSCANY, CORPORAL, JÄGER BATTALION, **1859** *A thoroughly Austrian uniform in character and detail, except for the red and white cockade at the front centre of the Corsican hat, behind the plume.*

◄ SARDINIA, CAPTAIN, 18TH INFANTRY REGIMENT, PARADE DRESS, **1849** *The regimental colour bears the cross of Savoy. The finial bears a crowned grenade, the staff was covered in red velvet, held by gilt nails.*

► FIELD OFFICER, GARIBALDI'S RED SHIRTS, **1860** *Initial stocks of these famous red shirts came from clothing that was intended to be worn by workers in a slaughterhouse in Buenos Aires. This officer wears the light blue and white colours of Sardinia and the cross on his belt plate. There was much variation in the uniforms of this volunteer corps.*

THE AMERICAN CIVIL WAR

ARMIES OF THE UNION

The American Civil War (1861–65) was an internal war in North America that began when 11 slave states declared their secession from the United States, to form the Confederate States of America (the Confederacy). Led by Jefferson Davis, they fought against the Federal government (the 'Union'), which was supported by all the free states and five border slave states in the north. The Union Army that fought and won the Civil War grew around a cadre of regular units, peacetime militia units, and a huge influx of volunteers dedicated to saving the Union. Forming a professional service from these three elements was a challenge, but by 1863 the Union had a trained and dedicated army led by inspiring and able generals.

▲ *Union general officers often wore what was practical and comfortable. The officer on the right is more or less uniformed according to regulations. The officer on the left, however, has his own ideas of comfort in the field.*

◄ *A cavalry charge into ranks of infantry in the age of the rifle musket was extremely risky for the cavalryman, but there were instances in the war where good cavalry defeated veteran infantry, such as in the Shenandoah Valley in 1864. This was done on more than one occasion during that campaign and has generally been overlooked by historians.*

RALLYING AROUND THE FLAG

Life for soldiers in the American Civil War was hard. Not only did they have to contend with the rigours of campaign and the frightening horrors of the battlefield, but also with disease, which was treated by a medical corps that had not progressed much beyond what the Romans had known about infection and tending wounds.

Recruitment

The Civil War volunteers came from all walks of life and many who came from isolated rural areas had no natural immunity to diseases. An infantry regiment might begin by mustering 1,000 men in camp, but be down to as little as 500 present for duty marching out for their first campaign.

Mustering such a large army, which the United States had never done before, was a monumental task –

▼ The 6th Maine Volunteer Infantry Regiment in 1862. Uniformity was a chance thing in the field. This company is generally in the same uniform with the exception of the drummer and the officer on the left.

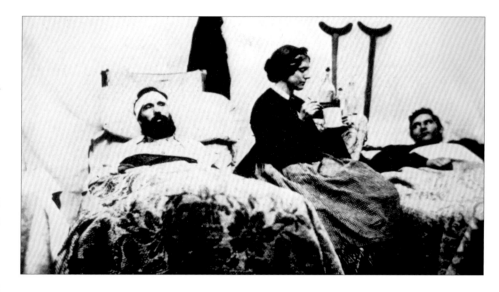

▲ A nurse tending the wounded at a Federal hospital in Nashville, Tennessee. Medical care was crude, and many on both sides died from disease and infection.

100,000 men probably served in the Mexican War of 1846 to 1848 whereas in the Civil War, the Union mustered 2,128,948 men for active service during the war. The war also strained the remount service, for the supply and movement of horses, as well as the clothing services, medical services, and the services of supply.

Equipment

Uniforms had to be made in quantity, along with headgear, shoes and boots, leather equipment to carry the soldiers' load and ammunition, and other regimental accoutrements (such as flags, standards and colours, as well as saddles and harnesses). Many manufacturers were dishonest and sought to make their fortune from the United States Government (many of the 'great' entrepreneurs of a later period first made their fortunes exploiting the war effort). While some manufacturers provided excellent materials, others supplied substandard goods, using cardboard for shoe soles, for example, and making trousers, coats and overcoats out of cloth known as 'shoddy' (made from scraps of other material), which quickly fell apart in the field.

The supply of livestock was just as open to corruption and opportunism. Cavalrymen, artillerymen and remount officers had to deal with unscrupulous horse dealers who would sell sick, old or infirm mounts to the army. Artillerymen actually had a harder job maintaining their mounts than the

cavalry did. Gun teams had to be carefully matched as to size and strength in pairs, one artillery driver to each two-horse team. On campaign, as the horses lost weight, harnesses had to be constantly refitted so that they would not cause injury. Horse losses in combat could be catastrophic.

Food and Supplies

The food eaten by the Civil War soldier was not the healthiest to be found. The staple item was hardtack, a twice-baked, hard square cracker also known as ship's biscuit, that would keep for years and could break the teeth of the unwary. Coffee was a necessity, and

▼ *The Union Army mortar gun known as the 'Dictator', was built to fire a shell weighing 200 pounds; here it is mounted on the train car required to transport it.*

every time the army came to a halt on the march, coffee would be broken out and boiled. Hardtack soaked in coffee or fried in bacon grease was a common meal on campaign.

Weaponry

The main long arm of the Civil War infantryman was the rifle musket that fired a .58 calibre round and could hit its target at 1,000 yards (914m). It had an effective range of between 500–600 yards (457–548m). It was 56in (140cm) long and could be fitted with a triangular socket bayonet that added another 15in (38cm) to its length. It fired a lead 'Minié' ball, named after the French officer that developed it, and was a weapon that could be fired in bad weather, something the older flintlock muskets could not do. Two of the most popular models of rifle

▲ *President Lincoln at General McClellan's HQ after the Battle of Antietam in September 1862. Lincoln later relieved McClellan for his failure to destroy Lee's army.*

musket (sometimes referred to as a rifled musket) were the Model 1861 Springfield (so-named because of the armoury where they were manufactured) and the imported British-made Enfield. Both were excellent weapons and ended up with the dubious distinction of being the biggest killer of the war. Other firearms were the .52 calibre Sharps carbine for the cavalry, along with various models of revolvers and edged weapons.

▼ *While Union troops generally began well-uniformed and equipped, as here, uniforms wore out quickly on campaign in the largely wooded American countryside.*

GENERAL OFFICERS AND STAFF

General and staff officers of the American Union forces usually dressed after their own fashion, though some definitely kept to the regulations. Some generals merely wore an enlisted man's uniform with general officers' epaulettes on the shoulders for ready identification. The purpose was comfort, utility and simplicity, and not for instant recognition. Others made it a point to be properly uniformed even on a day of battle.

Regulations

The regulation general officers' dress was a double-breasted frock coat of dark blue with two rows of gold buttons down the front. Sash and general officers' dress sword, belt and accoutrements would accompany this simple, elegant uniform and the hat was the regulation Hardee hat.

What was usually worn in the field was either the frock coat, or the enlisted man's sack coat, with the sash left in the baggage wagons. Shirts and vests were usually worn under the coat and the coats were frequently worn open for comfort. Slouch hats of dark blue or black were worn in the field as well as the forage cap, or kepi, that was modelled on the French headgear of the period. Branch insignia and unit designation were also worn on the forage cap by both officers and enlisted men.

Topographical engineers were a specialized section charged with making maps. The uniforms of officers of the topographical engineers and the medical service were generally the same as those of any other branch. The only distinctions were the colour of the epaulettes or shoulder straps, which would also indicate the individual's rank. The background colour of the epaulette would be in the individual's branch colour so that anyone could recognize to which organization the officer belonged. These are still

in use today in the Dress Blue uniforms of the United States Army.

One item of clothing that was very popular among the mounted arms (cavalry and horse artillery), was the short shell jacket that would also be worn by senior cavalry officers. The short jacket was much more convenient to wear when mounted than the frock or sack coat. The officers' version did not have the branch colour lace (red for artillery and yellow for cavalry) that was a feature of the enlisted man's version of the jacket, but it was still a handsome piece of uniform, both neat and somewhat dashing, while being quite functional.

▶ GENERAL GEORGE CUSTER, OFFICER OF CAVALRY, 1864 *General officers were allowed to design their own uniforms. This figure of General Custer depicts one of the definite show-offs of the war. He designed his own uniform and certainly intended that it should make him noticeable to both friend and enemy on the battlefield.*

Individual Expression
Cavalry officers on both sides were often highly conscious of their personal appearance. Some officers designed their own distinctive style of uniform, as Custer did, and these could be completely different from the regulation uniform, the oft-stated excuse being that the troops would be better able to identify their commander at a distance. Many

▶ GENERAL HENRY JACKSON HUNT, 1863
General Hunt was an artillery officer of unusual skill and devotion and he was arguably the best artilleryman the United States ever produced. He is uniformed here as required by regulations. As the artillery chief of the Army of the Potomac, he was responsible for the artillery concentrations at Malvern Hill and Antietam in 1862 and again at Gettysburg in July 1863.

◀ OFFICER, TOPOGRAPHICAL ENGINEERS, 1863 *Topographical engineers were responsible for accurate map-making. Engineer officers were also responsible for reconnaissance, were masters of many trades, and were indispensable to the war effort.*

general officers, Sheridan and Custer particularly, also had their own guidon carried so that their location on the battlefield could be found and followed by their commands, especially in a mêlée.

Staff officers would usually be uniformed by the example set by their commanding general. If the general officer was not too fussy, such as Grant, Sherman and some of the other northern generals, the officers assigned to their staffs were usually left to their own devices as to how they would dress

and what type of uniforms and accessories they would wear. If the general officer was particular about his dress, such as the meticulous Winfield Scott Hancock, the dress of the staff would naturally follow that example. Hancock, known as 'Hancock the Superb' because of his outstanding combat performance, was always in proper uniform and put on a clean, white shirt every morning. Even in the worst conditions, he was immaculate.

▼ SURGEON, 1863 *This surgeon wears the regulation uniform for his branch of the service. In the field, the tunic, sword and gloves would be discarded. Surgeons operated in the most primitive conditions and medical knowledge of the day had not progressed much past that of the Napoleonic period. Many wounded were lost to infection, especially the dreaded and deadly gangrene.*

PRE-WAR MILITIA

The militia system of locally raised civilian troops was by this time embedded in the American psyche. Militias were first raised to defend the first English settlements in the New World in the 16th century. A distrust of a standing army, which could be used as an instrument of oppression by a national government, preserved the popularity of the militia system.

Historic Traditions
In the Revolution, thoughtful officers such as Washington (who termed the militia a 'broken

reed'), Wayne, Greene and others knew from bitter experience that the militia could not stand against a well-trained and organized force, and they pressed for the establishment of an effective regular army. The resulting Continental Army was the backbone of American resistance in the Revolution, but upon its disbandment at the end of the war, the militia system was again resorted to by the government.

Militia units, some expensively and handsomely uniformed, were maintained throughout the country between the War of 1812 and the Civil War. While militia units remained in existence in the north throughout the war, their military usefulness and effectiveness was questionable.

Military Value of the Militia
The militia system did provide a pool of trained men that could be called on either as whole units or as individual replacements for existing units, but their contribution to the northern war effort is, at best, marginal. After the disaster at First Bull Run in 1861, Abraham Lincoln decided to fight his war with volunteer regiments

◀ OFFICER, 2ND REGIMENT, NEW HAMPSHIRE STATE MILITIA, 1861 *New Hampshire militia units were smartly uniformed and resembled the regulation American Army uniforms in a general way, though with particulars that set them apart, such as the colour and adornments on the kepi. These units, if and when they were mustered into Federal service, usually adopted the much more simple and practical field uniforms worn by much of the Union Army.*

▶ Private, 6TH REGIMENT, MASSACHUSETTS STATE MILITIA, 1861 *The 6th Massachusetts, which would look very much like a regular unit on parade, received its 'baptism of fire' from pro-southern rioters while marching through Baltimore in 1861. The shako and overcoat are typical of the 1850s look of the US Army, the shako being French-inspired.*

raised by the states, and not by calling up militia units into Federal service as was common practice.

There were generally two types of militia in the United States – the standing militia, which was supposed to incorporate every able-bodied male 'capable of bearing arms' – and the volunteer militia. While the first might not be of much military value, the

◀ **PRIVATE, 7TH REGIMENT, NEW YORK STATE MILITIA, 1861** *The 7th Regiment was known as a crack parade unit and was mustered in for temporary service in the first emergency call in 1861. The unit was uniformed in the popular grey colour, which was common to both sides early in the war. This tendency caused confusion in unit identification on the field of battle.*

▶ **PRIVATE, 12TH REGIMENT, NEW YORK STATE MILITIA, 1861** *The 12th Regiment was uniformed in the popular French 'chasseur' style, which typified French light infantry units of the period. The French influence was heavy among the volunteer and militia units of the period, though much of this would disappear with the combat units as the war dragged on.*

volunteer militia was useful and had provided excellent service in the field during the War of 1812.

The Volunteer Militia

This section of the militia was organized in units that varied from as small as a company or artillery battery to as large as a regiment. There were no militia brigades or divisions.

Some states had definite regulations concerning the formation, organization and uniforms for their volunteer militias, but these were frequently ignored. Unit designations could range from a simple numbering system, as with New York's infantry regiments, to fanciful names which incorporated colours, city names or

state mottos in the unit title. There were some more exotic formations of French-inspired zouave and chasseur units. There were many examples of 'Blues', 'Greens', 'Cadets', Fire Zouaves, Zouave Cadets and Rifles. Boston sported a red-uniformed unit of lancers and many of the more colourful cavalry units rode proud in European hussar-style dress, complete with pelisses, and colpacks for headgear.

One interesting American habit was the effect European-style uniforms had on the military forces in the United States, regular, volunteer and militia. Whichever was perceived as the leading European power at the time usually set the tone for the uniform styles in the United States.

At the time of the Civil War, the French were considered the leading military power in Europe and that influence was directly reflected in American uniform styles. French zouave and chasseur uniforms blossomed in the volunteer militia units all over the United States. Baggy trousers of sky blue and red, French-style shakos with multi-coloured round pompons, kepis and chasseur forage caps were all in evidence in the plethora of uniform styles present in the militia units. Colours of uniforms also varied greatly, though dark blue, grey, red and dark green were the predominant ones.

Philadelphia Light Horse

One particular unit of volunteer militia stood out from the mass of colour, cloth and bearskin to maintain a tradition of excellence throughout its existence. The Philadelphia City Troop of Light Horse was founded before the Revolution, and served gallantly in that conflict, though only a company in strength. It was called up twice during the Civil War, for the First Bull Run and the Gettysburg campaigns and it continues in existence today as part of the Pennsylvania National Guard. It always set a standard of efficiency and smartness, and has maintained itself throughout the existence of the nation when most of the other volunteer militia units have all but disappeared.

THE REGULAR ARMY

The US Army was very small in 1861, and its officers lacked much experience of leading or operating large forces. The United States had not fought a major war since the Mexican War of 1846–47, but did have the tradition of

▼ **NCO, Regular US Infantry Regiments, 1858** *This is the full dress for US infantry regiments during the 1850s, clearly showing the French influence that would change, particularly the shako, shortly before war broke out, becoming more 'American' in character.*

employing divisions in combat, though no commander that would rise to a major position in the Civil War had served at higher command levels during that conflict.

A Learning Process

The 16,000-strong US Army (on 1 January 1861 the strength of the United States Army was 1,098 officers and 15,304 enlisted men), true to American tradition, was unprepared for the outbreak of the Civil War. Not only was it too small, even by the standards of the period, but none of its officers had ever commanded any organization larger than a regiment, and there were few regiments in the

service that had all been together for any substantial period of time.

Neither side was prepared militarily. Most of the army was scattered across the great expanse of the American West, attempting to keep hostile tribes of Plains Indians in check and, at the same time, keeping a wary eye on the encroachment into Indian territory of land-hungry Americans. As most of these units were recalled eastward, they straggled into Washington and began to form the basis of the armies that would be sent south

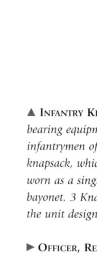

▲ **INFANTRY KIT, 1858** *This is the load-bearing equipment for the US regular infantrymen of the period. 1 Belt and knapsack, which was attached by straps to be worn as a single unit. 2 Waistbelt and bayonet. 3 Knapsack, or backpack, featuring the unit designation on the back.*

▶ **OFFICER, REGULAR US INFANTRY REGIMENTS, 1858** *This smartly dressed officer is in the regulation US Army uniform of the mid-1850s, before the change in headgear to the Hardee hat. With the exception of the large gold epaulettes and the shako, however, this is the uniform that was worn during the Civil War.*

to subdue the rebellion. Some of the officers of the US Army literally 'went South' and joined the Confederate Army. As southerners, they were torn by loyalty to their country, to their native state, and to the army they had served for years. Other southerners, such as John Gibbon (who would one day win his general's stars and command the famous Iron Brigade of the Army of the Potomac), stayed loyal to the Union while his family fought for the South.

Organization

The infantry was excellent, as were the five, soon to be six, cavalry regiments, but the artillery was in poor condition. Few of the companies in the four (later five) artillery regiments were properly equipped with either field pieces or horses and they were either employed as infantry or to man coastal forts. Most of the Regulars were recalled and either served as complete units or were used as cadres to train the new rush of volunteers that were determined to save the Union. Retired officers or those that had resigned came back into the service, usually to serve with fresh volunteer units.

When war started, the 5th and 9th infantry regiments were retained in the west to keep a wary eye on the Indians. Part of the 3rd Artillery Regiment was kept with them. Shortly after Fort Sumter fell to the Confederate bombardment in Charleston harbour, South Carolina, the authorized strength of the regular army was increased. Congress voted to expand the United States Army to 19 infantry regiments, 6 cavalry regiments, 5 artillery regiments, an engineer battalion, and various 'ash and trash'

▶ OFFICER, HORSE ARTILLERY, 1859 *The light, or horse, artillery was the elite arm of the US Army. The horse artillery had achieved that status in the war with Mexico from 1847–48 and the uniform adopted gave the overall appearance of the dash and élan of a mounted unit. In combat, the shako would be replaced by the kepi and shoulder scales (epaulettes) would be replaced by shoulder straps which would indicate the officer's rank.*

units of service troops. Not all of these units, however, were recruited up to strength, and regular infantry battalions in the field were sometimes commanded by the unit's most experienced or senior captain.

The advantages and experience the regular army gave to the Union armies is immeasurable. Congressional parsimony and the inherent distrust of a large standing army hurt the Union's war effort and prolonged the war into the bitter, bloody struggle it became. While it can never be said for certain that a larger, concentrated force of regulars could have subdued the southern

rebellion more quickly, the presence of a large, competent regular army ready to march south in 1861 would definitely have had an effect on southern morale and the will to fight.

Regular Infantry

Infantry dress for officers and enlisted men in the 1850s showed French influence but this uniform was replaced in 1859 with a frock coat, light or dark blue trousers, and the famous Hardee hat. Fatigue wear was now the sack coat, a ubiquitous uniform item that the greater majority of the infantry wore during the war.

The branch colour of the infantry was originally white, but had been changed to light or sky blue and this was the distinctive colour seen on the uniform for rank badges and the trim or braid used by musicians on the front of their dress uniform coats. While the dress uniform for all ranks was the frock coat with brass buttons, this was seldom worn, the usual practice being reliance in the field on the more comfortable and practical sack coat. Light blue trousers, the NCOs having a blue stripe along the outside trouser seam, were the norm and these were worn without leggings. Boots were not worn by infantrymen, with the exception of mounted officers, but the issue shoes were sturdy and had to be thoroughly broken-in. Most soldiers would tuck their trousers into their socks as a sort of 'field gaiter'. This was intended to keep dirt, pebbles and other debris out of their shoes on the march and in combat.

The personal equipment worn by the infantryman was of black leather and consisted of a waist belt with brass buckle, which held his bayonet and scabbard and his cap box (which contained the percussion caps for his rifle musket). A crossbelt was worn over his left shoulder, which was attached to the black cartridge box. His pack was held with black leather straps, which were usually seen intertwined across his chest in an unusual arrangement that had to be awkward at best. This was done because there was an error 'produced' with the leather equipment system that gave the pack 'extra' straps that were supposed to be attached to two small ammunition pouches on the front of the belt. As this never occurred, this left the soldiers to 'attach' the straps as best they could. The error was made because the two departments responsible for producing and designing equipment neglected to co-ordinate their efforts. As usual, it was the soldier in the field that had to live with the consequences.

As the war went on, most soldiers would discard their knapsacks or packs and make up a blanket roll with their personal items in it. They would take their blanket, wrap all of their personal items, which veterans would keep to a bare minimum (some to the extent that between two men, one would carry the coffee and the other the sugar), inside. This would be worn crosswise over one shoulder and fastened at the opposite hip. This arrangement left essential field equipment, such as ammunition, easily accessible.

One essential piece of equipment was worn using a shoulder strap over the right shoulder and that was the haversack. In this would be carried items the soldier might need or want immediately, for example during a break on the line of march. Over the

◄ TROOPER, US 2ND CAVALRY, 1862 *This is the uniform as it was supposed to be worn by regular US cavalrymen during the period. Note the double lace bars on his collar, which were supposed to be a distinction of regular US mounted troops, but were used by both regulars and volunteer units during the war. This trooper is reasonably well-equipped, though he would usually also be armed with a pistol and carbine in the field.*

◀ **OFFICER, FIELD ARTILLERY, 1863**
This is the regulation uniform for artillery officers in the field during the war. The frock coat was worn, but many artillery officers would wear the shorter shell jacket, as they were usually mounted, as indicated by the riding boots. The hat, as here, or the kepi would be worn in the field.

by the forage cap and perhaps by a slouch hat, but the general appearance of cocky jauntiness would be maintained. The horse artillery batteries prided themselves both on their efficiency and their dress. They considered themselves the elite of the army, and had won high repute for efficiency in the War of 1812, and skill and dash in the Mexican War.

Field artillery officers might wear a kepi, or fatigue/forage cap instead of the slouch hat, and might also wear an enlisted man's sack coat with his rank sewn on instead of the frock coat. As the war went on, uniforms became simpler. Throughout the war officers of all arms carried a sword as both a badge of rank and as a sidearm.

Cavalry

When war broke out in 1861 the cavalry arm had two regiments of dragoons, two regiments of cavalry, and a regiment of mounted rifles. That year another regiment of cavalry was formed and shortly thereafter all six of the mounted regiments were reclassified as cavalry and renumbered one to six. Naturally, this caused some resentment in the old regiments as their uniforms and designations were traditions to be items of pride within the regiments. Old distinctions were kept as much as possible in the regiments, regulations being things that could be ignored.

▶ **FIRST SERGEANT, REGULAR CAVALRY REGIMENTS, 1861** *This nattily uniformed sergeant major of cavalry is in the regulation dress prescribed at the beginning of the war. The Hardee hat has by now replaced the shako, and with that exception (usually replaced by the kepi), the shoulder scales and gloves, this is the uniform worn in the field. Boots would also often be worn.*

Dragoon Regiments

The two dragoon regiments had a full dress uniform (for parades) and a modified version of it in the field. Trousers on campaign would probably be tucked into boots, and there might be a pistol stuck into a boot for good measure, as it was easier to get to than one in the holster on the waist belt. The orange braid and trim, which was the distinctive colour of the dragoon arm, was officially changed when all of the US Army's mounted regiments were redesignated as cavalry, but the two regiments undoubtedly kept it until it wore out, as they were loathe to be termed mere cavalry.

same shoulder was the strap for his canteen, the strap usually being white, which was interesting; as all of the other infantryman's equipment was dark in colour this white strap was quite visible on the dark blue background of the soldier's uniform.

Artillery Dress

The light artillerymen wore uniforms which resembled those of the cavalry, being a mounted arm, with the short coat with red braiding in place of the yellow or orange of the cavalry and dragoon regiments. In the field and on campaign, the artillery wore basically the same uniform, especially if the battery was designated horse artillery. The full dress shako would be replaced

THE VOLUNTEER INFANTRY

The best infantry without a doubt on either side of the American Civil War were the regular army infantry regiments that could manoeuvre on the battlefield better than any, and upon whom the volunteer units looked with envy.

The Strawfeet

Many men in the volunteer infantry were literally right off the farm and this was their first exposure to urban life. Some did not even know left from right. What they did know was the difference between hay and straw, and an inspired instructor ordered his new recruits to tie some hay to one foot and straw to another when they were drilling, and that is how

cadence was called. Hence, 'strawfoot' became the nickname of any new soldier, or rookie, but most especially a particularly innocent one.

The volunteer infantry regiments were a varied lot. The popular view of their uniform is of light blue trousers, a blue coat or blouse, and black leather equipment, topped off by either a kepi or a slouch hat. While this is true for much of the infantry regiments, it is not for a great many who wore specialized uniforms of some type, and who strove,

◄ PRIVATE, 42ND PENNSYLVANIA VOLUNTEER INFANTRY REGIMENT (BUCKTAILS), 1862 *Also known as the 13th Pennsylvania Reserves, this regiment added the flash of a deer tail to their headgear, whether it be kepi, slouch hat, or whatever they happened to be wearing at the time. Their outstanding combat performance was rewarded by the army by the forming of a 'Bucktail Brigade of Light Infantry' later in the war. The regiment was also known for its creative and effective foraging capability.*

▲ *The Battle of Murfreesboro or Stones River, fought in January 1863, was an indecisive draw, but the strategic initiative remained with the Federals.*

because of pride and esprit de corps, to maintain it even in the most horrible conditions in the field.

Uniforms of both the volunteer and regular regiments were influenced by styles popular in Europe. In the 1850s the French Army was thought to be the best in Europe, and victories in northern Italy over the Austrians in 1859 tended to reinforce this belief. Therefore, American uniforms reflected that influence. The regular army infantry uniforms of the 1850s were definitely French inspired, and the zouave fashion spread through the north, and many militia units dressed themselves in either zouave, modified zouave, tirailleur or chasseur uniforms based on those units then serving in the French Army.

Zouave Style

The American zouave units that blossomed during the Civil War were modelled on the elite troops that evolved from the French campaigns in Africa. These new French troops generally wore baggy red trousers, short blue jackets, short gaiters, topped off by a red fez, sometimes wrapped in a turban. The short jacket was brightly embroidered in yellow lace, the entire picture presenting a striking uniform.

▼ PRIVATE, 165TH NEW YORK (2ND BATTALION, DURYEE'S ZOUAVES), 1864 *Duryee's Zouaves, the 5th New York, was back up to strength by 1864, but so many recruits were available that a second battalion was formed. The new regiment was uniformed almost exactly as the original and these two regiments, along with the 114th Pennsylvania, came closest to the French original.*

The zouave craze swept the north before the war and it was by far the most popular of the foreign-inspired uniforms. The most famous of the pre-war units was Ephraim Ellsworth's Zouave Cadets who travelled around the country giving demonstrations of zouave-style drill, dash and élan.

▼ PRIVATE, 146TH NEW YORK VOLUNTEER INFANTRY REGIMENT, 1863 *This zouave-style uniform was adopted by the New York Volunteers mid-1863, and worn for the rest of the war. While the regiment was known as a zouave unit, this dress is actually a form of the uniform of the Tirailleurs Algeriens of the French Army, known as the Turcos. The officers of this regiment were not uniformed the same as the enlisted men and wore a variety of uniforms.*

▼ SERGEANT, 14TH BROOKLYN, 1862 *The 14th Brooklyn dressed in its version of the French chasseur uniform and held an excellent combat reputation throughout its service. The regiment's official designation gave it the number '84' on the list of New York volunteer regiments, but the unit preferred, and was usually referred to as, the 14th Brooklyn, its old militia number and designation. The small flag is an infantry guidon, attached to a smooth piece of wood that fitted easily into the barrel of the rifle musket, a French practice from the 18th century.*

◀ PRIVATE, 155TH PENNSYLVANIA VOLUNTEER INFANTRY REGIMENT, 1864 *This volunteer regiment began the war in the usual uniform of sky-blue trousers and dark blue coats and kepis. In mid-1863 the brigade was 'converted' to zouave drill and uniform, and this handsome dark blue uniform in traditional zouave style is what the regiment was issued in early 1864. From then on, this is what was worn both in the field and in garrison until the war was over.*

▶ PRIVATE, 114TH PENNSYLVANIA VOLUNTEER INFANTRY REGIMENT (COLLIS' ZOUAVES), 1864 *From its inception in 1862 this regiment wore zouave dress that was one of the closest to the original French design in the US service. This outstanding unit suffered heavily at Gettysburg in July 1863. The next year the regiment was assigned as the provost guard of the Army of the Potomac and it also provided the band for army headquarters.*

under the jackets. Rank insignia was worn on the upper sleeves by the enlisted men and on the epaulette straps of the frock coat by the officers.

Some of the regiments that wore full zouave dress in a variety of colours were the 10th New York Volunteer Infantry Regiment whose short coattees were first dark blue and then brown, with red fezzes and white turbans and sky blue trousers tucked into white gaiters. The officers again wore the usual frock coat and the regiment eventually 'converted'

American zouave dress took many forms. Some such costumes were quite simple and not as flamboyant as the 'full' zouave dress adopted by so many volunteer regiments at the start of and during the war, such as the 11th Indiana Volunteer Infantry Regiment, also known as Wallace's Zouaves. The officers wore dark blue frock coats and trousers along with the ubiquitous kepi, and the enlisted men wore short grey zouave-style jackets, kepis, and light blue trousers sometimes tucked into short tan gaiters and blue shirts

▶ *A Union bivouac showing the troops of a zouave regiment around the campfire. Only officers would have had tents of this size.*

into the usual infantry dress of dark blue sack coat over sky blue trousers.

The 146th New York Volunteer Infantry Regiment wore a complete zouave uniform but in sky blue with yellow lace and trimming. Both the red fez and turban were worn along with white gaiters. Officers wore a natty semi-regulation uniform of dark blue shell jacket and trousers with yellow trim along with a red kepi trimmed in gold lace. The enlisted man's uniform resembled the French tirailleurs uniform, which was in zouave style but in the light blue colour worn by native Algerian troops in French service.

The 155th Pennsylvania Volunteer Infantry Regiment was in complete zouave uniform, but in dark blue jackets and trousers, again with yellow trim and white gaiters. The officers wore the same uniform but with a kepi in place of the fez. There were some regiments who wore the same colour of zouave uniforms as their French brethren. The 114th Pennsylvania was one of these with the dark blue short jacket, red trousers along with fez and turban (the 5th and 9th New York Volunteer Infantry Regiments also wore this general overall uniform). The jacket was laced in red trim.

▶ *Mary Tebe, vivandière of the 114th Pennsylvania, wore a zouve-style short jacket with red trim, a blue dress with red trim, and red trousers underneath.*

Following the French tradition the 114th had a *vivandière*, or sutleress, called Mary Tebe. She accompanied the regiment on campaign and on the battlefield, supplying them with provisions, dressed in modified zouave style. Interestingly, while she is mentioned in various personal memoirs and writings about this famous regiment, she is not mentioned in any official account or record.

Some of the units that originally wore zouave style eventually, as noted, converted to the usual 'regulation' dress of the Union infantry. Some, however, in the famous Army of the Potomac for example, were rewarded for excellent combat service by being granted permission to convert to zouave-style dress as the mark of an elite unit.

◀ **PRIVATE, 7TH NEW HAMPSHIRE VOLUNTEER INFANTRY REGIMENT, 1863** *This regiment, like the five regiments of the Iron Brigade, wore a variation of US Army regulation dress with dark blue trousers, frock coats and Hardee hats. Drummers were probably uniformed in the usual regulation musician's dress but probably wore the kepi, at least in the field. This regiment fought in South Carolina, where the uniform must have been hot and uncomfortable.*

▶ **PRIVATE, 2ND WISCONSIN VOLUNTEER INFANTRY REGIMENT (IRON BRIGADE), 1863** *The 2nd Wisconsin volunteer regiment, one of the regiments of the famous Iron Brigade, was re-uniformed by the commander that moulded the unit, General John Gibbon. He selected the regulation uniform of the regular infantry, which consisted of the frock coat and the Hardee hat. The hats, which were black, gave the brigade its first nickname, the Black Hat Brigade. The uniform shown here is the one worn on active service after some time in the field.*

Chasseur Style

French-style chasseur uniforms were adopted by some volunteer units and while they are similar to zouave units in general, there are particulars in style and detail which make them stand out. In general the chasseur-inspired uniforms were more trim and simple than the full-trousered zouave style and were much more in line with the regulation uniforms as worn on campaign. Generally speaking, the American version of the French uniform can be termed 'modified' chasseur style.

The 12th Regiment, New York State Militia, wore a handsome dark blue uniform coat with white piping on

▶ Drummer, 2nd Wisconsin Volunteer Infantry Regiment (Iron Brigade), 1863 *This drummer belongs to the Iron Brigade and could represent any of the four infantry regiments that made up the brigade. Initially the brigade was issued short, white gaiters by General Gibbon, but these eventually either wore out or were discarded by the men on campaign. Sometimes infantrymen would tuck their trousers into their socks on campaign instead, which served the same purpose as gaiters.*

the collar and cuffs as well as white rank insignia on the upper arms (it should be noted that this was the 'old Army' branch colour for infantry). A light blue kepi was the regulation headgear which matched the sky blue chasseur trousers; though full they were not as voluminous as the zouave version. The coat came down to the upper thigh, and though not as long in the skirt as the frock coat, it was sufficiently long in the skirt to be evident. Officers wore the usual dress of frock coat and sky-blue trousers, along with a sky-blue kepi.

Drummers wore the same general uniform as the enlisted men, but did have a short zouave-style jacket with white and sky blue trim. The regimental drum major wore a frock coat literally dripping in gold lace with heavy gold fringed epaulettes on each shoulder and gold lace across the front of the coat. His baldric was sky blue and the whole ensemble was topped with a magnificent black bearskin cap and white plume.

The 44th New York Volunteer Infantry Regiment was also known as The People's Ellsworth Regiment, sometimes also referred to as Ellsworth's Avengers. The regiment's

◀ Officer, Union Infantry Regiments, 1861−65 *This is how a well-dressed infantry officer would appear in camp and in the field. The kepi was a popular and comfortable piece of headgear and appeared in many variations throughout the war, some modelled exactly as the original French design, others in a more 'Americanized' style. The epaulette straps for officer rank indication are shown clearly here.*

first dress was a modified chasseur uniform, all in dark blue, with kepis as the headgear. Later, they were re-uniformed in the regulation US infantry uniform of dark blue coat and sky-blue trousers, but there is evidence that the chasseur uniform was still being worn in 1864.

The 14th Regiment, New York State Militia, was taken into federal service as the 84th New York Volunteer Infantry Regiment. However, soldiers' pride being what it is, they always referred to themselves as the '14th Brooklyn'. They were uniformed in a colourful chasseur uniform of short blue coattees, red trousers, white gaiters and red kepis. They maintained this uniform for their entire service with the Army of the Potomac. Their drummers had short blue jackets with a red plastron on the front, red kepis and red trousers.

The 83rd Pennsylvania Volunteer Infantry Regiment was apparently first uniformed in a blue jacket and trousers with yellow shirts. There are no pictures of this uniform. They were then issued the uniform worn by the French Chasseurs de Vincennes, which consisted of a dark blue coattee over grey trousers, white gaiters and chasseur-style shakos with falling feather plumes. French style fatigue caps were also worn. Apparently this uniform did not last past March 1862 when they were ordered into the regulation US Army field dress.

It should be noted that field equipment, personal equipment and weapons were all standard US issue for the zouave and chasseur units. Officers and NCOs, as in the usual uniform, all wore red sashes, and senior NCOs were authorized the wear of swords.

Other Distinctive Uniforms

The 42nd Pennsylvania Volunteer Infantry Regiment was also known as the Kane Rifle Regiment and the 13th Pennsylvania Reserves. The unofficial title of The Bucktails was inspired by the regiment's habit of wearing a deer tail on the front of their headgear, officers included. The regiment consisted of crack-shot Pennsylvania backwoodsmen, adept at skirmishing and fighting in open order.

A brigade of light infantry, known as the Bucktail Brigade of Light Infantry was organized and consisted of the 149th and 150th Pennsylvania and was the 2nd Brigade of the 3rd Division of the I Corps of the Army of the Potomac. This brigade was organized in late 1862. The uniform of the Bucktails was the normal dark blue

▶ INFANTRY EQUIPMENT, 1861–65
1 Pistol holster. 2 Bayonet scabbard and frog.
3 Haversack. 4 Canteen, cover and strap.
5 Cap pouch to carry the percussion caps that fired the rifle musket when struck by the hammer. 6 Ammunition pouch, closed.
7 Ammunition pouch, open.

coat or blouse with light blue trousers. Headgear consisted of either kepis or slouch hats, with the famous bucktails. In the summer of 1862 the regiment received Sharps rifles and were later issued Spencer repeating rifles.

In early 1862 artilleryman John Gibbon was promoted to brigadier general of volunteers and was given command of the only western brigade in the Army of the Potomac. The brigade consisted of 2nd, 6th and 7th Wisconsin Volunteer infantry regiments as well as the 19th Indiana Volunteer Infantry Regiment (later the 24th Michigan Volunteer Infantry Regiment would be added to the brigade). Gibbon was impressed with the raw material that made up the

brigade, but that was about it. He was determined to make it into the best trained, toughest brigade in the army.

After initial resistance to his Regular Army methods, the officers and men of the brigade settled down to hard work. Gibbon also procured a distinctive uniform for the brigade. White gaiters

▼ NCO UNION FIELD UNIFORM, 1861–65
This corporal shows the 'normal' and traditional look of the Union Army during the Civil War. The coat is a 'sack coat', comfortable and easy to care for. It was worn by both officers, including generals, and enlisted men. The regulation pack was often discarded and the personal equipment carried in a blanket roll worn across the body.

Brawner's Farm just before the Second Battle of Bull Run (Second Manassas). The fight was a draw, but the strawfeet of the soon-to-be-christened Iron Brigade had made their reputation. At the end of the war when records were being compared between units, it was

◀ **PRIVATE, US SHARPSHOOTERS, 1862** *The two regiments of US sharpshooters were regulars, though volunteers, and all had to be expert marksmen. They initially wore infantry green, and were armed with the Sharps rifle.*

▼ **ENLISTED DRUMMER, UNION INFANTRY. 1861–65** *The overcoat is regulation, and the lining of the cape would be the same colour as the outside, branch distinctive colours not being used until after the war. His drum is also regulation.*

found that the Iron Brigade had the highest proportion of men killed and wounded than any other brigade in the Union Army.

Two regular regiments of sharpshooters were recruited and formed at the beginning of the war. Known as Berdan's Sharpshooters after the man that raised and organized

▼ **OFFICER, 9TH REGIMENT VETERAN RESERVE CORPS, 1864** *The Veteran reserve corps was issued a regulation-style uniform in the colour shown here, though this was never popular, especially among the officers. Enlisted men were allowed to wear the regulation fatigue uniform of dark blue sack coat and sky-blue trousers on fatigue duty. The officers eventually went back to the dark blue frock coat.*

and gloves were issued, as were Regular Army frock coats and the tall regulation Hardee hat, which was black and turned up on one side with an eagle pin. The drummers of the brigade wore the same uniform though in the infantry branch colour of light or sky blue, with the usual musician's lace on the front of the frock coat.

The troops took to their new uniform with pride and became if not the best brigade in the Army of the Potomac, then one of the top two. Their combat reputation was legend in the army. Their first action was a meeting engagement with the famed Stonewall Brigade at the Battle of them, they were officially the 1st and 2nd regiments of United States Sharpshooters. They wore a distinctive uniform of dark green frock coats and trousers, with dark tan gaiters and usually a kepi, though slough hats were also worn. If it became difficult to maintain the all-green uniform in the field, sky-blue trousers would be worn with the distinctive green frock coats. Overcoats were either regulation light blue or could also be medium grey.

One interesting unit fought in the western theatre of operations and was unique in the Union armies. To answer the multitude of Confederate units that plagued the lines of communication in the Union rear areas, an infantry brigade commanded by Colonel John T. Wilder was mounted and equipped like cavalry but operated in the old dragoon style as mounted infantry, to move quickly by horse and fight on foot. Eventually, Colonel Wilder's own infantry regiment, the 17th Indiana Volunteer Infantry Regiment, followed by four others, the 72nd Indiana, 98th Illinois, 123rd Illinois and the 92nd Illinois (in that order) were uniformed and mounted as cavalry. They were not issued sabres as they were mounted infantry, but they were issued cavalry shell jackets without the lace. Their drums were traded for trumpets and they probably were later issued guidons. By all accounts they were a successful unit and did well in purging the Union rear areas of guerrillas and enemy cavalry.

Veterans

The Veteran Reserve Corps, originally designated the Invalid Corps, was organized in April 1863. Eventually reaching a strength of 24 regiments, each of two battalions, these units were intended to release able-bodied men on garrison duty to the field armies. The first battalion was to be made up of men still able to bear arms, the second battalion of men who still had the use of one arm. As originally organized, there were also to be third battalions in each regiment, the men constituting these units to have the use of one leg. There were insufficient numbers of the latter to organize these companies, so they were never organized at all.

The prescribed uniform was to be light blue coatee and trousers for enlisted men and light blue frock coats and trousers for officers. The officers' uniform was unpopular and they were allowed to wear the regulation dark blue frock coat. The enlisted man's coattee was almost identical to the cavalry jacket with the exception that it had cloth epaulette straps. For fatigue details and guard duty, the first battalion men wore the usual dark blue sack coat and light blue trousers.

▶ **PRIVATE, THE LIGHTENING BRIGADE, 1863**
This unit, the brainchild of Colonel John Wilder, was re-uniformed and re-equipped as mounted infantry to purge the Union rear areas of guerillas and other annoyances. The shell jacket has had the cavalry distinctions removed, but other cavalry equipment was retained, such as bugles and guidons.

ETHNIC REGIMENTS

A good portion of the infantry regiments raised for the Union at the outbreak of the war were 'ethnic' in nature. There were Irish, German, Scottish and French units, and an Italian regiment, that also had specific dress to highlight their alleged ethnicity and which added colour and panache to the army.

Many of the German troops had an unhappy history, and remained unpopular with native-born American units. The Germans might have spoken in a sharp accent or in broken English, but they fought willingly. Some soldiers, including some of their generals, were former army officers from the various German states, knew their profession well and proved to be thorough and inspirational officers, such as the expert artilleryman Hubert Dilger, whose men, native born or not, followed him repeatedly into the fire.

The XI Corps of the Army of the Potomac was made up in large part by German regiments, termed 'Dutchmen' by native-born Americans. The corps as a whole had a bad reputation, not helped by being stampeded by Stonewall Jackson at Chancellorsville in May 1863 and retreating again, albeit with heavy losses, on the first day of the Battle of Gettysburg.

early on in the conflict.

The 79th New York, for example, was raised as a Scottish regiment in flavour and uniform, the full kilt being issued but probably not worn in the field. Scottish trews, however, were worn in the field. This lively regiment was guilty of gross insubordination early in the war and had their colours taken away as punishment. The disgraced regiment was given a new commander who reshaped the unit.

Generally speaking, these colourful uniforms adopted by

Variations in Dress

Most of the regiments composed of particular ethnic groups wore the standard infantry, cavalry or artillery uniform. There were, however, some interesting variations, especially

◀ **PRIVATE, 79TH NEW YORK STATE MILITIA, 1861** *This regiment had both the kilt and the trews in its uniform inventory. Initially understrength when volunteers were called for, the unit did recruit enough men to be able to participate in the First Battle of Bull Run in 1861. Curiously, the Scottish uniform was not worn, but the usual dark blue uniform of the army. However, there is evidence that the Scottish uniform was retained during the war.*

▶ **55TH NEW YORK VOLUNTEER INFANTRY REGIMENT, 1862** *Raised in 1861 and commanded by the Frenchman, Baron Philippe Regis de Trobriand, this was another ethnic regiment, this time made up of Frenchmen – or at least pseudo-Frenchman. Its uniform was unique, as shown here. The regiment was reduced to a four-company battalion by 1862 and was amalgamated with the 38th New York Volunteer Infantry Regiment.*

The Irish Brigade

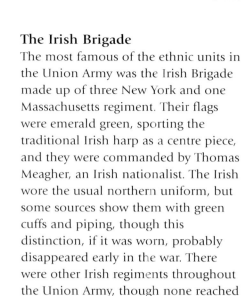

The most famous of the ethnic units in the Union Army was the Irish Brigade made up of three New York and one Massachusetts regiment. Their flags were emerald green, sporting the traditional Irish harp as a centre piece, and they were commanded by Thomas Meagher, an Irish nationalist. The Irish wore the usual northern uniform, but some sources show them with green cuffs and piping, though this distinction, if it was worn, probably disappeared early in the war. There were other Irish regiments throughout the Union Army, though none reached the fame of this brigade.

sharpshooters. Generally speaking, this was for two reasons. First, it was too hard to get adequate replacement uniforms to the troops in the field for such a small, specialized 'order'. Second, it was easier as the war went on to replace worn out clothing with what was readily available, and the regulation uniform was much easier to care for in the field. This wasn't always the case, as tradition after a few years took hold, as with the desire to keep uniformed zouave regiments with the army, but active service in the types of terrain in which the armies fought quickly wore out uniforms and equipment.

The Garibaldi Guard was named after the Italian patriot that fought so hard to unify his country in the 1850s and 1860s. Their striking uniforms consisted of frock coats of dark blue, matching trousers piped in red. They were also issued red undershirts and they wore round felt hats decorated with feathers on the left side which was akin to the famous Italian light infantry, the Bersaglieri of the Sardinian Army. They quite possibly also wore a red shirt as an outer garment, which was probably inspired by the Garibaldists during the Italian Wars of Unification.

▲ **39TH NEW YORK VOLUNTEER INFANTRY REGIMENT, 1861** *This regiment had a rocky start and a protracted shakedown period. After internal turmoil, the regiment received a new commanding officer and eventually became a good combat unit. By that time, however, the original uniforms – shown here – in the style and manner of the famous Italian Bersaglieri, were gone. The regiment was then issued the usual dark blue coats and sky-blue trousers that were the common field uniform for the Union infantry.*

newly raised units at the beginning of the war gave way to the usually seen and pictured blue sack coats and light blue trousers of the Regular Army. This even happened to such specialized units as Berdan's two regiments of

▶ **PRIVATE, 88TH NEW YORK VOLUNTEER INFANTRY REGIMENT (IRISH BRIGADE), 1863** *The Irish Brigade, an outstanding combat unit, was assigned to the famous II Corps originally commanded by General Edwin 'Bull' Sumner, one of the old army stalwarts whose point of pride was that his army corps never lost a flag or a gun. The Irish Brigade was a large part of that reputation and distinguished itself at Antietam and Gettysburg.*

AFRICAN-AMERICAN REGIMENTS

There was much opposition, both political and within the army as a whole, to the employment of black troops. Officers and government officials, however, who were dedicated both to the advancement of black Americans and their employment as combat troops forced the recruitment of both former slaves and northern freedmen and over 180,000 black troops served the Union from late 1862–65. Generally, they were employed in secondary theaters where the fighting was just as deadly as in the

▲ *This period print shows the storming of Battery Wagner outside Charleston, South Carolina, in July 1863. Colonel Shaw is shown falling at the head of his men.*

main theatres of war, but their participation proved that black Americans could and would fight; their regiments are among the 300 fighting regiments of the Union.

The most controversial troops on either side during the war were those raised from the black population of the nation. Invariably, they were northern units and did not exist at the beginning of the war. Not until late

1862 was the first regiment consisting of northern freedmen raised to fight for the Union. Massachusetts was the first northern state to step up to the plate and recruited the famous 54th Regiment of Massachusetts Volunteer Infantry. Officered by white combat veterans, it was a picked regiment that became the darling of abolitionist Boston. Its commander was Robert Gould Shaw, the son of abolitionists who was a wounded combat veteran. There were so many volunteers among the

◀ COMMANDING OFFICER, 54TH MASSACHUSETTS VOLUNTEER INFANTRY REGIMENT, 1863 *This figure of Colonel Robert Gould Shaw shows the regulation uniform for Union field grade officers during the war. The regimental commander of the famous 54th Massachusetts, Shaw led his regiment against Battery Wagner, South Carolina, and was killed in action at its head. Respected and beloved by his troops, his was the first black regiment in the north during the war.*

▶ SERGEANT MAJOR, 54TH MASSACHUSETTS VOLUNTEER INFANTRY REGIMENT, 1863 *This NCO is Lewis Douglass, the elder son of Frederick Douglass, the man who was instrumental in the formation of the 54th Massachusetts. As sergeant major of the regiment Lewis fought in and survived the bloody assault on Battery Wagner.*

▲ FIRST SERGEANT, 1ST SOUTH CAROLINA VOLUNTEER INFANTRY REGIMENT, 1863 *The 1st South Carolina regiment was formed from former slaves by Thomas Wentworth Higginson who, like Robert Shaw, was from a prominent New England family who were staunch abolitionists. His unit was smartly uniformed and disciplined. Like most of the black units formed from former slaves, getting qualified NCOs was a problem, as they had to be able to read and write.*

black population that a second regiment was formed, the 55th Massachusetts. The 1st South Carolina, formed by Thomas Wentworth Higginson, was another such unit. Its uniform was a distinctive combination

of styles in use in the army. Higginson undoubtedly designed it himself, and in photographs of the regiment, it is obvious they took pride in their appearance, more so than the usual white regiments. The uniform probably did not stand up to hard campaigning, however, and by the end of its service, the regiment was probably in standard dark blue coat and sky-blue trousers. They did so well that four black regiments, two cavalry and two infantry, were raised for service against the Plains Indians after the Civil War was over. All of them were excellent outfits, and the cavalry regiments, the 9th and 10th, are particularly famous as the Buffalo Soldiers.

▲ GUNNER, HEAVY ARTILLERY BATTERIES, UNITED STATES COLORED TROOPS, 1864 *The black units of the US Army in the Civil War were mostly infantry, but there were artillery and cavalry units among them. This heavy artilleryman, who would man the siege guns in the field, is uniformed correctly for his branch and rank. He holds the rammer and sponge staff used to both swab the gun tube and ram home the charge and round, as well as the ubiquitous water bucket.*

The heavy artilleryman would actually be uniformed in a light artillery uniform, which was probably easier to maintain, undoubtedly more dashing, and probably much more comfortable that the regulation coat.

ARTILLERY

Field artillery had been the *corps d'elite* of the United States Army since Washington had praised its performance at the Battle of Monmouth in 1778, stating to its commander, General Henry Knox, that "no artillery could have been better served than ours".

Union Dominance

The Union artillery dominated the battlefields of the first half of the war. The Battle of Antietam was described by southern General D.H. Hill as an "artillery hell", the Confederate artillery quite literally being blown off the battlefield. George Pickett's famous, futile and bloody charge at Gettysburg the following year was destroyed by the fire of General Henry Hunt's artillery. The small remnant of

▼ CAPTAIN HUBERT DILGER, BATTERY I, 1ST OHIO LIGHT ARTILLERY, 1863 *This figure of Captain Hubert Dilger shows the uniform he usually wore in combat. His coat is draped across his saddle and he is shown wearing enlisted trousers. One of the best battery commanders in the service, Dilger was a German immigrant, formerly of the Baden horse artillery. Allegedly, he emigrated to the United States in a hurry after being 'involved' with the Grand Duke of Baden's sister.*

Confederate General Armistead's brigade of Pickett's Division that actually managed to reach the Union position on Cemetery Ridge was destroyed by both Union infantry and short-range artillery fire.

Field, Horse and Heavy Artillery

There were three types of field artillery in the US Army of the period: field, horse and heavy. The field artillery, sometimes referred to as light artillery, was also called foot artillery and the gunners were actually expected to walk beside their pieces, but with the design of the excellent limber and caisson of the period, the gunners rode into combat on the ammunition boxes which doubled as seats and had handles for the gunners to hold onto when the batteries moved faster than a walk. At the war's beginning there were 4 regiments of regular artillery, each of them having 12 companies. Generally speaking, no more than two companies in each regiment were equipped as field or horse artillery, usually because of the sacred word 'economy'. The remaining companies of a regiment would be serving either as garrisons of the coastal defences of the country or as infantry. Sometimes, they also served on the frontier as cavalry, being as familiar with horses as the cavalry regiments. The 5th US Artillery Regiment was authorized in July 1861 just as the shooting started. It was during this period that the term 'battery' for a company-sized artillery unit came into general usage instead of the time-honoured term 'company'.

Horse artillery, also termed flying artillery, was the elite of the elite, they accompanied an army's cavalry and all of the gunners were individually mounted. One man in four was a

▼ GUNNER, HORSE ARTILLERY, 1861–65 *This horse artilleryman is holding a worm, and standing by his piece. While the 10-pounder Parrot rifle is depicted here, horse artillery were more usually equipped with the excellent 3-inch ordnance rifle. The Parrot had a tendency to burst at the breech, which made it somewhat unpopular with the gun crews. It was made of iron, and the bulge at the breech was a reinforcement, designed to prevent the field piece from bursting.*

horse holder, as in the cavalry, and the northern horse artillery was undoubtedly the best of any artillery of the war. They were equipped with the superb 3-inch ordnance rifle, which the Confederates especially prized when they captured one.

The heavy artillery was trained to man siege, fortress and seacoast pieces. They were dressed and equipped as infantry and late in the war after the gruelling battles in the Wilderness and Spotsylvania, many of the heavy artillery regiments were taken out of the defences of Washington where they had been sitting for over two years and put into the field. These regiments were huge compared to the veteran infantry regiments reduced by casualties, but they were soon depleted in the intense fighting.

Both the field and horse artillery batteries wore light artillery uniforms with a tunic which resembled the short cavalry jacket, except that the braid trim was in the artillery branch colour of red instead of the yellow of the horsemen. Trumpeters were uniformed the same as the cavalry, the

braid again being in red, and they rode whites or greys to be distinguished and easily identified in the smoke, roar and mess of combat.

Guns and Gunnery

Artillery had made definite advances since 1815 and the end of the Napoleonic period. Sights had improved, as had the casting of the gun tubes themselves, and rifled artillery had been introduced. Where before most field pieces were cast in bronze or brass, many were now cast and constructed with iron and the two most-used rifled artillery pieces, the 3-inch ordnance rifle and the 10-pounder Parrot rifle, were made of iron. The Parrot was reinforced in the breech by built-up iron, which gave it a non-aesthetic appearance, and the lines of the gun tube were not clean. It also had the tendency to burst on occasion, but for all that it was still an excellent field piece. The 3-inch ordnance rifle was light, had clean lines, and was an excellent horse artillery piece, and was

favoured by both sides, the Confederates especially valuing captured pieces. It may have been the best field piece of the war. The 1857 12-pounder model Napoleon, named such after the French Emperor Napoleon III, who designed it, was a brass smoothbore much favoured by field artillery batteries. Although it didn't have the range of the rifled pieces, it could handle a larger canister round, which was helpful in the close-range warfare typical in heavily wooded areas, such as the Wilderness and Spotsylvania.

► **OFFICER, HORSE ARTILLERY, SERVICE DRESS, 1861–65** *This horse artillery officer is unusually depicted in a frock coat, which would not be worn in action, but replaced by the shorter shell jacket specified for mounted troops. This uniform might be worn in camp and garrison or while on leave.*

▼ **12-POUNDER NAPOLEON GUN HOWITZER, MODEL 1857** *This field piece, a smoothbore, was popular on both sides during the Civil War. Commonly referred to as the Napoleon, it was designed in the late 1850s by Emperor Napoleon III of France. It was an excellent weapon, though it lacked the range and accuracy of the rifled field piece.*

▲ **GUNNER, HORSE ARTILLERY, 1861–65** *This artilleryman, in the regulation shell jacket piped in the artillery branch colour of red, holds an implement called a 'worm'. This was used to extract any refuse left in the gun tube after firing so as not to impede the ramming of a new round. In action the shell jacket might be set aside, the gunners working in their shirtsleeves.*

▼ GUIDON BEARER, 9TH MASSACHUSETTS, 1863 *The guidon bearer marked the place the battery commander was located. This guidon belonged to the Union battery that held off the Confederate infantry on the second day at the Battle of Gettysburg.*

▶ TRUMPETER, HORSE ARTILLERY, 1861–65 *This trumpeter, without spurs, was the voice of a mounted unit. The trumpet could be heard, like its companion drum in the infantry, above the noise of combat, and its place in action was with the battery commander.*

Ammunition

Artillery fired round shot, which was a cast iron ball effective against fortifications and troops in formation. It was still effective after it hit the ground, as it continued on its way with an amazing amount of kinetic energy. This type of firing, called 'ricochet firing', effectively doubled the range of the round and was dangerous to individuals and formations. A 12-pounder ball could still take off a foot, leg, or otherwise mangle an individual or group. It was only safe when it stopped rolling.

Exploding shell was another round that was a hollow cast-iron sphere filled with powder and detonated by a fuse that was lit when the round was fired. A more effective round was spherical case shot, otherwise known as shrapnel, which was similar to exploding shell, but filled with iron balls. It was deadly to troops in the open, especially if it detonated in the air. Lastly, there was the ubiquitous canister, often wrongly termed 'grape' or 'grapeshot', which was a very effective anti-personnel round, especially at close range. It was basically a tin can filled with cast-iron balls that ruptured when fired, giving the field piece the effect of a large shotgun.

▶ US 3-INCH ORDNANCE RIFLE 1861–65 *This was arguably the best field piece of the war. Specifically designed for the horse artillery arm, it was light and accurate.*

CAVALRY

The cavalry arm of the United States Army had always been small if it existed at all. Cavalry was expensive to raise and maintain, and it took much time and effort to train a competent cavalryman, not to mention commanders of large units of horsemen. Furthermore, the heavily wooded terrain of much of eastern North America was not conducive to cavalry operations and the recommendations of the venerable commanding general of the US Army, Winfield Scott, kept the regular

cavalry arm small, restricted to only six regiments for the duration of the war. While these six regular regiments of cavalry were excellent and had a proud tradition, the rapid expansion of the army led to much inexperience in the raising and training of volunteer cavalry regiments and their newly promoted commanders.

By the summer of 1863, under such hard-riding commanders as Mississippi-born 'Grimes' Davis and John Buford, the Yankee cavalry was coming into its own. The well-planned and executed raid on Brandy Station, where the Federal horsemen surprised and almost defeated Confederate cavalry icon J.E.B. Stuart, the commander of the cavalry arm of the Army of Northern Virginia, 'made' the

◄ OFFICER, 6TH PENNSYLVANIA VOLUNTEER CAVALRY REGIMENT, 1863 *This officer of the 6th Pennsylvania is uniformed per the usual regulations, and it is interesting that this regiment's officers wore dark blue trousers alongside the sky-blue type. The usual short shell jacket is shown, and the officers' model is not piped in the branch colour as those for enlisted men and musicians were.*

▲ *The all-or-nothing charge of the 5th US Cavalry at the Battle of Gaines' Mill during the Seven Days Battles in June 1862. The cavalry suffered heavy losses in a charge that was doomed to failure from the start.*

▼ *General John Reynolds was an outstanding commander. His loss on the first day of the Battle of Gettysburg was a grievous blow to the Army of the Potomac.*

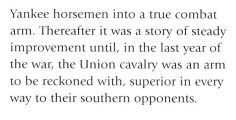

Yankee horsemen into a true combat arm. Thereafter it was a story of steady improvement until, in the last year of the war, the Union cavalry was an arm to be reckoned with, superior in every way to their southern opponents.

Cavalry Reforms

There was no shortage of volunteer cavalry regiments raised for the Union, but a cavalryman is much more than a man and a horse. The average northern boy was a poor rider. Undoubtedly these newly-minted horse soldiers faced their newly 'conscripted' mounts with considerable trepidation, and equally the new trooper's horse no doubt had similar reservations about his new master.

Considerable time would be needed not only to mould man and horse into fighting trim, but also the regiments, brigades and divisions of cavalry that would be formed for the war.

The basic dress of the Union mounted regiments would be dark blue shell jackets and either dark or light blue trousers and riding boots with spurs. The shell jacket was

◄ TROOPER, 6TH PENNSYLVANIA VOLUNTEER CAVALRY REGIMENT (RUSH'S LANCERS), 1862 *This was the only cavalry unit on either side that was organized and equipped as lancers during the war. When the lance was finally abandoned, the regiment performed outstandingly. The uniform is typical of cavalry units at the beginning of the war. The shoulder scales would soon be discarded as impractical.*

► NCO, US REGULAR CAVALRY REGIMENTS, 1862 *This no-nonsense NCO – a necessity for every efficient unit – is uniformed in the prescribed manner, including the sash that his rank was authorized to wear. Gauntlets were authorized for mounted troops. The sash would disappear as the war wore on, and trousers would later be tucked into spurred riding boots, possibly with a pistol tucked into one of them.*

popular, dashing enough for a cavalryman, and practical for mounted service. Kepis or slouch hats would be worn and generally speaking, any outstanding uniform styles might disappear as the war dragged on, though it would be the cavalry that would keep natty distinctions longer than the other combat arms.

The traditional cavalry branch colour was bright yellow and this was highlighted by braid on the shell jacket. The collar, cuffs and seams on the back of the shell jacket would be picked out with braid and one or two short pieces of braiding would highlight the collar lace, usually along with a brass button.

Generally speaking, volunteer units would use one piece of braid and the regulars two, but this distinction was not always followed, which could irritate the regular units and send some rookie volunteer cavalrymen back to their units with bloody noses and hurt pride. Long service and gradual proficiency gained on campaign and battle would eventually dim the distinction between volunteer and regular, the regulars actually accepting the 6th Pennsylvania Volunteer Cavalry Regiment as one of their own in skill and proficiency.

Weaponry

Cavalrymen were usually armed with sabre, carbine and pistol. Pistols were carried on the waistbelt in a holster, negating the need for saddle holsters that had been attached to the front of the saddle on either side. Both officers and men preferred revolvers, and many would carry more than one, extra pistols sometimes being carried tucked into the belt for easy access. Many models were carried but the ubiquitous Colts the were favourites. Repeating carbines were popular and became more evident as the war progressed. This gave cavalry regiments a great advantage over infantry in the volume of fire that could be delivered and this, combined with the cavalryman's mobility, enabled cavalry to wage effective delaying actions against larger numbers of infantry, holding positions until their own infantry could arrive. An outstanding example of this was General Buford's two-hour stand against greater numbers of Confederate infantry on the first day of the Battle of Gettysburg in July 1863.

Quite naturally, the cavalry was armed with a heavy sabre and the ideal for any ambitious cavalryman was to make a decisive charge, knee to knee, either against opposing cavalry or to overrun hostile infantry. In actuality, the sabre could be a hindrance and pistols were generally preferred in an engagement. The sabre would be worn either on the pistol belt or attached to the saddle, which was a better arrangement if the troopers were to do any dismounted fighting. There were, however, several mounted engagements during the war in the old style. The cavalry and horse artillery fight at Brandy Station, Virginia, in June 1863 saw lines of sabre-swinging cavalry having at each other for a long afternoon, the surprised Confederates later stating that the engagement 'made' the Union cavalry arm. In the Shenadoah Valley in 1864 the veteran Union cavalry divisions made sabre charges against unbroken Confederate infantry, overrunning and shattering them on the field. The day of the cavalryman was not over.

◀ TRUMPETER, 2ND UNITED STATES CAVALRY REGIMENT, 1863
Trumpeters were traditionally mounted on whites or greys, so that they could be recognized in combat. Cavalrymen had to care well for their horses if they did not want to end up dismounted.

◀ NCO, THE MICHIGAN CAVALRY BRIGADE, 1863 *The Michigan Brigade came under the command of George Custer shortly after he gained his stars. By all accounts it was an efficient unit. Custer later issued red scarves as a unit distinction. This NCO would probably wear his carbine in a boot attached to the saddle, rather than hung on the regulation shoulder strap.*

▶ 3RD NEW JERSEY VOLUNTEER CAVALRY REGIMENT, 1864 *This regiment, nicknamed The Butterflies, was uniformed in hussar style, after the Austrian hussars. They came late to the war, not being recruited to strength and organized for field service until early 1864. Assigned to the cavalry corps of the Army of the Potomac, the regiment compiled an excellent service record and fought in the Shenandoah Valley. Officially the 1st US Hussars, the regiment preferred to be called the 3rd New Jersey.*

The 3rd New Jersey, officially the 1st US Hussars, were uniformed hussar-style, allegedly copied from the Austrian hussar regiments of the period. Their dark blue short coattees were laced across the chest with yellow lace, and their forage cap had no peak and was worn jauntily cocked to one side. Their interesting headgear was worn in place of either the kepi and slouch hat and was unique to this regiment. Their cloaks, or talmas, were worn pelisse- or coat-style and were

▼ *Lieutenant Custer (right) with his prisoner, and former West Point classmate, Confederate Lieutenant Washington in May–June 1862.*

not worn in combat. A relative late-comer to the Army of the Potomac, they were an excellent regiment and established a war record that few regiments could match.

The Michigan Brigade

This was George Custer's first command as a general officer, and he gave them a distinctive red scarf that could identify them on the battlefield. That, along with his personally designed general officer's uniform and the brigade's reputation for efficiency in the field, made them just a cut above the normal cavalry unit. Contrary to Custer's later reputation, the war record he established as a cavalry commander was excellent.

The 6th Pennsylvania and 3rd New Jersey

Two colourful volunteer regiments made a name for themselves during the war: the 6th Pennsylvania and the 3rd New Jersey. The 6th Pennsylvania was also known as Rush's Lancers, for they were the only US cavalry regiment to be equipped with the lance. Though they held onto it for a year, it was found to be nearly useless in the heavily wooded terrain in which the armies operated, and was discarded, the troopers then being issued carbines like other cavalry regiments. The lancers were uniformed as a volunteer cavalry regiment. Though they probably wore dark blue trousers initially, they would later wear sky-blue.

NAVAL FORCES

The United States Navy at the beginning of the Civil War was a small, professional service with well designed ships and an excellent reputation, which had been established as world class in the War of 1812, and the Mexican War of 1846–48. The Civil War saw the navy pass from a steam-powered force to a much more modern force of armoured warships that would eventually produce a navy that was able to project power around the globe by the turn of the century as the 'Great White Fleet'.

Full Dress

Prior to the Civil War navy officers wore a handsome dark blue cutaway tailed coat with dark blue trousers. All ranks up to captain (the highest permanent rank in the US Navy, the first true admiral being named and promoted to that newly created rank during the war) wore gold bullion epaulettes in the style of the day and the rank insignia system for the navy was somewhat complicated, being a combination of gold lace of varying lengths on both collars and sleeves. All officers had gold trouser stripes varying in width from 2.5cm (1in) for lieutenants to 4cm (1½ in) for captains. Hair was supposed to be worn short, along with short and neat facial hair. However, as was common in the army, facial hair was treated as optional and down to personal preference, and this was one of the regulations that was ignored by anyone who chose.

Service Dress

As the Navy expanded during the war, the uniform regulations and requirements were somewhat 'relaxed' because of the influx of new officers

◄ OFFICER, US NAVY, 1861–65 *This was the typical sea service dress for commissioned officers of the United States Navy during the war. Off-duty and ashore, the officer might wear the collar of his coat open, the open portion of the coat forming lapels. Straw hats were frequently worn on-board ship by all ranks in hot weather.*

► SEAMAN, SERVICE DRESS, US NAVY, 1861–65 *The navy's dress regulations for enlisted men was vague in many areas, and variations would exist from ship to ship and even among the same crews. Beards and moustaches were allowed, but hair was generally worn short. Sailors also served ashore in naval landing parties with the Marines, and would be armed and equipped accordingly.*

and the employment of many of them from the merchant service. The full dress uniform was expensive and the new officers, who would be in the navy only for the war, generally complained about the added expense. What was decided was to modify the service dress of the frock coat and trousers, a handsome uniform in itself, to replace the pre-war full dress (though it would be reinstated after the war) and most naval officers wore this throughout the war. The complicated rank system on

▲ MIDSHIPMAN, US NAVY, 1861–65
Midshipmen's uniforms were officer-like in appearance, but not quite. The cap was different from that of the enlisted men and the bow tie was common throughout the navy for midshipmen, the 'young gentlemen'.

device. This rank system would remain after the war and, in a modified form, is still in use today.

Enlisted Men

The enlisted sailor wore a regulation uniform that was similar to those worn by navies around the world. The basic colour was dark blue and the trousers had blossomed into the ubiquitous 'bell bottomed' style that is still employed by some navies. These were semi-form fitting at the thigh and widened as they passed the knee to their widest point at the ankle.

The pullover 'shirt' or jersey was practical and comfortable for shipboard wear and duties and was worn with a tie that was loosely fastened at the neck. A cloth flap hung down the back of the shirt to just below shoulder level and the uniform was topped off by a jaunty sailor cap, usually embroidered with the name of the man's ship on the cap band. Rank devices and naval rating specialities were worn on the upper arm denoting the man's 'branch' aboard ship.

▲ *Captain John Winslow and officers aboard the USS* Kearsarge, *the ship and officers that sank the Confederate raider CSS* Alabama.

the uniforms was simplified during the war. New ranks were created: rear admiral, commodore, as well as lieutenant commander and a new rank system implemented. The cuff rings of gold would now be one for ensigns and eight for admirals, the other officer extremes falling in between those two grades. Sea officers would now wear a gold star above their rank on the cuff and staff officers would not have that

▶ PETTY OFFICER, US NAVY, SUMMER SERVICE DRESS, 1861–65 *The only rank insignia for enlisted seamen was for petty officers and was either worn on the left sleeve, as shown, for most petty officers, but on the right sleeve for boatswain's mates and other senior petty officers. The hats were generally the same for ratings and petty officers, but these too would vary from ship to ship as to the size of the tops and the length of the ribbons that hung from the back.*

THE MARINE CORPS

The United States Marine Corps was a very small organization charged with guarding naval installations and providing the US Navy with detachments to serve aboard warships and to provide landing parties for amphibious operations.

Naval Troops

The strength of the Marine Corps in 1859 was 2,000 officers and men and this almost doubled during the war to 3,900. There

▶ DRUMMER, FULL DRESS, UNITED STATES MARINE CORPS, 1861–65 *In full dress, the Marine Corps retained the French-style shako and the old custom of reversed colours for musicians. The Marine full dress uniform was elaborate and quite handsome and was retained in service to 1875.*

was a Marine battalion at the First Battle of Bull Run (First Manassas) in 1861, but the next major land operation the Marine Corps engaged in was not until the assault on Fort Fisher in late 1864. The first assault was a failure, but the second was successful.

It should also be noted that the Marine Corps was not part of the United States Army. It was a separate service under the auspices of the United States Navy. It had its own Colonel Commandant and was headquartered where it still is today, in Washington DC, though that is now split between Washington and Quantico Virginia, about 30km (20 miles) south of the capital. The Commandant lives at the Marine Barracks, Washington DC, at the intersection of 8th and I Streets (commonly referred to as 8th and Eye). The Commandant's house has been occupied continuously since 1804 and was the one public building in the capital that was not burned by the British when they took Washington in 1814. Legend has it that it was because of the respect they had for the fight the sailors and Marines put up against them at the Battle of Bladensburg in front of Washington.

◀ OFFICER, UNITED STATES MARINE CORPS, SERVICE DRESS, 1861–65 *At first glance, the Marine officer might be taken for an army officer, but the Marine Corps field (as well as full dress) uniforms had several distinctive features. The braided epaulettes to show the officer's rank and the 'M' surrounded by a wreath on the front of the fatigue cap were two immediately recognizable features of a Marine officer's uniform.*

French Style

The uniforms of the Marine Corps had the same overall colours as those of the US Army, dark blue coats and light blue trousers. However, besides the insignia of the services being different, there were many significant differences apparent in the uniforms of the two respective services. Marine NCOs' chevrons were pointed upward as they are today, while those of the Army of the period were inverted with the chevrons pointing downward. The Marine Corps had not yet adopted the famous eagle, globe and anchor insignia so familiar today (that would not be adopted until 1868), and the usual insignia was a light infantry hunting horn with a capital 'M' inside it, which had been adopted in 1859. Officers and staff NCOs wore heavy

▼ **NCO, United States Marine Corps, Field Service Dress, 1861–65** *The Marine Corps still used the older white leather cross belts, as well as a waist belt, during the Civil War. Marine NCOs, like their army brethren, were also supposed to carry a sword with the rest of their equipment. This NCO is fully equipped and armed but by the standards of 1862 he is carrying too much equipment.*

gold epaulettes on their dress uniforms, and there was gold lace on both the collar and cuffs, along with red piping on the dress frock coats.

The dress headgear was a French-style shako that the army had also worn in the 1850s, and the enlisted men's cross belts were white (and therefore made a perfect target over the chest in the field). The enlisted fatigue uniform consisted of blue or white duck trousers (white if aboard ship in hot weather) and the fatigue 'shirt' was not a coat like the Army's but resembled a pullover shirt. The undress, or fatigue, cap was a variation of the French Army's kepi, though it was more of the chasseur pattern with a straight rather than a curved or shaped peak.

Overall for field service, Marine infantry detachments would look like an Army unit at a distance and only a trained eye could tell if they were Marines. Drummers and musicians were often uniformed in the traditional reversed colours of military musicians. Red was the traditional facing colour of Marine uniform since 1779 and the Marine Band in Washington DC at the Barracks at 8th and I Streets, along with the Marine Drum and Bugle Corps, are still uniformed in these colours today.

Service in the Civil War

The Marine Corps served as they usually did, long and uncomplaining, supporting the navy at sea and in

▶ **Officer, United States Marine Corps, Summer Service Dress, 1861–65** *This uniform, complete with straw hat, was designed for use in the summer or in tropical regions aboard ship. Enlisted men would also have a uniform modified for tropical use or for summer service, which would include at least white trousers. The uniform shown is the same cut and style as the blue dress uniform but is of different, lighter and more comfortable material.*

amphibious landings. However, they were an auxiliary force during this war and were not the dominating factor that they would become by World War II. Marines fought in small detachments, doing their duty one way or another and soldiering on as professionals and not winning much glory as they did it. The US Navy fought the largest war in its history, co-operating with the army in their land campaigns. They also performed the tediousness of blockade duty, as did the Marines aboard ship. The Marines' day would come in another war, in another century, and in far more deadly campaigns.

UNION FLAGS AND COLOURS

Flags and colours carried by infantry and cavalry units are the visible symbol of a regiment and men will fight and die in their defence. It is a dishonour for the regiment to lose their colours in combat unless there is no one left to defend the colours, all being killed or wounded. It was common for units to have to replace colour bearers during an action because of casualties; some units had as many as eight colour bearers shot down in combat as the colours made an excellent target for ememy artillery.

A system of corps, division and brigade flags was devised for the Union army early in the war by General George McClellan. It was a worthy aim, but a complex sytem, as were most of that officer's ideas. It was soon abolished and a much simpler system replaced it.

▶ *1 National Colour, 2nd Minnesota Volunteer Infantry Regiment (Iron Brigade).*
2 I Troop, 6th Pennsylvania Volunteer Cavalry Regiment.
3 Company A, 'California Hundred', 2nd Massachusetts Volunteer Cavalry Regiment.
4 Battery L, 1st US Artillery.

◀ *5 National Colour, 2nd Wisconsin Volunteer Infantry Regiment (Iron Brigade).*

▼ *6 Regimental Colour, 3rd US Artillery Regiment.*
7 Regimental Colour, 54th Massachusetts Volunteer Infantry Regiment.
8 Regimental Colour, 2nd US Cavalry Regiment.
9 Regimental Colour, 2nd US Infantry Regiment.

1

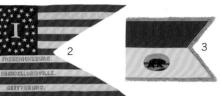

2

3

4

5

6

7

8

9

Colours

Union volunteer infantry regiments normally carried two colours, one being the national colour and the other being the regimental colour, usually a variation of the state flag that was adapted for use. Regular infantry regiments carried two colours, one again being the national colour and the other being the regimental colour, which would be dark blue for the infantry, bearing the unit's designation.

Some colours were so battle-damaged that they had to be replaced as all that remained attached to the staff were coloured rags. These revered colours were retired and replacement colours provided to the units. In the assault on Battery Wagner in July 1863 the state colour of the 54th Massachusetts was torn from its staff in

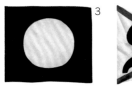

◀ *1 51st New York Volunteer Infantry Regiment.*
2 9th Conneticut Volunteer Infantry Regiment.

the ditch in front of the fort. Men died to recover it, but it was lost. The staff was saved, and when the regiment was refitting after suffering heavy losses, Massachusetts provided a replacement colour as there was no disgrace in losing the original. This colour is now in the State House in Boston.

Some units carried 'presentation' colours, which had been specially prepared by civilian organizations and were given to the regiment in a ceremony before they deployed for service. Some of these were quite elaborate, and sometimes units were issued three colours instead of the usual two.

Guidons
Light artillery units carried guidons, a smaller flag used for the battery to 'guide on' during parade or combat.

They usually were of the branch colour, red, and carried the unit's battery letter and the regimental number above and below crossed cannons, all of which were in gold.

Cavalry units also carried guidons which were a miniature version of the national colours during the war and were swallow tailed. Some volunteer cavalry regiments, however, still carried the older style guidon, which were red and white, in horizontal form, the red below and the white above, and carried the unit designation.

There were also marker or camp flags which were used to mark the unit's area when encamped or in winter quarters. Some infantry used company guidons attached to a small piece of wood that would fit in the barrel of a musket. It was the infantry form of a guidon.

In the artillery batteries, the loss of a gun in combat was the equivalent of an infantry or cavalry regiment losing its colours. Guns were fought to the last in combat, and some artillery units would only withdraw when ordered by the distance their guns would recoil when fired. Sometimes guns could not be extricated from a hopeless situation, and many lives were lost to keep the pieces from the enemy. Some, however, were lost honourably, such as those of the 9th Massachusetts Battery at Gettysburg, and there was no disgrace attached to actions such as those.

▲ *3 2nd Division, 1st Corps, Army of the Potomac.*
4 Chief Quartermaster, 2nd Corps, Army of the Potomac.
5 52nd New York Volunteer Infantry Regiment.
6 4th Brigade, 2nd Division, 2nd Corps, Army of the Potomac 'Clubs are Trumps!'
▶ *7 Camp Colour, 6th US Infantry Regiment.*
8 Camp Colour, 2nd US Artillery Regiment.
9 Company H, 1st Regiment, New York Volunteer Engineers.
10 3rd Division, Cavalry Corps, Army of the Potomac.
11 Horse Artillery Brigade, Cavalry Corps, Army of the Potomac.

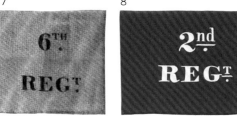

THE AMERICAN CIVIL WAR

ARMIES OF THE CONFEDERACY

During the American Civil War the Confederacy created an army that did not exist before 1861. In combining professional army officers that 'went South' in 1861 when their respective states seceded from the Union, the pre-war militia units, and the volunteers that presented themselves for duty at the first call, the Confederate government created an army out of almost nothing but promising raw material, enthusiastic amateurs, and a core of hardened professionals who had seen war in Mexico in the 1840s. The army they created came close to defeating the north, nearly achieved foreign recognition from Great Britain and France, and succeeded in establishing a legend that persists to this day.

▲ *A postwar photograph of General Robert E. Lee and two of his officers. Lee has been idolized postwar and he and other southern generals were heroes before the war had ended. Of all the Southern commanders, Lee had the highest percentage of casualties.*

◄ *General Winfield Scott Hancock (mounted), dubbed 'Hancock the Superb' for his cool under fire and the care with which he dressed, defeated Pickett's Charge on the third day of the Battle of Gettysburg July 1863, but sustained a wound from which he never recovered.*

BAND OF BROTHERS

The Southern soldier was tough, self-reliant, individualistic, resentful of what he perceived as northern interference and aggression into his homeland. Terrible in the attack, resolute and stubborn in the defence, these troops were some of the best soldiers in the history of warfare, led by some of the most famous commanders in military history.

Infantry

The Southern infantry was organized in the same manner as that of their northern counterparts. There was one very large difference though, and one which made a difference on the battlefield. It was the Confederate practice when replacing casualties that replacements were sent into an existing

regiment and those replacements would have the benefit of a veteran cadre to 'show them the ropes' and to be a steadying influence in combat. The Southerners enjoyed better cohesion in their combat units because of this system and this could make the difference on a day of battle.

Confederate infantry was solid in line of battle and an excellent force on the battlefield. They were also unyielding in defence and could stand toe to toe in fire-fights at relatively close range, closing ranks as men fell, determined to maintain their front.

Cavalry

The cavalry arm of the Confederate armies was excellent and well-mounted. For the first two years of the war they were vastly superior to their northern opponents, but suffered later in the war from the lack of remounts.

◄ *A well-equipped Confederate infantryman at the beginning of the war in 1861. The knapsack would soon be discarded in favour of the blanket roll and the bow tie would also disappear as it became obvious that the war would drag on beyond one battle or one year.*

▲ *A Union infantry attack at the Battle of Antietam against the Confederate left flank with the Dunker Church in the background.*

Artillery

Confederate artillery was good, but was affected by the lack of a southern manufacturing base, there being only two foundries in the southern United

▼ *General Nathan Bedford Forrest of "Get there first with the most men" fame. A driving, aggressive commander, he was one of the Confederacy's best cavalry commanders, but was finally defeated late in the war at the Battle of Selma, Alabama. He would later found the infamous and racist Ku Klux Klan.*

Bull Run and in the Iron Brigade's first fight), the 'shattered thunderbolt' of the 1st Minnesota, the regiments of the Irish Brigade of the Army of the Potomac and perhaps the entire II Corps of the Army of the Potomac along with the regular infantry regiments (which no infantry unit of either side could best in either drill or manoeuvre not to mention fighting ability) were just as good as, if not better than, their Southern opponents.

Northern artillery was superior to their southern opponents, but that had a lot to do with the artillery pieces, and not the artillerymen themselves.

The spirit of brotherhood in arms, immortalized in the marching song 'Bonnie Blue Flag', had a part to play in the initial Confederate success, as did the skill of the Southern cavalry, especially in the east, which was vastly superior at least initially to the Northern cavalry. The Northern horsemen, however, became excellent cavalrymen, and by 1864 were outstanding, riding over Confederate infantry in massed sabre-wielding charges not seen in North America before or since.

▼ Confederate General Robert Edward Lee (right) surrenders to General Ulysses S. Grant at Appotamax Courthouse, 9 April 1865, and ends the American Civil War.

States. Often Southern gunners would find themselves under-gunned, the calibres of their field pieces being less than that of their northern counterparts, and captured field pieces, especially the 3-inch ordnance rifle, were much prized. Some rifle muskets were imported from Europe, and the South imported two types of British breech-loading artillery in small numbers, the Whitworth and Armstrong rifled field pieces.

Difficulties
The Southern war effort suffered from the Union naval blockade, especially later in the war, when many vital supplies were cut or reduced. The Southern home front suffered from shortages of nearly everything in order to maintain their armies against what they considered to be invaders from the North and made herculean efforts to supply their troops in the field. Units were usually well uniformed or clothed, although toward the end of the war shoes were soled in cardboard, and made out of wood.

Military Reputation
There have been discussions on whether or not the Southern soldier was superior to his Northern counterpart but such a debate can never reach a reliable conclusion. Southern infantry was excellent, but so

▲ A stylized print of the Third Battle of Winchester in the Shenandoah Valley in September 1864 during General Phillip Sheridan's successful valley campaign. Sheridan thoroughly defeated Confederate General Jubal Early's army in the Valley, and then proceeded to devastate the area, which had been the bread basket of the South.

were their Northern opponents. Many Northern regiments, such as the five of the famous Iron Brigade (who defeated the equally famous Stonewall Brigade at the Battle of Brawner's Farm in 1862, just before the Second Battle of

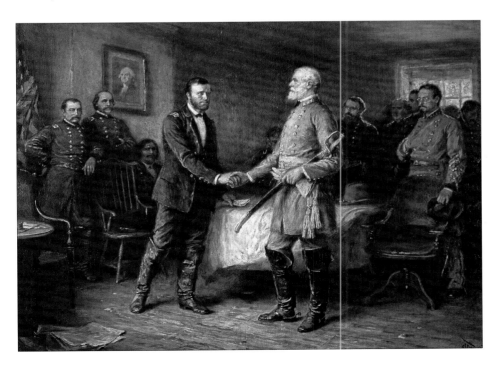

COMMANDERS AND STAFF

The Confederate Army did not have a formal general-in-chief until Confederate President Jefferson Davis took the role of commander-in-chief late in the war, and this lack of centralized control was a strategic weakness. The army did have its generals in the field, however, who were held up as heroes by the southern states they fought for, in particular Robert E. Lee, 'charged with the conduct of military operations in the armies of the Confederacy'.

The dress for general officers was prescribed by the Confederate uniform regulations. The rank system for the entire army will be described in the Regular Army section.

▲ *Jefferson Davis was serving as a Senator in the US government when war broke out. In 1861 he was declared President of the Confederate States of America, an office which he held until the end of the war.*

◄ **GENERAL JAMES LONGSTREET, 1863** *Longstreet was dubbed 'Lee's Warhorse', probably by Lee himself. He was arguably the best of the southern corps commanders and had originally been a supply officer, not a combat arms officer. His quiet competence was overshadowed by more flamboyant commanders such as Jackson and Stuart, but his competence in the field was one of the main reasons the war lasted as long as it did.*

Frock Coats and Tunics

The frock coat was the favourite of most general officers. Both the frock coat and the tunic had two rows of buttons down the front and these varied in pattern, most of them having an eagle as the centrepiece, although some had the 'battle flag' with the cross of St Andrew as the central device. Many of these were also imported from Britain. Stars were worn on the collar to denote the rank, reinforced with gold braid in elaborate

◄ **GENERAL ROBERT E. LEE, 1863** *Robert E. Lee wore a plain uniform that was, like Napoleon's, much simpler than those of his senior generals, and understated the esteem in which he was held by both his subordinates and peers. His jacket was grey and did not have a stand-up collar. His hat was non-regulation and his appearance, usually with his horse Traveler, became a southern icon.*

◀ **GENERAL AMBROSE POWELL HILL, 1863**
A.P. Hill is depicted here in regulation uniform, which he probably wore more often than not. The old story that he wore a red shirt in combat is probably apocryphal. An excellent division commander, he was probably out of his depth at the corps level. Like his fellow general Jeb Stuart, he would be killed in action in the last year of the war.

▶ **GENERAL JAMES EWELL BROWN STUART, 1863** *Jeb Stuart was the epitome of the cavalry commander of the Civil War. He became the darling of the Southern press and was one of the most flamboyant commanders of the war. His non-regulation uniform definitely has his personality stamped on it and until mid-1863 his cavalry command was superior to its opponents. After the pivotal cavalry battle at Brandy Station that year, the Northern cavalry began to surpass their Southern counterparts.*

French knots on the sleeves that usually would come up above the elbows. Some general officers, such as James Longstreet, preferred to wear the more form-fitting tunic that was not as full in the skirt below the waist but was much neater in appearance.

Regulations

The regulation dress for officers was to consist of a frock coat of grey wool and wool trousers of dark blue. The dress hat for the Confederacy was to be the kepi, but this varied later in the war, many general officers opting for the usual slouch hat. The colour of the uniform coat could come in a variety of shades from light to dark grey,

blue-grey even being seen in some examples. The material was supposed to be wool, but woollen denim material could be seen later in the war. As generals and staff officers were usually mounted, riding boots of various patterns were worn along with the usual spurs.

The distinguishing colour for general officers was buff, a bright, light tan. It was to be worn on the collars and on the cuffs of the coat. General officer sashes were also buff in colour. As with general officers in other armies and other eras, some general officers would either design their own uniforms or would have them tailor-made (many of them in England, something which was difficult to do because of the Union naval blockade, and expensive) and these might or might not conform to the more-often-than-not ignored uniform regulations.

Individualism

Some general officers, Robert E. Lee in particular, would wear a grey frock coat without either gold lace on the arms or buff facings. The stars denoting rank would be worn on a grey collar and the overall effect produced was simple, elegant and relatively businesslike. Lee has also been pictured in a uniform

coat that had an open collar, instead of the semi-high collar that is usually depicted for Confederate generals.

General officers might wear the sash, but also went without it more often than not. Some uniform coats would be more of a light brown than a grey, depending on the dyes used, and the stars denoting rank on the collar would frequently be surrounded by gold laurel wreaths. Buff piping might be used at the cuff without the entire cuff being in buff and the coat itself might be piped in buff down the front and at the rear seams. Generally speaking, the way in which a general officer would present himself would be up to the individual.

PRE-WAR MILITIA

The southern states had their militia units, and from these grew the quite formidable Army of the Confederacy, especially the famous Army of Northern Virginia commanded by Robert E. Lee.

Varied Styles

Most of the pre-war militia units were of one or two companies in strength and were colourfully uniformed in a variety of styles and colours, blue and grey being predominant.

One of the noteworthy facts about American uniformology of the 19th century is that American units, both regular and militia, usually adopted dress based on European uniforms, emulating that which was considered to be the pre-eminent power on the Continent at the time. Prior to and during the Civil War the French influence was very heavy and after the French defeat by the Prussians in 1870–71, Prussian styles took over, including the adoption of the spiked helmet by the US Army.

Jackets varied from the old, obsolete style of coat from the late 18th century, to the style of the 1840s – which consisted of a coattee with tails and cut straight across the front at the waist. Some of the early militia units, usually at company strength, had adopted the new frock coat that was both popular and practical and was the general style in Europe at the time. The shako with plume was a very popular headgear and

▶ OFFICER, 1ST REGIMENT, GEORGIA VOLUNTEERS (REPUBLICAN BLUES), 1860 *This spectacular uniform would not last long once the unit was mustered into Confederate service. The French style, from the shako to the plastron on the front of the tunic, is evident. This style of uniform was expensive and a luxury the Confederacy could not afford.*

◀ DRUMMER, 1ST REGIMENT, GEORGIA VOLUNTEERS (REPUBLICAN BLUES), 1860 *This drummer is in a much simplified form of the uniform of this unit. Many of the southern pre-war militia units were only in company strength when the war began and they were amalgamated with other companies from the same state to form regiments for field duty. For some time many regiments would look quite different in appearance from company to company. Only later, after service in the field, would the units' pre-war uniforms be replaced.*

was seen quite often in the militia units as they mustered in for service. The shako later proved to be unpopular and was replaced officially by the kepi and on active service by a variety of slouch hats.

Among pre-war militia units, there was an outstanding lack of uniformity even if they were from the same state. Before the Confederacy issued its own uniform regulations, regiments being mustered into the service of the

Confederacy would present a very varied appearance; sometimes described as 'motley'. Sometimes units were clothed by the local populace, with tailors being brought in as the unit mustered and clothing being made up on the spot as the troops waited to be outfitted and equipped. Examples of the militia units' uniforms are as follows.

The Lynchburg Home Guard, Virginia

This unit was a new unit, formed just before the outbreak of war. It wore a uniform of dark blue frock coat and sky-blue trousers topped by a sky-blue kepi. The enlisted men wore white waist and crossbelts. Officers wore gold epaulettes with gold fringe.

▶ PRIVATE, GUILFORD GRAYS, 1861 *This simple uniform was much more practical for active service than the more flamboyant styles prevalent during the pre-war years. The pompon on the kepi as well as the white crossbelt would disappear quickly, the crossbelt to be replaced by one in black leather. In general, except for the length of the tunic, this was the general appearance of the Confederate infantry during the war.*

The Richmond Grays, Virginia

This unit was formed in 1844 and had the reputation of a well-drilled unit,

although it was only a company in strength. Grey frock coats and grey trousers of the same shade were worn topped by a shako of the French pattern with a short white plume. Waist belt and crossbelts were white, and the epaulettes of the enlisted men were black with white fringe. Collar and cuff flaps were black.

The City Light Infantry Guard of Petersburg, Virginia

This milita unit was formed in 1852 and was attached to the 39th State Militia Regiment. It was uniformed similarly to the Richmond Greys, but in dark blue piped white. The shako with short white plume was of the same pattern and the crossbelts and waist belt were white.

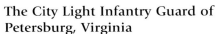

◀ PRIVATE, MARYLAND GUARD, 1861 *This Maryland unit was dressed in modified zouave style which was quite smart in appearance. The first thing to go would probably be the gaiters, as they were not liked by the majority of the infantrymen. Many times the peacetime uniforms fell apart on active service. The responsibility for equipping and uniforming the units fell to individual states, though central government often assisted in this process.*

The Washington Light Infantry, South Carolina

This was an older unit dating from before the War of 1812, having been formed in 1807. The unit's uniform consisted of a dark blue jacket with wings ending in gold fringe on the shoulders and a hunting horn device on the stand-up collar. The jacket had nine rows of black lace on the chest and four rows on each sleeve near the cuff. The lace on the cuff was in herringbone pattern. Dark blue trousers were worn and the usual pattern of French shako was also dark blue with a leopard-skin turban around the base and topped with a scarlet pompon. This unit was absorbed into Hampton's Legion, though some of the men from it went into the 25th South Carolina Infantry Regiment instead.

The Guilford Grays, North Carolina

Formed in 1860, enlisted men wore a single-breasted frock coat (the officers' coats were double-breasted) over trousers, both of which were grey. A black waist belt was worn with one white crossbelt. Headgear was a grey kepi with a short black plume. The unit's flag was of blue silk with yellow fringe and bore the arms of North Carolina on one side and a wreath bearing the motto of the Edgeworth Female Seminary on the other.

▶ **OFFICER, WASHINGTON LIGHT INFANTRY, 1861** *This officer is simply and elegantly uniformed in tunic, trousers and kepi. The French cuffs on his sleeves are noteworthy, and the fact that his rank insignia is worn on his shoulders, a detail that would change when the new Confederate rank system was adopted.*

The Clinch Rifles, Georgia

Formed in 1852, this unit wore a simple, elegant uniform of rifle dark green single-breasted frock coat and matching trousers. Green kepis were worn, the frontal device on the kepi being a laurel wreath with the initials 'CR' inside. The collar and French cuff flaps were outlined in the regimental colour for the enlisted men and gold for the officers. Black leather equipment was worn as befitted a rifle unit.

The Montgomery True Blues, Alabama

This was an artillery unit, and men were dressed in a very handsome dark blue uniform of coattee over trousers, the tails of the coattee hanging down at the back halfway down the thigh. Red full epaulettes were worn as was a black leather waist belt and white crossbelts. The French-style shako was black with a red falling feather plume and the cap device was a gold sunburst with crossed cannon embossed on it.

◀ **OFFICER INSTRUCTOR, THE CITADEL, 1861** *The Citadel was a southern military school in Charleston, South Carolina. Founded after West Point, it was a state rather than a national school and it provided its students with an excellent education. The cadets manned one of the batteries in Charleston Harbor that bombarded Fort Sumter to begin the war, and this officer is dressed differently than his cadets would be for easy identification. Their uniform was quite similar to the Federal pattern.*

The Tom Green Rifles (Texas)

Originally formed in 1858 as the Quitman Rifles, this unit wore grey instead of green, having a single-breasted frock coat over grey trousers, trimmed in dark blue, the rank insignia also being in dark blue. Black slouch hats with the Texan single star device on the front were worn.

The Iredell Blues, North Carolina

This unit wore dark blue coattees with white European lancer-type plastrons on the front of the coattees. The coattees had white standing collars and slashed cuffs and the men wore dark blue trousers with white stripes in the

The Sumter Light Guards, Charleston

This unit wore a dark blue uniform together with either white or sky-blue trouser stripes. The officers and NCOs wore a dark blue frock coat while the enlisted men wore a short shell jacket. All ranks wore the kepi. Eastern units, both North and South, were more likely to be more formally and expensively uniformed than units farther west. Some units on the nation's fringes even wore their own civilian clothes and were without uniforms of any type until the war was underway.

▲ *The Duplin Grays in formation before the war. This militia finery would quickly evaporate for the Confederate armies as it became obvious that the war was not a spectator sport but a serious business.*

winter and white trousers in the summer. Their caps were topped with large white plumes.

The Oglethorpe Light Infantry, Savannah, Georgia

Named after the state's founder, this was a relatively new unit founded in 1857. They wore a dark blue uniform, both coat and trousers, and the regimental colour was buff. The front of the coat had a lancer-style buff plastron and the French shako had a large white plume.

◀ PRIVATE, SUMTER LIGHT GUARD, 1861
This Georgia unit was elegantly and simply uniformed, but again this would quickly change due to the realities of life in the field and on campaign. The kepi would most likely be eventually replaced by a slouch hat and the coloured distinctions, such as the epaulettes, would disappear.

▶ PRIVATE, CLINCH RIFLES, 1861 *As a rifle unit, this outfit was initially uniformed in dark green, as seen here, but that pre-war finery would quickly disappear as the unit was absorbed into one of the state regiments that would eventually become Confederate regulars.*

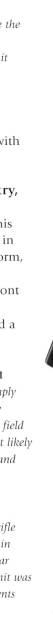

STATE TROOPS

The line between militia, state troops and Confederate regulars was blurred at best. With no regular army before the war, the Confederacy had to create one and it drew on both the militia and state units to do this. Both the states and central Confederate government clothed the field units, and uniformity among troops even in the same unit was variable at best. Some states had no uniforms for their troops, such as Missouri, whose troops were dressed in a style referred to as 'motley' and the men had to be identified by a field badge. This was a white flannel stripe on the left shoulder. Arkansas had no uniform regulations and their troops were required to wear a yellow flannel stripe on their left shoulder.

Some states troops, such as those of Maryland, which did not secede but did provide units, were uniformed by the Confederate government. The table right gives an overall approximation of the states that supplied uniforms to their troops and what they might have worn in the field. Variations were many, and civilian clothing was used if necessary, some units, such as Texas units in the west, preferring it.

Some of the southern states, such as Virginia, South Carolina, North Carolina and Alabama, had state uniform regulations which were thorough and quite specific. Generally speaking, even conscientious commanders would ignore them in order to keep their troops clothed and shod, it being sometimes necessary to get clothing wherever it could be found. Still, some units kept a sharp appearance through the war. Many regiments were organized from different militia companies with different uniforms. Many of the former militiamen were happy with their pre-war uniforms and were not about to change anything no matter what the regulations might say.

North Carolina, whose troops served gallantly during the war, was unique among its southern brethren, and assumed total responsibility for equipping and clothing its troops during the war.

◄ **NCO, 4TH BATTALION VIRGINIA VOLUNTEERS, 1861** *French influence is once again evident in this pre-war infantryman. The high collar was uncomfortable and would disappear.*

▲ **FIRST SERGEANT, 17TH REGIMENT VIRGINIA VOLUNTEER INFANTRY, 1861** *The bow tie was common on both sides, but disappeared quite swiftly among the enlisted men as the war progressed. The kepi with its waterproof cover is noteworthy and quite practical.*

Provisional Army

When the war started, the Confederate government established what was called the 'Provisional Army' which was separate and distinct from the

State Troops Uniform Distinctions

State	Coat/Jacket	Trousers	Head Gear
Alabama	dark blue	grey	shako
Arkansas	grey	various	various
Florida	grey	grey	various (straw hats)
Georgia	grey/blue	grey	various
Kentucky	grey	grey	various
Louisiana	blue/grey	grey/light blue	kepi/various
Maryland	grey	grey	various
Mississippi	grey	grey	black, slouch
North Carolina	grey/blue	grey/blue	various
South Carolina	grey (predominant)	grey	various
Tennessee	grey	grey	various
Texas	grey/civilian	grey/civilian	various
Virginia	grey	grey	kepi

still being carried by units in the field, along with the tradition of mounting the trumpeters of cavalry and artillery units on whites and greys, which made identification easier). Confederate units clothed in blue were mistaken for northern units by both sides, which resulted in other Confederate units opening fire on them. However, such confusion could prove to be advantageous, though dangerously so. One blue-coated Confederate unit at First Bull Run attacked and overwhelmed Union artillery units, the Yankees not recognizing them until too late. The Union gunners shifted trails and opened fire, but were overrun and the guns captured.

initially small Regular Army of the Confederacy. The Provisional Army consisted of troops drawn from both the pre-war militia units and from the myriad volunteer companies. These troops were not initially to be uniformed by the central government and like the pre-war militia companies, when they were formed into regiments, the variety of uniforms gave a most unmilitary appearance.

Some units were uniformed in blue before and (initially) during the war. This caused not only confusion on the battlefield, it also caused casualties from 'friendly fire'. The Civil War battlefield, like those in the wars that had preceded it, was usually cloaked in black powder smoke which made the identification of units difficult at best (and this was one of the reasons why regimental and national colours were

◀ **ADJUTANT, 17TH REGIMENT VIRGINIA VOLUNTEER INFANTRY, 1861** *With the exception of the three rows of buttons on his tunic, the epaulettes and the device on his kepi, this adjutant is close to regulation uniform requirements. The sash is a rank distinction for both officers and NCOs.*

▶ **NCO, ALABAMA VOLUNTEER CORPS, 1861** *This Alabama NCO could pass at first glance for a French infantryman. The single-breasted tunic, shako with plume and large epaulettes would disappear once the shooting started and survival become paramount.*

REGULAR ARMY

Confederate regulation uniforms for the Army, as well as for the Navy and Marine Corps, were similar to those for the US Army, Navy and Marine Corps, although generally grey in colour.

Grey Coats

In cut, style and overall impression, the uniforms adopted appeared to be identical to those worn by their northern foes, but there were, however, significant differences.

Overall, the regulation colour of the army's uniforms was to be grey, though blue still showed up regularly, especially in the first year of the war. Light to medium grey was specified for jackets, coats and frock coats, as well as overcoats. The colours that 'evolved' and that were used, however, ranged from a light to a dark grey, even blue grey being seen and accepted. The branch colours were designated as light or sky blue for infantry, yellow for cavalry and red for artillery. The regulation headgear would be the French-inspired kepi, which would either be trimmed in the branch colour or the colour would cover the entire top of the kepi. Trousers would be light or sky blue.

Rank Insignia

While the overall appearance would be very similar to that of the United States Army, the rank insignia for officers would be quite different. Rank would be indicated on both the collar and the sleeve of the jacket or frock coats. Company grade officers (second lieutenant, first lieutenant and captain) would have gold bars or slashes on the colours: one for second lieutenant, two for first lieutenant and three for captain. Field grade officers (major, lieutenant colonel and colonel) would have their rank indicated on the collar by stars, one for major, two for lieutenant colonel and three for colonel. General officers would have stars on the collar

surrounded by a laurel wreath. Collars would be in the branch colour, and general officers would be in light buff.

On the sleeves elaborate braid would also indicate the officers' rank. Lieutenants would have a single 'loop' of braid, captains two, and on up the chain to the quite thick and elaborate looping for a general officer. Cuffs would also be in the branch colour. Officers' headgear, especially the kepi, would have gold braid and trim to distinguish them from the simpler kepis of the enlisted men.

The rank of NCOs was displayed on the upper sleeve of the jacket or coat in a series of chevrons pointing downward. Corporals had two stripes, sergeants three, with the higher ranks of senior staff NCOs having the three basic stripes of a sergeant but with added stripes above the chevrons, called 'rockers'. First sergeants had a diamond added to their chevrons and ordnance sergeants a star. These all would be in the branch colour.

Uniform Regulations

Initially, a short, grey tunic was approved for wear by the congressional committee that was assigned to design uniforms for the Confederate Army. This was inspired by the uniforms of riflemen, or Jägers, of the Austrian Army. Nicola Marschall (a German-American artist who supported the Confederate cause) was asked to design the uniforms, and the tunic, which was shorter than the popular frock coat, met with immediate disapproval by the army. It was later abolished and the frock coat was made regulation.

Infantry uniforms were quite plain and handsome, but cavalry and artillery, especially horse artillery, might get a little fancy with braid or lace in the branch colour along the seams or collars and cuffs of the short shell jacket. This item of clothing was favoured among the mounted arms.

Tunics of all types and colours, sometimes matching the trousers in colour, were worn by many in the

◀ INFANTRY PRIVATE, REGULATION DRESS, 1861 *This is the regulation dress for Confederate infantry during the war, which was never achieved on a national level. The branch colour was sky blue, and rank insignia and the kepi would be in the same colour. Units that actually wore the frock coat probably dropped them by the end of the first year of the war in favour of the more economical shell jacket.*

◄ **ARTILLERY OFFICER, REGULATION DRESS, 1861** *Confederate artillery had the same branch colour as the Union artillery – red. This officer's collar, kepi and cuffs are in the branch colour. The short shell jacket is typical of mounted units, as this company-grade officer is a horse artilleryman.*

► **CAVALRYMAN, REGULATION DRESS, 1861** *Again, the cavalry had the same branch colour as their northern counterparts – bright yellow. Collar, cuffs, and kepi were supposed to be in red, but economy and other factors allowed variations throughout the Confederate army. This trooper is well-equipped, which would diminish as the war wore on.*

darker grey was seen often, especially among the officers. Brown or 'butternut' coloured uniforms might be seen, along with a liberal dose of civilian and non-regulation attire. Uniforms were supposed to be made from wool, but denim and any other sturdy material could and would be used to keep the Southern soldier clothed and in the field.

▼ **REGULATION COLLAR AND SLEEVE RANK INSIGNIA, 1861** *Contrary to the system of officers' rank employed in the US Army, the Confederate government issued regulations in 1861 that used a combination of collar and sleeve rank for its officers. Collars and cuffs were supposed to be in the branch colour to make identification of the officers easier. Collars: 1 General officer. 2 Cavalry colonel. 3 Staff lieutenant colonel. 4 Medical corps major. 5 Artillery captain. 6 Infantry first lieutenant. 7 Cavalry second lieutenant. Sleeves: 8 General officer. 9 Artillery colonel. 10 Cavalry captain. 11 Infantry lieutenant.*

Confederate ranks, as they were by their northern opponents. Cloth was made locally or imported from Europe by the blockade runners, and officers would sometimes embellish their uniforms to their own standards and preference, one notably outlined the braid on the sleeves in the branch colour which made a striking contrast to the rest of the uniform and was quite handsome.

These were the regulations, which soldiers have a habit of ignoring. The Southern regular also had additional problems with uniforms because of the inferior quality of the dyes that were used, and the supply of the uniforms themselves. The proper shades of grey may or may not be available and

ZOUAVES

While the South never adopted the zouave trend to the extent that the North did, they still fielded some colourful units in zouave costume.

Louisiana Units

The most famous Louisiana zouave unit was the Louisiana Tigers, also known as Wheat's Tigers, after their commander, the experienced, enigmatic and indefatigable Rob Wheat. Officially the 1st Special Battalion, Louisiana Infantry, Wheat's Tigers was a rough and

ready outfit that needed a firm hand. When war broke out, Wheat raised a company of infantry that later was incorporated into the Tigers and Wheat was elected major. The battalion served well at First Bull Run and in the Shenandoah Valley as part of Jackson's command, and fought in the Peninsular campaign. Wheat was badly wounded at First Bull Run, but recovered, but he took his death wound at Gaines' Mill. Wheat's death also spelled the death knell of the unit, which fell apart. The battalion was broken up and the surviving Tigers were sent to other units.

The other Louisiana unit that adopted zouave dress was the 1st Battalion Louisiana Zouaves, also known as Coppens' Zouaves. A polyglot outfit that had a good portion of the Coppens family in its chain of command, the unit was a hard-fighting but unruly unit that caused as much trouble to civilians as it did fighting against the Federals. Sent to Virginia at the beginning of the war, the unit

◀ LOUISIANA PELICANS, 1861 *This zouave looks like his northern counterparts, being uniformed in short blue jacket and wide red trousers. The headgear is also similar to northern zouave units. In the South, however, zouave dress disappeared quite early in the war as it was expensive to maintain, as were the units themselves.*

▶ ZOUAVE, 1ST SPECIAL BATTALION, LOUISIANA INFANTRY (WHEAT'S TIGERS), 1861 *The Louisiana Tigers have been pictured in either brown or blue short zouave jackets, though they were most likely to have been brown. The flamboyant trousers were made from bed ticking, as coveralls had been in the Revolution. This was excellent material for field uniforms as it wore well and long and it also gave an interesting view of the unit when it wore them.*

proved to be undisciplined off the battlefield, but went into action and suffered heavy casualties until it was unfit for further combat.

The battalion was part of the assault force that took Hampton, Virginia, in August 1861. It did well, and then did its best to burn the town down around the inhabitants' ears. Put into garrison duty until the next year, the battalion fought hard at Seven Pines, suffering heavy casualties. The battalion fought at Gaines' Mill and Second Bull Run,

▲ *A group portrait of the Charleston Zouave Cadets, taken in 1861.*

◄ Officer, Charleston Zouave Cadets, **1861** *This officer is typical of zouave officers on both sides during the war. Generally not uniformed as their men were, but in more usual uniform items, such as trousers and frock coats with kepis, they were conspicuous targets for the enemy.*

► Private, 1st Special Battalion, Louisiana Infantry (Wheat's Tigers), 1862 *This is the uniform finally worn by the Louisiana Tigers at the end of their existence. Straw hats were popular, especially in the hot and humid coastal areas of the south. This is a practical and easily maintained field uniform, though not all members of the unit wore it, a mixture of this and zouave dress being quite possible.*

where it was part of the 2nd Louisiana Brigade. At Second Bull Run, the zouaves and others of the brigade ran out of ammunition and ended up throwing rocks at the enemy.

The Battle of Antietam was their last fight. They were mauled and lost so heavily that they had to be pulled out of the line to reorganize, but they never recovered from the heavy losses and their combat career was over.

Zouave Costume

Both units wore the typical zouave uniform of short jackets over baggy trousers. The Tigers were unique in that their trousers were made from bed ticking, an excellent material for campaign and active service; this was white or off-white with blue stripes. They have also been pictured with dark blue or brown short zouave jackets – the brown is probably the correct colour. The Tigers probably also wore straw hats with the word 'Tigers' across the headband. One notable feature of the Tigers' uniform was the unique and unusual striped stockings that were worn under the leggings and that were visible above the leggings and below the striped pantaloons.

Coppens' unit looked like any typical Union zouave unit with the dark blue short jacket and baggy red pantaloons.

INFANTRY

The basic uniform colour for Confederate infantry (with a few exceptions such as the zouave units and those that were uniformed initially in dark blue or dark green) was grey, but even this came in various materials and various shades.

Branch Distinctions

The distinctive regulation branch colour for Confederate infantry was light or sky blue, but as with all regulations in time of war this usually went by the wayside and was probably seldom seen except in the officer ranks, and most likely

disappeared by the last two years of the war. Rank insignia for enlisted men was quite similar to that of the United States Army used during the period. Officers were very much the exception, however, as has already been noted.

Confederate uniforms were provided by the individual states and the Confederate infantry was probably better uniformed during the war than has usually been stated. On parade, the Confederate armies probably did not present a 'uniform' appearance because of the different types of uniform jackets worn, but these armies were field armies, inured to hardship and fatigue and were not parade ground troops. On campaign they have been described as tattered, smelling

◀ PRIVATE, 4TH GEORGIA INFANTRY, 1862 *This well-equipped infantryman has typical clothing and equipment for this period of the war. The success of the blockade runners in getting through the US Navy's increasingly effective blockade supplied the Confederacy with some of its best equipment and small arms. As the Confederate ports fell to the Union as the war went on, that source of supply dried up.*

▶ COLOUR SERGEANT, 17TH SOUTH CAROLINA INFANTRY, 1862 *Infantry regiments usually carried the battle flag of the Army of Northern Virginia. The infantry branch colour was sky-blue, which should have been used for his chevrons, but as the war progressed any available colour was utilized.*

bad, and as early as 1862 the vaunted Army of Northern Virginia was described as being completely non-uniform as to appearance. One civilian in September 1862 described the

'perfect uniform', including white gaiters, and presenting a soldierly appearance to a man. Apparently, it depended on the commander at the time and under what conditions the troops were seen.

Headgear and Jackets

Again, the most favoured headgear for officers was the kepi, while the enlisted men, including NCOs, usually wore some form of the ubiquitous slouch hat. Leather might not be used for brims or peaks, with oilskin being used instead as it was less expensive.

Confederate officers preferred the frock coat, and this could be made from wool, cotton or wool jean material. Colours would vary depending on the dye used and from which depot the clothing originated. Some of it came from the officer's home, and it could be done in crude homespun, sturdy and warm, but not

◀ PRIVATE, 17TH SOUTH CAROLINA INFANTRY, 1862 *This southern infantryman is well equipped and comfortably uniformed in what would become a typical uniform for the Confederate infantry. The forage cap, or kepi, is worn here.*

▲ *Private James Greer of the 4th Georgia Infantry – a poignant portrait of a nervous young man in his brand new uniform.*

nearly as neat and trim as wool uniforms perhaps should have been.

Early in the war, the jacket began to take the place of the frock coat. It was much plainer, shorter, used less cloth, was less expensive to produce and was also simpler to manufacture.

troops as being filthy in appearance and said they could be smelt as they marched along the road. In the same year the Army of the Mississippi Confederate troops were described as being well armed, well dressed and well shod. This latter is unusual as footwear was a constant problem for the South's armies. Boots wore out very quickly on the roads and dirt tracks, and were often poorly manufactured in the first place. The famous Louisiana Brigade during the same period was described as being in

▶ *An Arkansas infantry unit on parade in June 1861, with a partial band at its head. It is hard to find two soldiers in the same uniform even this early in the war.*

▼ PRIVATE, HOOD'S TEXAS BRIGADE, 1862
Some Confederate units would fight in their shirtsleeves on hot summer days, as well as doing so on the march. The Texas Brigade under General John Bell Hood established an excellent combat reputation in the Army of Northern Virginia early in the war. At the Battle of Antietam, they tore into attacking northern troops with great ferocity because their first meal in a few days had been interrupted by a Northern attack.

▲ PRIVATE, 14TH MISSISSIPPI INFANTRY, 1862
An excellently uniformed and accoutred infantryman with frock coat and kepi, this man would be unusual from about 1862 on. Southern infantrymen usually did not carry the knapsack. If they did, it was not for long. The usual practice was to carry a blanket roll instead, which was lighter, easier to carry on the march and carried as few personal items as possible.

▲ PRIVATE, CONFEDERATE INFANTRY, 1863
From some (perhaps biased) accounts by northern troops, some Confederate soldiers from Florida spoke with either so heavy an accent or in a particular type of dialect that they could barely, if at all, be understood. While this figure is uniformed quite well, the overcoat appears to be of civilian manufacture, which was common in the Confederate Army.

It was a simple, handsome design, along the lines of the Union Army's shell jacket, and was usually without ornamentation. It had a short, stand-up collar, and a single row of buttons.

This item, so common in the field and worn by both officers and enlisted men, gave rise to the term 'grey jackets' when referring to the Confederates. The shell jacket design was also used

by the Confederates and it is difficult to tell the difference between the shell jacket and the common uniform jacket worn by the men in the field. Sack coats were also worn by the troops.

North Carolina produced an excellent sack coat for issue to its regiments along with the ever-present jackets.

Coats and Shirts

Overcoats were produced in a variety of styles, both double-breasted or with a single row of buttons, with or without capes. Many of the overcoats followed the US pattern then being used in the Federal armies, something which caused some confusion. Some units wore shirts as outer clothing on campaign, and these came in a variety of designs and colours and were made of wool, cotton or homespun. Some were imported from Great Britain and these were the same as were worn by the British Army. Plaid material was popular, and some shirts looked quite exotic being made from such things as tablecloths.

Rank and Insignia

Officers were authorized to wear the sash, as were NCOs. Sashes came in three colours: yellow for cavalry, green for the medical department, and red for infantry, artillery, engineers and staff officers. There were myriad uniform button designs

◄ **NCO, HAMPTON'S LEGION, 1861** *This colour sergeant of Hampton's Legion from South Carolina displays an excellent example of the type and quality of uniform of units that were raised by an individual, in this case the wealthy Wade Hampton, who became one of the better southern cavalry commanders. The frock coat would be maintained as long as possible by units of this type and calibre as a matter of unit pride, though the gaiters may have been discarded early on. Note that the issue hat is the slouch hat and not the kepi. The legion was made up of both infantry and cavalry, hence the term 'legion' instead of 'regiment'. By all accounts it was an outstanding outfit and fought well. The flag identifies the unit as from South Carolina.*

► **PRIVATE, 20TH TENNESSEE INFANTRY, 1862** *This Tennessee private is dressed unusually in a frock coat instead of the shell jacket that by this date was more usual. He is very well equipped with haversack, canteen and bayonet, and his black leather equipment is in very good shape.*

▲ DRUMMER, CONFEDERATE INFANTRY, 1862
The ubiquitous drummers were usually, age wise anyway, boys. However, a teenage boy in 1861–65 was considered to be a man, and combat – if you survive – will age any youth in a hurry. Drummers were combat troops and accompanied their units into the roar and horror of ground warfare.

worn by the southern soldier. Each state issued its own particular design, and when the war started, the Confederacy did not have any button factories and so these items had to be imported. This was done in considerable quantity. The regulation button design called for a button with an eagle insignia for both general and

staff officers, with buttons denoting the branch of service for line officers, and enlisted buttons were to have the regimental number, but apparently these last were never issued. What the troops preferred was to wear their state buttons, the general cause for which they were fighting. State buttons had different versions of the state seal on them, sometimes modified with unit identification or branch of service identification embossed on them. Some were cast by the state, others were of local or community manufacture.

Equipment

The Confederate soldier's basic equipment was his musket with bayonet, a cartridge box and cap box (for carrying the percussion caps that fired the rifle musket), a canteen, and perhaps a haversack and a blanket roll for his personal items. This was made by placing all of his personal items on his blanket (which would vary from 'issue' blankets to a homemade quilt) and then rolling it up, then wearing it diagonally over his shoulder and across his chest. This may have given the soldier some additional protection, as well as being more comfortable than carrying a pack. The pack itself was seldom used by Confederate infantry and this lightened the load that was carried by each soldier considerably.

The cartridge box was supposed to be constructed of waterproof leather, but cloth was also used, as leather was very expensive. The haversack, also worn over the shoulder, was made of cloth, oilskin or other available materials, and essentials such as food

▶ PRIVATE, CONFEDERATE INFANTRY, 1863
This is a more usual appearance of a Confederate infantryman after 1862 in both theatres (east and west). Note the patched uniform trousers and the blanket roll, obviously sent or taken from home as it is a patch quilt probably made by one of the female members of the soldier's family. The headgear and beard are typical.

and coffee were carried there, as well as spare ammunition. Canteens, an essential piece of equipment, were of varied designs and could be made of wood or tin. Most were circular in design, some of the wooden 'drum' shape, and others either flask type or the ordinary round tin type. Personal items, or those sent from home or taken from the enemy, also made an appearance. All were carried over the shoulder by a strap.

Weaponry

A variety of swords and pistols were carried by infantry officers, and some enlisted men also

carried pistols as an extra weapon. The main weapon of the infantryman was the rifle musket, although this was not so when the war began. As with some northern volunteer units, the older, more inaccurate smoothbore musket was still carried, but the newer, more efficient and accurate rifle musket of various designs was generally carried by the Confederate infantry for most of the war. Three

types of long arms of US manufacture were used by the Confederates: the US model 1855 rifle musket, also known as the Harper's Ferry rifle, and the US model 1841 Mississippi rifle.

Some infantry weapons were imported from Europe, such as the excellent 1853 Enfield rifle musket, the Enfield rifle and the Austrian Lorenz rifle musket. Other rifles were made in the south and much use was made of

captured US material from the battlefield, which would also include individual equipment such as shoes, belts, cartridge pouches and the like.

The Depot System

Uniform depots, where the clothing was produced, were located in Richmond (Virginia), Athens (Georgia), Atlanta (Georgia) and Columbus (Georgia). They were given specific distribution areas. These depots were modelled on the excellent Federal depot at the Schuylkill Arsenal run by the United States Army. None of the Confederate depots could match the production output or standards of the Schuylkill facility, and each of them employed about 40 men in the arsenal itself and between 2,000 and 3,000 outworkers. These were mostly women who did the actual sewing. Usually, with a few exceptions, the uniforms produced were of the same colour for both coat and trousers, but the uniforms were often not of the regulation cut (frock coats, for

▶ **OFFICER, CONFEDERATE INFANTRY, 1863**
Officers were generally more completely equipped than the enlisted men in the Confederate Army and usually only field grade and general officers were mounted. This is the typical equipment, both personal and for the horse, that was used by the Confederacy during the war. Though an infantry officer, the saddle is a cavalry saddle, as is most of the mounted equipment.

▶ *Texas infantrymen in winter quarters,*
Quantico, 1861–62. As men moved into
camps for the winter, most units would build
log structures for protection from the elements.

example, could have one row of
buttons instead of the regulation two)
and the manufactured coat was the
plainer, shorter shell jacket or coat and
not the frock coat that was regulation
issue. The problem of colour was
further compounded by the instability
of 19th-century dyes. These would
sometimes run in wet weather or if the
wearer sweated, and would bleach in
strong sunshine. Even if the cloth
had started out as a uniform colour,
and had been correctly dyed, it
very quickly lost its original hue.

However, the depot system that had
been established by the Confederate
government was reasonably efficient
and by late 1862 clothing supply was
taken over by the government. The
initial products were of good quality
but as the blockade tightened over
time and the South was running out
of money and materials, the quality of
the issued uniforms began to slip.
Replacement of items became
increasingly difficult, although the
use of captured equipment and some
items of dress alleviated some of the

◀ **COLOUR SERGEANT, CONFEDERATE
INFANTRY, 1863** *This toughened veteran is a
member of the famous 'Stonewall Brigade'
which had been initially commanded by
Thomas J. 'Stonewall' Jackson. If a unit had
battle honours they were either painted or
sewn onto the colour by the units themselves.
Colour sergeants would become an enemy
target during combat.*

▶ **OFFICER, CONFEDERATE INFANTRY, 1863**
*This southern stalwart is in almost regulation
uniform, except for the colour of his trousers
and the slouch hat. After 1863, despite the
herculean efforts of the Confederate national
government, and the state governments, the
problems of supplying the Confederate armies
multiplied exponentially. More and more
civilian items of clothing were gradually
used by troops as well as uniform items
lovingly made at home for husbands and
sons in the field.*

▲ *Thomas J. 'Stonewall' Jackson, considered to be one of the most gifted tactical commanders in American history.*

▲ *Lieutenant General Wade Hampton, a plantation owner in the south, and a brave, audacious Confederate commander.*

Confederate government and the individual states made a conscientious attempt at keeping the troops in the field supplied with enough clothing and equipment to survive the hardships of camp life, on campaign and in the field of battle.

▼ PRIVATE, STONEWALL BRIGADE, 1862 *The Stonewall Brigade gave the Army of the Potomac its baptism of fire in early 1862, the day before the Second Battle of Bull Run at Brawner's Farm. The rookies of the then Black Hat Brigade held their ground and prevented the Stonewall Brigade from gaining any ground against them, clearly demonstrating the benefits of their Regular Army training.*

problems in the field. Troops engaged in support, such as guarding convoys, serving in garrisons or escorting prisoners, would initially have been uniformed in a basic manner and would only rarely be resupplied. This caused a problem if they were on active duty, but was less damaging in a garrison, for example. However, generally speaking, the Confederate soldier went on campaign and into combat reasonably well clothed until the end of the war, certainly when the supply situation is taken into account.

While the southern soldier may not have been as well equipped as his northern counterpart and may not have appeared all spit and polish on parade, they were generally well clothed and reasonably equipped. Regiments may have had a varied appearance as not all of the companies were uniformed or dressed alike, and there may have been more noticeable items of civilian dress among the rank and file, but both the

▶ PRIVATE, JACKSON'S 'FOOT CAVALRY', **1862** *Jackson was a no-nonsense commander who expected much from his troops. The men moved so fast in the field, especially during Jackson's famous Shenandoah Valley campaign in 1862 that they were dubbed 'Jackson's Foot Cavalry'. They were expected to keep on the march whatever their physical condition and however badly kitted out, even when they had no shoes.*

CAVALRY

The Southern cavalry at the beginning of the war was excellently mounted and led. The troopers, for the most part, were veteran riders, as most southerners were comfortable astride a horse, and because of this they dominated their northern counterparts for the first two years of the conflict.

Southern Advantage

Under commanders such as James Ewell Brown ('Jeb') Stuart, Wade Hampton, Fitzhugh Lee and Nathan

Bedford Forrest, the Confederate cavalry arm literally rode rings around the Federal horsemen for the first two years of the war, and bested them in cavalry on cavalry engagements.

Stuart, the *beau sabreur* of the southern cavalry arm, came to epitomize not only the ideal of the cavalryman, but he became famous for his raids in the rear of the Union armies in the east. Dressed in his short, double-breasted jacket with pointed Polish cuffs, piped in the buff colour for general officer's facings, buff collar and yellow sash, his élan and dash personified the picture of a cavalry commander. His uniform was finished off with a plumed hat and high cavalry boots along with his sabre, and he and his horsemen rode proud until he was surprised at Brandy Station, Virginia. Here, in the middle of a review, he was surprised by a determined Union cavalry attack, backed up by the excellent Federal horse artillery batteries, and was almost defeated by the newly trained and well-led Union

◀ OFFICER, 1ST VIRGINIA CAVALRY, 1861 *The 1st Virginia Cavalry was a show-horse outfit and this uniform is certainly indicative of it. The yellow sash, high cavalry boots, gauntlets and the slouch hat all indicate the Confederate cavalry officer. The unit maintained the frock coat with the black frogging, hussar style, across the front of the tunic, but after this wore out, the plainer, shorter shell jacket for mounted troops would probably be substituted.*

▶ NCO, 8TH TEXAS CAVALRY, (TERRY'S TEXAS RANGERS), 1864 *Compared to the finery of the Virginia cavalrymen, this Texas horse soldier is a relative poor cousin. Probably only the officers attempted to wear regulation uniform, but none of the members of the unit would be without the lone star insignia, as seen on this trooper's hat.*
Initially the rangers were poorly armed, but better weapons were picked up along the way.

cavalry of the Army of the Potomac. Pilloried in the southern press for being surprised and roughly handled, Stuart attempted to regain what he considered to be his sullied reputation with a repeat of a raid in the rear of the Army of the Potomac. Not only was his raid a failure, he deprived Lee of half of his reconnaissance capability in the Gettysburg campaign and Stuart himself was beaten by Union cavalry under generals Gregg and Custer on the third day of the battle and he had

to retreat with the rest of the Army of Northern Virginia the next day. Stuart himself would be killed in action in May 1864 in a large cavalry engagement at Yellow Tavern in northern Virginia.

Branch Colours

Cavalry uniforms followed the same regulations as the infantry, with the branch colour being yellow. Cavalrymen favoured the jacket or shell jacket, as it was less cumbersome to wear mounted. The buttons on the uniform generally were decorated with an ornate 'C' and sometimes with crossed sabres, the usual symbol of the cavalry arm in the American service.

Headgear was the usual slouch hat or kepi, some of the cavalrymen having bright yellow kepis, which added colour to the overall appearance of the units and to the general grey colour of the uniforms. Riding boots were worn, if they could be procured, by the cavalry arm and saddles could be of the Federal type then in use – the McClellan saddle, a model of which was manufactured in the south. Another type used was the Jennifer saddle, which was similar to the McClellan saddle but with a higher comb in the front of the saddle. Saddle bags came in at least two types, and captured Federal horse furniture was highly prized.

Trumpeters

The equivalent of the infantry drummer in the cavalry was the trumpeter. This was the commander's radio operator of the period. A bugle could carry much farther than the word of command on the battlefield so a good trumpeter was worth his weight in gold. The cavalry trumpet was very simple in design and had no valves during this period. Trumpeters not only echoed the commander's intentions through music, but also covered the commander's back in a mêlée. They also had to be recognizable in the noise and mess of combat, and if at all possible rode white or grey horses for easier identification.

▼ NCO, 1ST VIRGINIA CAVALRY, 1861
This standard bearer of the 1st Virginia is dressed like the ideal cavalryman he was supposed to be. The plume in the slouch hat is also typical of how the southern horse soldier saw himself. The standard is typical of Confederate battle flags. The St Andrew's cross with either 11 or 13 white stars was the battle flag of the Army of Northern Virginia, though other Confederate armies also used versions of that flag. Unfortunately, this flag, which was carried with honour into combat by the Confederates as a symbol of their freedom and independence, has since been appropriated by racist groups such as the Ku Klux Klan and has become a banner of hate and prejudice, which was not the original intent.

Weapons

The Southern cavalryman was supposed to be armed with pistol, carbine and sabre, but not all of the cavalry carried the complete range of weapons because of various problems in supply and procurement. Sabres should have been worn by all ranks, but there was not one model that really could be considered the standard issue sabre for the Confederate Army. There were many designs, some foreign and some domestic, and some captured from the northern armies, but all had the same feature of a protected hilt and a long, curved blade.

Pistols came in various models, again locally procured or brought in from Europe. The favoured ones were usually the various Colt models, especially the .36 calibre Navy model. The firms of Griswold and Gunnison, as well as Leech and Rigdon, made excellent revolvers on the Colt model for the Confederate Army during the war.

As the war progressed, breech-loading long arms came into service. While this is especially true for breech-loading carbines issued to and used by the Federal Cavalry, it was also true for the southern horseman. Sharps carbines were found among the Confederate cavalrymen as well as older pre-war models, such as the unpopular Colt repeating carbine, which had a revolving cylinder much like that found on a revolver. Some southern cavalrymen carried sawn-off shotguns and the Mississippi Rifle mentioned in the infantry section was also a popular cavalry long arm. In firearms, however, the southern cavalry lagged behind the Union horse, and when some Federal cavalry units began to be issued with magazine-fed Sharps and Spencers later in the war, the Confederates said the Yankees had a carbine that they could load on Sunday and fire all week.

▶ OFFICER, HAMPTON'S LEGION, 1861 *This officer represents the cavalry element of Hampton's Legion and is uniformed even more flamboyantly than his comrades in the 1st Virginia Cavalry. Everything about this officer, from the plume in his hat, the hussar-style frogging on his short cavalry jacket to his boots and spurs spells 'southern cavalier' and the unit served loyally and well.*

◀ TROOPER, 7TH VIRGINIA CAVALRY, 1864 *This Confederate trooper is dressed for cold weather in a grey overcoat. The same style of overcoat was used by the Confederates as by their northern enemies, and while not waterproof, it did provide warmth and protection in the cold. A version of this style of overcoat is still worn by the cadets of the United States Military Academy at West Point. This is the appearance of a Confederate cavalryman from late 1862 through to the end of the war.*

Confederate cavalry could be uniformed in any manner from the nattily uniformed Hampton Legion to the come-as-you-are Texas Rangers who were dressed in different styles of civilian clothes and could be mistaken for militia or the notorious guerrilla units that may or may not stand to fight. Mistaking the indifferently uniformed Texas Rangers for a motley guerrilla unit might be a fatal mistake.

Cavalry Style

While the overall colour for Confederate cavalry was grey, the branch colour of yellow, at least in the first two years of the war, would be prominently displayed, especially by the officers. Frock coats were regulation wear, but most, if not all, of the Confederate cavalry officers preferred the short jacket without tails for mounted wear. It was handsome, practical, and did not become encumbered with either weapons or horse furniture when mounting or dismounting, especially in combat. In addition, it gave a dashing appearance

▼ **TROOPER, 12TH VIRGINIA CAVALRY, 1862**
Unusually, this trooper is wearing a shortened tunic instead of the usual short shell jacket for mounted troops. He is excellently equipped and his horse is well cared for, which was a marker of the good horsemanship of the trooper, and the care which the unit's officers took of the unit's mounts.

when the wearer was mounted, and when topped by a rakish slouch hat adorned with plume or feathers stuck in the side it gave an overall picture of a 'beau ideal' of the mounted arm. Cavalry breeches, yellow silk sashes and riding boots, some thigh-high with spurs, completed the cavalry officer's highly dashing uniform.

The enlisted men wore a much simpler uniform. The jacket usually or sometimes, depending on the availability of yellow cloth or the foraging abilities of the troops and NCOs to get it, had a yellow collar and cuffs. The kepi was worn, but the slouch hat became more common as the war wore on. Knee-high riding boots were usually worn with spurs.

The horse furniture first used was the southern version of the English riding saddle. While an excellent saddle, it had the tendency to rub the horse raw as the mount would lose weight on campaign, so the McClellan saddle was used in the second half of the war, a saddle that was designed to be more comfortable for the horse than the rider, as more than a few cavalrymen on both sides could attest.

Uniform coats for both officers and enlisted men also varied from state to state. Those furnished by North Carolina were longer than the usual round jacket or shell jacket, sometimes looking like a modified frock coat. Some states also issued sack coats instead, so a Confederate cavalry regiment in the field or on parade could be varied in appearance, much to the chagrin to the officers and NCOs who might be sticklers for neat and uniform appearance.

ARTILLERY

The Confederate artillery served well throughout the war. The artillery unit of the Army of Northern Virginia fully earned their title 'The Long Arm of Lee' for their superb performance, sometimes under crippling handicaps, throughout its service.

Supply Problems

However, the Confederate artillery arm was not as numerous nor as well handled as that of their northern opponents. They were, however, better organized for combat and as a supporting

arm, at least initially. Confederate artillery units were organized in battalions of four batteries each, each battery usually being of four guns. This allowed better command and control, critical for artillery units in combat, and allowed greater flexibility in their employment on the battlefield.

The greatest problem faced by the Confederate artillery arm was supply of weapons and ammunition. The South was not a manufacturing society, but an agrarian one. There were only two manufacturing centres in the Confederacy and at the beginning of the war there were no artillery foundries. This led to critical shortages of field pieces and the vehicles, such as limbers and caissons, to move the pieces and carry the ammunition. Another problem that was aggravated

by this handicap was the uniformity of field pieces in the artillery battalions and sometimes in the batteries. Additionally, older field pieces had to be employed, such as the obsolete 6-pounder, and this put the southern gunners at a distinct disadvantage when facing their well-equipped northern opponents.

One of the ways in which shortfalls were made up was by employing captured northern equipment and field pieces. The northern-designed and produced 3-inch ordnance rifle, favoured by

◀ NCO, THE WASHINGTON ARTILLERY OF NEW ORLEANS, 1861 *This smartly uniformed NCO would be the backbone of any good artillery unit. The Washington Artillery began the war with one company only, but soon recruited to battalion strength (four companies). At this time the term for a company-sized artillery unit was still transitioning to 'battery' instead of the usual and soon-to-be-obsolete 'company'. The Confederates organized their artillery arm in battalions, which gave them an organizational advantage over their northern counterparts.*

▶ OFFICER, THE WASHINGTON ARTILLERY OF NEW ORLEANS, 1861 *The Washington artillery would eventually transition into grey uniforms from the original smart blue uniforms, undoubtedly by necessity and to avoid confusion on the battlefield. The gaiters would be kept with the new grey uniforms after the transition from blue. The standard issue sabre for enlisted men would soon be discarded, though all ranks would be armed with pistols for battery defence in tight situations. The red kepi, not shown here, was retained as long as possible as an artillery distinction, artillerymen having the notion that they are elite troops.*

◀ **GUNNER, FIELD ARTILLERY, 1862** *This is an excellent view of what an enlisted Confederate artilleryman was supposed to look like and how he was armed. The short shell jacket was worn by enlisted men of both horse and field artillery and the kepi was as usual, as was the slouch hat. The bucket was a vital piece of equipment, and was used in combat to wet the swab that was used to clean out the gun tube after every round to ensure there was no premature detonation of the next round, which would be catastrophic to the artilleryman with the rammer.*

▶ **OFFICER, FIELD ARTILLERY, 1862** *This field artillery officer wears the regulation frock coat with a double row of brass buttons, and his rank is quite visible above his sleeves. His branch colour is also quite obvious on cuffs, collar, and kepi, so there is no doubt that he is an artilleryman.*

northern horse artillerymen, was much prized by the southern gunners and was deemed to be the best horse artillery piece of the war.

Southern Redlegs

The artillery branch colour was red, just as it was for their northern opponents. The Southern 'Redlegs' were a cantankerous lot and utilized their guns as well as their northern opponents, but were generally outclassed despite their superior organization and the skill which they repeatedly demonstrated on the battlefield in both theatres. Artillerymen were uniformed similarly to their cavalry comrades with the

yellow distinctions of the cavalry being replaced by the red of the artillery. Short jackets and shell jackets were the usual wear for artillerymen, as the horse artillery was a mounted arm and at least some of the field artilleryman – the officers, guidon bearer, trumpeter and gun team drivers – were also mounted. Uniform buttons had a distinctive 'A' embossed on them and red kepis were usually a distinction of great honour among the artillery.

Not all artillerymen were uniformed the same. The famous Washington artillery of New Orleans was originally uniformed in dark blue in a handsome uniform that they at least attempted to keep up during the first half of the war. Some artillery units had red collars and cuffs, some were merely piped in red.

As in the United States Army, the Confederate horse artillery arm was considered to be a *corps d'elite*, especially the units assigned to the Stuart Horse Artillery. Horse artillery batteries were organized to be entirely mounted on their own horses, each gunner having his own horse and no artillerymen were supposed to ride on limbers or caissons (the ammunition boxes on both the limbers and caissons, which carried one and two ammunition boxes respectively, were

designed to serve as seats for gunners and were used as such in the field artillery where the gunners were not individually mounted). Additional gunners were supposed to be assigned to act as horse holders in action. As the battery was emplaced and the gunners took their places on their assigned guns, additional gunners for every three or four artillerymen would hold the horses of their comrades while they served the guns.

Crews and Guns

Gun crews were seldom armed with their own sidearms, though pistols were much prized by artillerymen. Their weapons were the guns

◄ GUNNER, HORSE ARTILLERY, 1863 *This is another view of what a southern gunner would look like in the field. It was unusual for enlisted men to be armed with a pistol. For all practical purposes, their personal weapon was the field piece they served. Some of the field pieces that the Confederate gunner would service would be produced by the Confederate government, especially the favoured 12-pounder Napoleon gun-howitzer, which was copied from the Federal model. Some of his ordnance would be captured northern pieces, and if he was a horse artilleryman the battery might be equipped with the much-prized US 3-inch ordnance rifle.*

► OFFICER, HORSE ARTILLERY, 1863 *This battery officer is prepared for field service and wears his rank insignia on sleeve, collar and kepi. The red sash is a further insignia of rank. Armed with sabre and pistol he is prepared to command his gun section and keep up with the cavalry he is to support.*

themselves, and the field pieces served by Confederate artillerymen were both smoothbore and rifled models, the rifled pieces being more accurate and capable of longer range than the venerable smoothbores. Smoothbore artillery pieces were usually cast bronze (sometimes referred to as brass) and the rifled pieces were usually made from iron in a variety of ways. The most famous field piece of the war was the 12-pounder brass Napoleon, which was an excellent field piece and reputedly the favourite of the gunners of both sides during the war. The two most common rifled pieces for field artillery were the 10-pounder Parrott

rifle and the 3-inch ordnance rifle, an excellent piece that was specifically designed as horse artillery. It was a northern design, probably the best field piece of the war, and was light, accurate and reliable and not prone to splitting or exploding on its crew as the Parrott rifles had a reputation for doing. Southern artillery units usually gained possession of this field piece by capturing it from Federal units, and it was a much-valued prize among southern gunners.

Gun crew drill had not changed too much from that used in the Napoleonic period (in fact it has not changed much through the present time – the main difference being that the round is loaded from the breech and not the muzzle). A major difference in crew drill and firing the piece was that the friction primer had been developed and gunners no longer had to use the portfire and slow match to set off the primer to ignite the powder train and fire the piece. The friction primer was ignited by pulling a length of rope, the lanyard, which ignited the primer. It was much safer using the lanyard and primer combination as the gunner could fire the piece safely away from the wheels

and the recoil of the piece when fired. The southern artillery arm was handicapped by a lack of modern ordnance and obsolete types and calibres, such as the 6-pounder that had been used in the Mexican War, and this definitely cut down on the throw weight of an artillery battery, as well as its range, which was taken advantage of by the Federal artillery on more than one field.

There were a few imported field pieces from Great Britain that were breech loaders, both the models produced by Whitworth and Armstrong being used (there were two Whitworths used by the Confederates at Gettysburg in July 1863). While it was an advantage to be able to load a field piece from the breech, it was not necessarily quicker, some maintaining it was as fast to load the Whitworth from the muzzle, which could be done with both British models.

Sidearms

The gunner's tools, or sidearms, were basically the same as they had been for decades. Sponges and rammers, worms and brushes were still used to clean and ram the rounds, or extract excess material after firing rounds from the piece. Vent picks, gunners' haversacks, and gunners' pouch belts and pouches were virtually the same as during the Napoleonic period. What had changed was range and accuracy, and

▲ *This is a line of gun limbers with the ammunition caissons attached to them. Each held one ammunition box and each caisson carried two; the boxes doubled as seats for the gunners. All of the standard field pieces were pulled by the same limbers and caissons. This photograph shows the position that the ammunition caissons of Cushing's Battery A, 2nd US Artillery, held during Pickett's Charge at Gettysburg, 3 July 1863.*

the lethality of the ammunition. Spherical case shot, commonly known as shrapnel, could now be fired from cannon as well as howitzers, and canister was still a lethal round at point-blank range. Optics, the sighting tools, had also improved, and the beginnings of modern gunnery could be found on the Civil War battlefield. This was the epitome of muzzle-loading artillery and the last great war in which it would be employed.

◀ GUNNER, HORSE ARTILLERY, 1863 *This cannoneer has a shot bag slung over his shoulder. This leather case was used to bring rounds from the ammunition chests on the limbers and caissons to the field piece when they were in action. One round was carried at a time, and in action this gunner was a very busy man. As shown by his boots and spurs, this gunner is a horse artilleryman.*

▶ OFFICER, HORSE ARTILLERY, 1864 *This horse artillery officer is dressed for bad or cold weather and he wears his sabre belt on the outside of his overcoat. Junior officers and enlisted men would generally wear the same overcoat.*

SUPPORTING ARMS

The Confederates were supported by a small number of technical branches providing a range of services.

Engineers

As originally formed in 1861 the Confederate engineer arm had neither enlisted men nor lieutenants. It was an organization of officers from captain to colonel and if fortifications had to be built, or other pick and shovel work had to be done, it was done by forming provisional pioneer brigades. However, in late 1863 two engineer regiments were formed and the 1st Regiment was assigned to the Army of Northern Virginia in time for the Wilderness campaign along with two companies of the 2nd Regiment. The remainder of the 2nd Regiment was sent to the western theatre.

Officers wore grey sack coats and slouch hats; apparently this was typical wear for staff officers in the field. If mounted they would wear the usual riding boots and spurs. When serving dismounted they undoubtedly wore trousers over shoes. Rank insignia and designation was as for the other branches of the army.

Enlisted men probably wore an all grey uniform of short jacket and trousers with a grey kepi. They were equipped as infantry and though their branch colour was buff, they could have their rank insignia in white.

Signalmen

The Signal Corps was formed in April 1862. It was a small organization consisting of only 60 personnel, half officers, half NCOs. If enlisted men were needed for duty, they were assigned from the line units on temporary duty. They were uniformed as other staff personnel and undoubtedly by the last half of the war were uniformed as the engineers with the same branch colour distinctions. Unlike the other branches, however, the signal corps apparently had a cap badge modelled on the signal corps in the Union Army, though silver-plated and not in colour.

Invalids and Medics

As with the Union Army, the Confederates formed an invalid corps early in 1864 to relieve fit men of guard duty. There was not a designated uniform but frock coats were usual for issue and wear.

◄ OFFICER INSTRUCTOR, VIRGINIA MILITARY INSTITUTE, 1864 *The Virginia Military Institute (VMI) was a military school situated in the Shenandoah Valley. The cadets and their officer-instructors fought in the Valley campaign. This instructor is in regulation Confederate dress for infantry officers.*

► CADET, VIRGINIA MILITARY INSTITUTE, 1864 *This interesting and different uniform is that of the VMI cadets for field service. It was in this uniform that they took the field to face the 'invading' army in the Shenandoah Valley in 1864. They fought valiantly and well to defend their home state and school.*

The Confederate medical department had surgeons and medical personnel assigned to combat units and higher level headquarters. Officers were authorized a knee-length frock coat with collar and cuffs in the branch colour. Rank distinctions were as for the other branches. An unofficial cap badge of a gold wreath with the letters 'MS' within it was worn on the front of the hat or kepi.

Irregulars

Guerrilla warfare played a significant part on the fringes of the war. Missouri was ravaged by gangs of outlaws operating under the guise of southern guerrillas, who were nothing more than murderers, thieves and thugs.

They hit soft targets of civilians, killing innocents with an enthusiasm that was reminiscent of the bitter civil war in the South during the War of the American Revolution. One excellently led and disciplined guerilla unit was Mosby's rangers in the Shenandoah Valley, who were uniformed as Confederate cavalry (which they had previously been). Colonel Mosby's uniform consisted of a grey jacket and riding breeches and boots. His equipment consisted of a leather belt for sword and pistol and he is often pictured carrying

binoculars. His usual headdress was a slouch hat. At the other end of the scale to Mosby's rangers were the criminals and outlaws who under leaders such as William Quantrill raided, burned and looted through the war, spawning such famous outlaws as Jesse and Frank James. These bandits wore regular civilian clothing, undoubtedly with military accoutrements.

Scholars

There were two military academies in the South, both of which supplied troops from among their student body and staff, to the field armies when necessary. The Virginia Military Institute and the Citadel, both still in existence today and turning out commissioned officers for the Armed Forces of the United States, were excellent institutions of higher learning and they added combat laurels to their institutions by their performance when summoned during the war. The cadets of both of these institutions wore variations of the Confederate Army uniform and these were worn into combat.

◀ COLONEL JOHN SINGLETON MOSBY, 1864 *John Singleton Mosby was a thorn in the side of Union operations in the Shenandoah Valley throughout the war. Originally in command of a regular cavalry battalion, he converted them into 'partisan rangers' and used them to control a significant portion of the Valley. His men were not in the strict sense guerillas, though they did fight in that manner, but were uniformed troops who fought honourably and long for their cause.*

NAVAL FORCES

The Confederate Navy was nonexistent when war broke out in the spring of 1861. Regular officers from the United States Navy 'went South', however, and were instrumental in establishing an effective fleet.

The Navy would prove proficient in the defence of Confederate coastal waters and also put raiders to sea which wreaked havoc with Northern seaborne commerce, the most famous ships being the *Alabama* and the *Shenandoah*. The CSS *Alabama* was finally run to ground by the USS *Kearsage* and sunk off the coast of France in a dramatic sea battle, where the better-trained northern crew literally shot the *Alabama* to pieces. The *Shenandoah* was never run down and was still at sea when the war ended.

Blue or Grey

Initially, like the Confederate Marine Corps, the Confederate Navy wore dark blue. When the official uniform became grey, many of the navy officers did not want to wear it as no other navy in the world wore grey. Generally speaking, most navies wore dark blue as a uniform and those in the Confederate service wanted nothing different. However, grey was the official colour and the specified uniform for the Navy was to be a grey frock coat and matching trousers for officers and the usual 'naval dress', also in grey, for enlisted men. They wore the pullover blouse with the large white collar that fell down the back between the shoulder blades along with a tie. The tight cuffs on the blouse were also white. Except for the overall colour, they undoubtedly looked like their Federal counterparts.

Rank for the officers was worn both on the sleeve and on the shoulder. A tunic, also in grey, was usually worn with the long-sleeved shirt under the coat. The navy frock coat was cut full and long, and probably went down to the knee. Headgear was the typical 'navy cap' that was similar to that worn in the Mexican War. Enlisted headgear clearly resembled that worn in the United States Navy, but in grey cloth.

The men who organized and built the Confederate Navy were generally former officers of the United States Navy, and many of them were old 'sea dogs' who knew exactly what they had to do to defeat the US Navy. However, the economy of the South

◀ **OFFICER, LOUISIANA STATE NAVY, 1862**
Some of the southern states had their own navies. This officer is uniformed in typical naval fashion for the period and his rank is displayed on his shoulders with epaulette straps. He is uniformed for summer or for tropical service with white trousers and the ubiquitous straw hat.

▶ **OFFICER, CONFEDERATE STATES NAVY, 1863**
The Confederate Navy was officered by the men who 'went South' when their respective states seceded from the Union in 1861. The uniform they adopted was similar to that of the US Navy, but in grey. Rank is shown worn on epaulette straps on his shoulders.

▲ *The capture of the Confederate ironclad* Tennessee, *pounded into submission by Admiral David Farragut's Federal fleet in the Battle of Mobile Bay, on 5 August 1864.*

◄ **SEAMAN, CONFEDERATE STATES NAVY, 1863** *Dressed in the typical naval uniform of the period, this Confederate seaman is armed and ready for service ashore or in a raiding party. Like the US Navy, sailors joined Marines for such operations and were also used to garrison and man forts along the coast, such as in Charleston Harbor and at Fort Fisher.*

in the first two years of the war, but too many of these captains brought luxury goods and items, which hampered rather than helped the southern war effort. Some of these men became rich or well-off during their careers, but more were caught, sunk, or deprived of a friendly port. In early 1865 when Fort Fisher fell and Wilmington, North Carolina, was taken – the last open port of the Confederacy, and her last communication centre with the outside world – the Confederacy became isolated from outside help.

Blockade runners were civilian seamen and wore either civilian dress or the usual dress, if any, worn by civilian crews before the war.

was agrarian, and not manufacturing, and they had to scrimp and scavenge to get material to construct their ships, especially their ironclads. Theirs was a poor-man's navy, but one which did well against long odds and added further laurels to American seamen.

Blockade Runners

One aspect of the southern effort at sea did not belong to the navy. The blockade runners, daring captains with fast ships designed to outrun the US Navy ships on blockade duty, operated more or less successfully while southern ports remained in southern hands. Vital arms and ammunition were brought in through the blockade

► **SEAMAN, GEORGIA STATE NAVY, 1862** *Except for the colour of the uniform, this state sailor is uniformed similarly to his regular counterpart. State navies were not large, but even so they drained the regular service, and ultimately the Confederate war effort, of valuable manpower as well as precious assets and supplies.*

THE MARINE CORPS

The Confederate Marine Corps, like its northern counterpart, was a small organization employed on various naval missions.

Ship and Shore
The main purpose of the Marines was to serve aboard ship as detachments, or man coastal fortifications, and form the nucleus of landing parties to both go ashore in an amphibious landing or to be part of boarding parties that would attack Union ships

on blockade. The Confederate Marine Corps, like its northern counterpart, was small and generally served in either detachments or company strength, but seldom above the battalion level in any campaign or engagement. In action the Confederate Marines made a name for themselves in cutting out operations where they would attack and board Union ships on blockade duty. They were particularly noticeable in the defence of Fort Fisher in late 1864 and early 1865 where they engaged the Union fleet, and the Federal landing forces that tried, failed – but were finally successful – in assaulting and taking the fort. The landing force also consisted of United States Marines and sailors. The loss of this strategic southern seaport, effectively shut down the blockade runners.

Uniform Details
The original uniform for the Confederate Marines was blue, usually worn by those who had left the United States Marine Corps and 'transferred' into the Confederate service. As this

▶ OFFICER, CONFEDERATE STATES MARINE CORPS, 1864 *This is the regulation uniform prescribed for Confederate Marine officers after the dark blue uniform was abolished. The uniform with its rank insignia on both the collar and the sleeves would make this officer very hard to distinguish from an army officer at a distance, though there would be no difficulty in determining whether or not he was an officer.*

◀ OFFICER, CONFEDERATE STATES MARINE CORPS, 1862 *Initially, the Confederate States Marine Corps was uniformed in dark blue as many, if not most, of its officers had been in the United States Marine Corps and brought their old uniforms with them. Rank insignia, like the Confederate Army, was worn on the sleeves in gold braiding. Needless to say, this colour of uniform could cause problems in combat.*

state of affairs would undoubtedly cause confusion and casualties in action, this was changed to a handsome grey uniform that made it easier to distinguish friend from foe. However, there is evidence that dark blue, usually flannel, shirts were still issued and worn by the Confederate Marines later in the war.

The new grey uniform was neat and handsome and consisted of a grey and sometimes a blue-grey frock coat

▲ Fort Fisher guarded Wilmington, North Carolina. It had to be assaulted twice before being taken by the Union, slamming shut the last southern door to Europe.

with dark blue at the collar and cuffs for officers. The shade of grey would vary with the dyes being used and sometimes the grey could be quite dark. This is indicated in surviving photographs. Rank insignia was the same as for the Confederate Army, being denoted at both the collar and in the voluminous gold lace on the sleeves. Black leather equipment was worn and the regulation kepi was dark blue with gold lace.

Enlisted men wore a simpler single-breasted grey frock coat without dark blue facings and they wore their rank on the upper sleeves in dark blue. As with the officers, their kepis were dark blue, though without the gold lace. The leather equipment was black and at a distance it would be difficult to distinguish the Marines from army units purely by the uniform worn. Sometimes the enlisted Marines wore naval dress. This would most probably consist of a grey blouse, without collar, and white trousers, topped by a navy cap without the ribbons that hung down the back of the cap. As in the Confederate Army, a mixture of uniforms would be worn on active service, even within the same company, no matter how hard the officers and NCOs tried for uniformity and smartness.

Still, the uniform of the Confederate Marine Corps, whether they were the original dark blue or the newer grey-faced dark blue, was a handsome uniform in keeping with the traditions that the Confederate Marine Corps inherited from its parent unit, the US Marine Corps.

◀ **PRIVATE, CONFEDERATE STATES MARINE CORPS, 1864** *The prescribed uniform for enlisted Confederate Marines went to grey, instead of the initial dark blue, quite swiftly after the first year of the war. There is no doubt, though, that Confederate Marines continued to wear dark blue when necessary and this undoubtedly would cause confusion in a close action.*

▶ **PRIVATE, CONFEDERATE STATES MARINE CORPS, 1862** *The Confederate enlisted Marines were also initially uniformed in dark blue, but that changed within the year, at least by regulation. As the Confederate Marines served in small detachments across great distances, uniform standards, and the availability of suitable clothing and material, gave them a variable appearance.*

CONFEDERATE FLAGS AND COLOURS

Confederate colours and flags generally came in two types: national flags and unit colours.

National Flags

There were three evolutions of national flag. The first – the 'stars and bars' – consisted of three large horizontal stripes, alternating red and white with the white stripe in the middle, a blue field in the upper left-hand corner with a circle of 11 white five-pointed stars.

The second national flag was completely different, undoubtedly because the first one at a distance bore a resemblance to the United States national flag. It was mostly white, with a red square in the upper left-hand corner which had a dark blue St Andrew's cross outlined in white and 13 white five-pointed stars inside the cross, three on each portion of the cross and one in the centre.

The last flag was of the same general pattern as the second, but ended on the fly with a broad red vertical stripe.

These flags were made of either wool or cotton 'bunting' for strength and were usually of three sizes as garrison flags: 5 × 7m (16 × 24ft); 2.5 × 3.5m (8 × 12 ft); and 3 × 4m (10 × 15ft). The latter two smaller sizes were usually the ones used as these flags were expensive to produce.

Battle Flags

Confederate unit or 'battle' flags can be further subdivided into two groups: those used by the western armies and those by the eastern armies. Some of the colours, as with those in the North, were presentation colours by citizens of towns or cities and also from civic groups. These were the most varied and colourful types of colours issued and used and they could be made of bunting, silk or other material with the crests, mottoes and other designs on them either painted on or sewn.

In the eastern armies, particularly the Army of Northern Virginia, the most common unit colours became what is known as the battle flag of the Army of Northern Virginia. It was usually, but not always, a red flag with a blue cross of St Andrew, sometimes outlined in white, with either 12 or 13 five-pointed stars within the arms of the cross. Battle honours were sewn or painted on the colours and they were made of either bunting or silk.

The Army of Northern Virginia also had headquarters flags, the most famous probably being that of Jeb Stuart, Lee's cavalry commander in the Army of Northern Virginia.

The colours of the western armies were more varied, and some of the earlier 'models' were patterned after the 'stars and bars' of the first national flag, while some of the regimental colours were also presentation flags or modelled on the state flags. There were also some of the pattern employed by the Army of Northern Virginia. However, there were also colours of blue with a white St Andrew's cross with no stars, as well as flags that had a vertical and horizontal bar cross, some with stars and some without. The colours in the western theatre were more varied and much more colourful

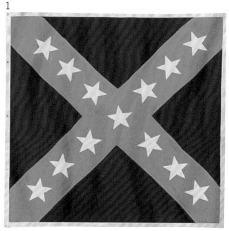

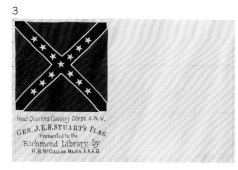

▲ 1 18th Georgia Infantry.
2 1st or 3rd North Carolina Infantry.
3 Headquarters flag, Cavalry Corps, Army of Northern Virginia.

◄ 4 6th and 7th Arkansas Infantry.
5 Regimental battle flag, Walthall's Brigade.

6

7

8

9

10

than those in the east and this would give a western army a colourful appearance in battle or on parade.

In addition, personal flags were also evident in the western theatre, and one Confederate general, Patrick Cleburne, objected vehemently when it was

suggested that all the western regiments replace their colours with the pattern used in the east. Cleburne's protest was so vocal and angry that his command was allowed to keep the older colours which they had fought under for so long.

▲ 6 1st Louisiana Infantry Battalion.
7 King's 22nd/20th Arkansas Infantry.
8 2nd Virginia Infantry.
9 1st Arkansas Infantry.
10 16th Alabama Infantry Regiment.

11

12

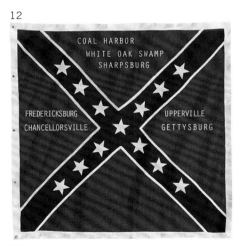

13

▲ 11 11th Alabama Infantry Regiment.
12 King William Artillery Battery, Virginia.
13 28th North Carolina Infantry Regiment.

► 14 3rd Tennessee Infantry.
15 Dobbin's 1st Arkansas Cavalry Regiment.

14

15

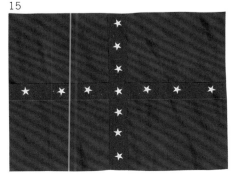

THE BOER WARS

The 'collision' of the Dutch settlers (Afrikaners or Boers) and the British during the 19th century in South Africa became inevitable after the Napoleonic Wars. The Boers wanted to be independent of any allegiance to a European state and to determine their own destiny, but British interests in South Africa grew exponentially after the defeat of Napoleon and the growth of the overseas British empire. Africa had immense natural resources and was rich in diamonds, assets which the British government felt could not be relinquished. The Boers were essentially farmers and had fought the African native tribes for their right to survive and expand their territories on the continent. In the wars that ensued, the Afrikaans settlers fought the British to the bitter end, but were eventually defeated and for a time South Africa became part of the empire 'upon which the sun never set'.

▲ *Boer commanders were tough, intelligent and independent. This is a photograph of Boer General Christian de Wet (centre) after his capture by the British. Others, such as Jan Smuts, would later serve the British in other wars, as would the citizens of South Africa.*

◄ *British officers offer each other congratulations upon meeting at the lifting of the siege of Ladysmith in February 1900. The Boers became adept in the early portion of the war at cutting off and besieging isolated British garrisons. Not only were the Boers good riflemen, they were also excellent artillerymen and proved it against the British on more than one occasion.*

THE BRITISH IN SOUTH AFRICA

British ambition for South Africa led to confrontation with European settlers and native peoples. The result was a series of brutal wars.

The British Army in Africa

The British incursion into South Africa, which occurred over the period of about 100 years (from the beginning of the French Revolution to the Napoleonic Wars, and culminating with the end of the Second Boer War), covered not only a period of violent colonization of the southern portion of the African continent but also a period of development in the British Army. Not only were technology and weapons affected, because of the Industrial Revolution, but tactics, organization and uniforms changed immensely. This was not only as a result of the wars the British waged in South Africa, but also because of the continuing series of wars the British conducted around the world from Africa to the Far East, as Great Britain became the most powerful nation and

▼ *Field Marshal Lord Kitchener, who along with Sir Garnet Wolsely, Lord Roberts and other commanders, held the British empire.*

▲ *The epic defence of the mission station of Rorke's Drift against 4,000 Zulus on 22–23 January 1879 earned 11 Victoria Crosses for one British infantry company and the troops assembled there to support them.*

empire in the world and her queen, because of the changes in the empire, also became Queen Empress.

Most of Great Britain's wars of empire were not fought against another European power. From the end of the Napoleonic Wars until the beginning of the Great War in 1914, Great Britain only fought one 'European' nation, Russia in the Crimea in the 1850s (some historians and writers, not the least of whom is Rudyard Kipling, the Bard of the British soldier during the late Victorian period, considered Russia to be an Asian and not a European nation). While the British Army, as well as the Royal Navy on both land and sea, was engaged almost continuously during the period concerned, the warfare they conducted was usually against

▲ *A Boer skirmish line in a temporary entrenchment in the field, c.1899–1902.*

indigenous peoples in Africa and Asia. These peoples were equipped differently, fought differently, and were as different culturally from each other as they were from the British.

The British, who had fought until at least 1881 in their red service dress modified for field service, learned to wear khaki uniforms (first used in India in the 1850s) to blend in with the countryside, emphasized rifle marksmanship, modified their tactics to fit the enemy they were fighting, and learned counter-insurgency techniques that the French had been taught long before in North Africa.

Troops employed in the field force fought as the Boers fought, and their uniforms changed to fit that role. The long-used foreign service helmet largely disappeared in favour of the slouch hat which later became known as the bush hat. Boots would disappear to be replaced by puttees, which were in use in India, and shoes. These were worn even by mounted troops who wore spurs attached to their shoes.

For the first time, large contingents of empire troops were employed and Canadians and Australians made their way to South Africa, as did entire units of volunteers from Britain who were also used as replacements in regular units. The Second Boer War was a time of great change for the British Army and it was also a preparation for a long and more bitter war that would not only take place in Europe, but around the world in 1914.

The Zulu Nation

In the wars in South Africa the two most formidable opponents the British faced were the Zulus and the Boers. At the hands of these two very different enemies the British learned some hard lessons in defeat. The Zulu victory at Isandlwana in January 1879 was a shock to the British empire and self esteem. The British force was annihilated with very few escaping, with the British infantry standing in place to die to a man. However, the overall campaign in Zululand was successful and was concluded somewhat rapidly after that initial, devastating defeat, and the Zulus were ultimately defeated and their king taken prisoner.

Boer Settlers

Descended from Dutch Calvinist, Flemish and Frisian Calvinist as well as French Huguenot and German Protestant origins, the Boers were an entirely different proposition. The descendants of these original settlers in the Cape were a formidable opponent with their inherent knowledge of the terrain and native peoples. They were fighting on their home turf for what they believed were their territorial rights. Collectively, the Boers were tough fighting men who gave as good as they got in the first year of the Second Boer War until the British used overwhelming force and adapted themselves to the environment.

The war became something of a 'total war' in that all facets of the Boer homeland were attacked. Civilians were forcibly removed from their farms and placed in camps. The farms themselves were burned to separate the Boer units from their support base, and troops were employed in garrisons, as well as line of communication security, to secure British gains.

▼ *The Battle of Blauwkrantz in 1838, one of the many actions the Boer settlers fought against the indigenous populations of southern Africa as they carved out a homeland.*

FIRST BOER WAR: BRITISH TROOPS

The British had come to southern Africa during the early 19th century, and, as an expanding empire, were determined that they had come to stay. The army came with the settlers and governors and that army had to adapt itself to warfare in a new land. This was not a novel experience for the British soldier, for the occasions upon which the British Army had fought overseas against a variety of enemies were myriad, and the British soldier had proven himself more than able to adapt to changing times, methods of warfare and enemies.

British Infantry

As would happen in the Second Boer War at the end of the century, British infantry would wear a modified version of their dress uniforms in the field. The full dress uniform for the British infantry consisted of a red tailed coattee that was cut across at the waist. There was white lace across the front of the coattee for the enlisted man and it was of a single-breasted design. Officers and NCOs had scarlet double-breasted coattees without the white lace across the front and had a double row of brass buttons down the front. Headgear was a straight shako which was worn with coloured pompons denoting battalion, light or grenadier companies. The coattee had a high collar that must have been uncomfortable if worn in the field. Bandsmen wore a white double-breasted coattee with a high collar and a double row of buttons down the

◀ **OFFICER, 27TH FOOT, 1845** *This infantry officer is in undress uniform, which was used as the 'service' uniform on campaign in southern Africa during this period. It was more comfortable than the dress uniforms, but was not entirely suitable for campaigning in the climate prevalent in southern Africa. The jacket, sash and trousers must have been hot, uncomfortable and restricting.*

▶ **GUNNER, ROYAL ARTILLERY, 1845** *Where the British infantryman went, the British artilleryman generally accompanied him, following British General William Phillips' old adage that "where a goat can go, a man can go; where a man can go, he can drag a gun". The all-dark blue artillery uniform was a sign of the gunner's profession just as his field guns would be and the British artilleryman, like his infantry brethren, would modify the uniform as necessary for field service for comfort and not the parade field.*

front of the coattee. Dark blue trousers were worn over shoes. Officers' badges of rank were gold epaulettes, while NCOs had the usual array of stripes on their sleeves which was becoming common in all armies in Europe and the United States.

On foreign service and on campaign the coattee was usually replaced with the plainer, shorter shell jacket which would at least be more utilitarian for wear in combat, although it still had a

high collar. The shako would be replaced by the regulation forage cap, especially in hot weather. Overcoats were still of a slate grey shade and had not changed much in appearance from the Napoleonic Wars.

On campaign the British soldier wore whatever he could get his hands on. Surviving records and the photographs that became more common as the century wore on, depict British infantry, even in the same battalion and sometimes down to the same company, in a variety and mix of uniforms which gave the army a very varied appearance on campaign. Even units that were uniformed smartly at the beginning of a campaign would have their appearance deteriorate depending on how hard the campaign would become (such as the different campaigns in Afghanistan during the period) and how long between the issue of new clothing and equipment as the original uniforms wore out.

▼ **INFANTRY KIT, C.1840**
1 Cap pouch for the musket lock.
2 Haversack.
3 Canteen.
4 Knapsack and blanket roll.
5 Bayonet frog.
6 Cartridge pouch and shoulder belt.

▲ **PRIVATE, RIFLE BRIGADE, 1845**
The famous Rifle Brigade was formed during the Napoleonic Wars and established a reputation second to none in the British Army of the period. Traditionally dressed in the dark green uniform of rifle units, the Rifle Brigade distinguished itself in every action in which it participated. As a rifle and light infantry unit, it did not carry colours and used the bugle instead of the drum to communicate in the field and in combat.

Combinations of dress and undress uniform items were worn, but equipment was regulation issue.

Uniform issue and replacement would be difficult in the wars of the

▼ **PRIVATE, 27TH FOOT, 1845** *While the British infantryman would usually maintain his undress tunic in the field, he was concerned about his comfort on campaign and would not only use civilian items for wear, such as the comfortable corduroy trousers, but might also 'liberate' Boer clothing items, such as shoes, for wear on campaign. The brown leather equipment is unusual, as is the 'belly box' for carrying cartridges for his personal weapon. The belly box was usually found as a piece of cavalry equipment, but was a common-sense item for use by infantry fighting against a skilled enemy in the bush.*

British empire, and the longer a war or expedition lasted, the more ragged in appearance the British troops would appear. British infantryman might favour undress caps to regulation headgear, especially the hot and top-heavy shakos, and officers often ignored dress regulations completely, which also happened many times in India, especially during the Indian Mutiny. Comfort and survival, as well as the practicalities of campaigning in a hostile environment, both in terms of climate and against ready and determined enemies, became much more important than strict compliance with Queen's regulations.

Rifles

The Rifle Brigade was a product of the Napoleonic period and was part of the British Army's drive for more well-trained light troops after having suffered repeated reverses in the 1790s by the French. These light infantrymen were uniformed in green and armed with the excellent Baker rifle, and had black equipment instead of the usual white belts. These traditions continued after the end of the Napoleonic Wars.

Dark green continued to be the uniform colour of the Rifle Brigade and later the King's Royal Rifle Corps as the Rifle Brigade was reorganized along with the rest of the British infantry in 1881. Black leather equipment was habitually worn, and the rifle companies were manoeuvred by bugle instead of drums. Being a light infantry unit, no colours were used by the regiment.

Volunteers

There were never enough British regular units in the field during the colonial campaigns of the British empire period, at least at the start, especially in South Africa and at the beginning of the Indian Mutiny. However, there were always civilian volunteers who stepped forward to partially or temporarily fill the breech and usually they served both gallantly and well. The civilian population of the British colony in South Africa organized temporary units that volunteered for service with the British regular units. These

◀ PRIVATE, 3RD BATTALION, 60TH RIFLES, 1881 *Like the rifle brigade this infantry unit was dressed in rifle green and the 60th Rifles was originally raised in the mid-18th century as the 'Royal Americans' a title that eventually was found to be uncomfortable after the success of the United States in gaining its independence from Great Britain in 1783. The 60th Rifles seldom served together during its active service and for a long time was overwhelmingly German in make-up, though British in character. As a rifle unit, it gained an outstanding reputation.*

▲ GENERAL OFFICER, 1845 *This is full dress for a British general officer of the period. It is indicative of the period with the double-breasted tailed coat, sash indicating rank and status, the feathered bicorne, which would stay in fashion and use for quite some time in the British Army, and the heavy epaulettes and gold on collar and cuffs.*

volunteers eventually organized themselves into either paramilitary or volunteer units and continued to serve with the British Army in the successive wars in South Africa.

▲ *The Battle of Isandlwana after which the victorious Zulus overran the camp, killing everyone in sight. Wounded were not spared and the Zulus took no prisoners. Those who could not escape were hunted down and killed. It was the worst British defeat in the colonial period. This painting shows the last stand of the 24th Foot Regiment.*

British Cavalry

Regulation dress for British line cavalry was either a red or dark blue coattee with short tails (for mounted troops), light dragoons wearing a double-breasted coattee with a double row of brass buttons down the front, and

◄ OFFICER, 21ST FOOT, 1881 *This is how a 'properly' uniformed and accoutred junior British infantry officer might appear in the field. The sword still might be carried, even for dismounted officers, but some officers might leave it in the unit's baggage wagons and might also use rifle and bayonet to supplement the usual pistol in combat.*

► PRIVATE, 94TH FOOT, 1881 *Even though the slouch hat was not common among British troops at this early date in the wars in South Africa, some units did 'adopt' it, as it was cooler, afforded more protection against the sun and was undoubtedly more comfortable and easier to maintain under campaign conditions. The regulation undress tunic is shown here along with locally bought civilian trousers, probably made of corduroy.*

as they were more comfortable. British regular cavalry employed in South Africa was probably more 'formal' than the infantry and would even go to the extreme of wearing their helmets in the field, though they would be bereft of any plumes or other distinctions. Undoubtedly, this was hot and uncomfortable and provided little or no protection from the sun.

Regarding horse equipment, there was little change from the end of the Napoleonic Wars until 1853. Up to that time the saddlery and harness were different for light and heavy cavalry, and shabraques and the older style valises common in the Napoleonic period were still in service. Carbines for the cavalry only changed from flintlocks to percussion caps, so their outward appearance was virtually the same. A new weapon for light cavalry, the lance, was brought into use, the British Army having being introduced to it somewhat roughly by the French in Spain and at Quatre Bras and Waterloo.

Four light cavalry regiments were converted to lancers beginning in 1816. The lance would be used on active service in India, Afghanistan and southern Africa.

British Artillery

The Royal Artillery would conform to the exigencies of campaign like their infantry brethren and wear what was comfortable and/or serviceable, happily ignoring uniform regulations if the situation called for it.

The artillery regulation uniform of the period was almost identical to that of the infantry with the exception

that it was in the traditional artillery colour of dark blue. However, there was no lace across the front of the enlisted man's coatee and all ranks wore a double-breasted coatee with a double row of brass buttons down the front of the garment. The tail length of the coatee in the rear was identical to the infantry version, but lined and faced with red for all battalions as that was the traditional facing colour of the arm. The same pattern shako was worn. Officers' rank distinctions were gold epaulettes, and NCOs wore chevrons on their upper sleeve. Shell jackets were worn as undress and in the field on campaign and in combat,

▲ CIVILIAN COLONIAL VOLUNTEER, 1881 *This volunteer is dressed in typical civilian clothes of the period – riding breeches and boots, civilian coat and hat – and armed with his own personal weapon. These individuals organized themselves into either paramilitary or volunteer units and served with the British in the wars in South Africa.*

dragoons and dragoon guards wearing a single-breasted coatee. This handsome uniform was worn in the field but usually without the spectacular full dress headgear that some, especially 'heavier' regiments, wore. On foreign service in Africa and India, undress forage caps were worn

▶ OFFICER, CAPE MOUNTED RIFLES, C.1845 *This was a volunteer unit of mounted infantrymen, dressed in dark green as was now the British tradition, which would fight as infantrymen when engaged. They uniformed themselves in British-style uniforms, patterned after British regular units. Combat units of this type usually gave a good account of themselves in action, if well led.*

Naval Brigade

Great Britain being a maritime power, there were never enough ground troops to go round for the colonial wars during the 19th century. The Royal Navy, besides being the senior service, gave great strategic mobility to the British Army in the colonial campaigns, being able to land army units wherever they were needed and providing the necessary naval gunfire support to operations within range of the fleet units that were available. The Royal Navy also supplied badly needed manpower to the numerous land operations engaged in during the Crimean War and the Indian Mutiny in the 1850s through to the Boxer Rebellion in 1900. Both seamen and Marines were supplied by the fleet and wherever the Royal Navy could float, naval landing parties and naval brigades were deployed. Operations ashore became as common to the sailors of the Royal Navy as they were to the army units they served alongside.

If the army had a shortage of artillery, the Royal Navy sometimes came to the rescue, sometimes supplying rocket units ashore and sometimes, as happened in the last Boer War, dismounting naval guns, fashioning artillery gun carriages for these large guns out of boiler plate, and supplying sailors and Marines to serve as gun crews.

Naval troops suffered all the hardships and losses of their army brethren, sometimes engaging in costly frontal assaults on prepared Afrikaner positions in the Boer Wars, and serving ashore against the Russians in the Crimea. The naval brigades supplied by the fleet were a vital addition to the land forces available in the campaigns of the 19th century.

As an interesting footnote, although the Royal Marines (which consisted of two branches in different uniforms, the Royal Marine Light Infantry uniformed in scarlet like the army, and the Royal Marine Artillery uniformed in dark blue like the Royal Artillery) were a naval asset, their personnel were not considered naval personnel. Alongside their sailor comrades, they were numbered on the Army List, and they were granted precedence on parade after the 49th Foot.

▲ TROOPER, 7TH DRAGOON GUARDS, C.1845
This regular unit of heavy cavalry was noted for wearing their full dress helmet in South Africa, at least initially. The uniform was not modified much, if at all, for service in a hot, humid climate, and the helmet must have been miserable to wear in the heat.

usually accompanied by some type of headgear, either regulation or not. The forage cap was worn, but so were various types of civilian hats, depending on availability and individual taste. Civilian shirts and coats were also worn when uniform replacements were not available, which gave the artillery as varied an appearance as the rest of the army.

▶ SEAMAN, NAVAL BRIGADE, 1881 *In Britain's series of colonial wars there was usually a contingent of sailors of the Royal Navy that served ashore with the army. They would wear their naval uniforms, which were usually modified for land service by foreign service helmets, as shown here, or perhaps straw hats. They would also be issued with either army or Royal Marine personal equipment.*

FIRST BOER WAR: BOERS

The First Boer War, which lasted in reality until the second one began, at the end of the century, clearly defined the relationship between the British and the Boers.

Expansion

The British generally left the Boers alone until after the mid-century and were more concerned in pacifying the areas of South Africa under their control. The Boers during this period were also establishing their small states and

▶ **BOER VOORTREKKER, C.1840** *This man is in a more suitable 'uniform' for fighting both the British and the native peoples of southern Africa. The hat with feather would have been a personal affectation, but his more military appearance is enhanced by the powder horn and ammunition pouch slung over his shoulder with a military-type shoulder belt.*

encroaching on the lands of the Bantu peoples. It was natural, however, that the British and Boers would come into conflict, even though they had common enemies among the indigenous peoples of South Africa. Limited assistance from the Boers during the Zulu War of 1879, when the Zulus were the enemies of both the Boers and the British, and were determined to keep what they had won under their great leader, Shaka, clearly underlined the differences between Great Britain's aims in South Africa and self-determination by the Boers. Neither side would compromise and the issue had to be settled on the battlefield. This was not finally accomplished until 1902 with the defeat of the Boers in the Second Boer War.

Boer farmers were hardy, independent, determined and extremely protective of their autonomy. They were also experienced in fighting and had waged war against the Zulus for generations.

Dress and Equipment

Initially, the Boers who took the field against the British were dressed in civilian clothes and armed with their

◀ **BOER, 1870–80** *Boers fought in civilian clothes and were armed with their personal weapons. Take away the rifle and the ammunition bandolier, and this man would look like any other civilian in southern Africa during the period.*

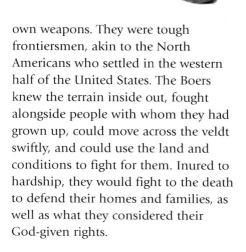

own weapons. They were tough frontiersmen, akin to the North Americans who settled in the western half of the United States. The Boers knew the terrain inside out, fought alongside people with whom they had grown up, could move across the veldt swiftly, and could use the land and conditions to fight for them. Inured to hardship, they would fight to the death to defend their homes and families, as well as what they considered their God-given rights.

The Boers had no standing army and were essentially farmers. They were religious, individualistic, intolerant of interference from native African and Briton alike, and crack shots. Their traditional enemies were the indigenous peoples of South Africa, especially the Zulus, the most warlike and efficient of the Bantu peoples who had migrated south into the South African veldt.

During this period the Boers wore no uniforms, but civilian clothes, sometimes with some type of 'rank' insignia to designate who was in command of a particular commando. 'Commando' was a Boer term which generally meant a group of mounted riflemen who were extremely mobile and armed with various weapons

that were all owned by the individual Afrikaner. Top hats were popular, sometimes with a pompon, rosette or small plume in the Boer colours, usually orange, which derived from the settlers' Dutch ancestry and was the traditional colour of the House of Orange, from which the Stadtholders of the Netherlands came to serve and rule Holland.

There was no fixed commando organization and the members generally came from the same 'community', organized by one of the leaders of the community who would lead the commando on campaign and into battle. Being hardy frontiersmen, who feared God and practically nobody else, the Boers lived a hard life that could end at any moment from the 'knock' of the Zulu or any other of the Bantu tribesmen with whom the Boers had picked a fight.

Field Kit

In the field, the Boers wore civilian clothes consisting of trousers, shirts and jackets, as well as coats, and their 'military' kit was also owned by them. Generally speaking Boer equipment was kept to a minimum, just enough for the members of the commando to be able to fight and live in the field

◄ BOER COMMANDANT, 1881 *This lightly but otherwise well-equipped Boer is a member of a Boer commando. His leggings would be useful in the bush and his ammunition bandoliers at both the waist and over his left shoulder give ready access to ammunition, something at which the Boer commandos became expert. The pouch on his left hip is a haversack, probably homemade, to carry belongings and rations.*

▶ BOER FREE STATE COMMANDO, C.1860 *This well-equipped stalwart is a member of one of the well-organized and well-led commando units that became the scourge of the British Army. He is armed with rifle and knife. The canteen on his left hip is a vital piece of equipment on the veldt. The colour of his clothing helped him blend in with his surroundings.*

against whatever enemy they were arrayed against. Ammunition could be carried in pockets and saddlebags, but eventually cloth bandoliers were used, which were utilitarian and are still employed to this day by modern armies. Some Boers used a vest-bandolier, where the loops for individual rounds were sewn to a civilian vest for use on campaign.

The Boer went to war much as he farmed, ready for anything and equipped lightly and practically. He was a formidable foe and the organization of the commando meant that he could move fast, hit hard, and be deployed alongside his friends and neighbours. The name 'commando' has come represent elite units trained for special operations missions.

ZULU WAR: BRITISH INFANTRY

The war between the British and the Zulu nation was the result of tensions generated by British imperialism in southern Africa, the situation with the Boers, and how both groups interacted with the Zulus.

Friction into War

All three groups wanted to expand, and both the Zulus and the Boers were fiercely independent, and they were also mortal enemies. That situation was not going to change until one or the other was utterly defeated and broken.

The British wanted dominion over the gold- and diamond-rich area held by the Dutch and they wanted no interference from either Boer or Zulu. Sooner or later, fighting between the British and the Zulu was inevitable.

The British invaded Zululand with a force under the command of Lord Chelmsford and the first big battle with the Zulus was an unexpected attack on the British encampment at Isandlwana on 22 January 1879. An army of over 20,000 Zulus, armed with shield and spear (the *assegai*), launched a well-disciplined and determined attack against the troops left at Isandlwana. These consisted of companies of the 24th Foot along with auxiliary units. The British infantry companies formed in line of battle away from the camp, and while their ammunition lasted they inflicted heavy losses on the Zulu regiments (*impis*) attempting to get to grips with their enemies. However, ammunition was not brought up to

◀ **COLOUR SERGEANT BOURNE, 24TH FOOT, 1879** *Colour Sergeant Bourne was the senior non-commissioned officer of Liuetenant Gonville Bromhead's B Company, 2nd Battalion, 24th Foot, which garrisoned the mission station at Rorke's Drift. This group of men successfully defended the station against the 4,000 Zulus that attacked it almost immediately after the Zulu victory at Isandlwana. He was typical of the British NCOs, that backbone of civilization that made the British infantry so formidable in combat. Surprisingly, Colour Sergeant Bourne was not awarded the Victoria Cross for his gallant performance at Rorke's Drift. Perhaps that was because, despite his valiant efforts, it was considered that he was merely 'doing his duty', which was expected of the British NCO.*

▶ **GONVILLE BROMHEAD, 24TH FOOT, 1879** *Bromhead was the commanding officer of B Company, at the Battle of Rorke's Drift. By the time the battle took place he was almost deaf. Though he commanded the infantry company that made up most of the garrison of the mission station, he was not in overall command. Lieutenant John Chard of the Royal Engineers, who happened to be at Rorke's Drift at the time, was senior to Bromhead and was responsible for the overall defence. Both officers received the Victoria Cross for holding the mission station, and their gallant conduct in combat.*

the firing line in support of the infantry companies, and as the troops ran out of ammunition they were overrun and wiped out to a man by overwhelming numbers of infuriated Zulus. The *impis* then turned their attention to the camp itself, overrunning it and killing most of the troops who stood and fought. It was a disaster of unexpected proportions. Needless to say, back at home, the British were appalled.

A corps of 4,000 Zulus who had largely missed the victory at Isandlwana then moved on to the mission station at Rorke's Drift on the Buffalo River. There, one company of the 24th Foot was stationed. On learning of the disaster that morning from terrified survivors running past the station, the two junior officers in charge of the station, Lieutenants

Bromhead (the company commander) and John Chard (an engineer with the main column that had been destroyed but was on detached duty), decided to fortify their post and stand and fight. In an epic battle that lasted from one in the afternoon, through the night, and into the next morning, they defeated the Undi Corps, inflicted

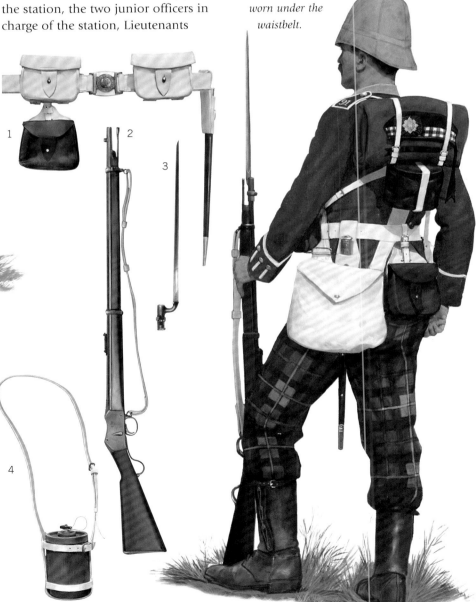

▼ **PRIVATE, 91ST FOOT, 1879** *This British infantryman, belonging to a Scottish regiment, is shown in the regulation trousers, in the regimental tartan. Of note here is how the equipment was attached and worn on the back, as well as how the bayonet was worn. The haversack, probably the most important piece of equipment used by the troops as it carried rations as well as personal items, is worn under the waistbelt.*

▲ **PRIVATE, 99TH FOOT, 1879** *This at ease but battle-ready British infantryman is from a regular line regiment and is uniformed and accoutered according to Queen's regulations. The leather leggings are attached above the shoes and, interestingly, his ammunition pouches are black not white leather, as was usual. The foreign service helmet, however, is in the regulation white and it also has the regimental crest in brass attached to the front of the helmet.*

▶ **INFANTRY KIT, C. 1879**

1 Belt and ammunition pouches.

2 Martini-Henry rifle.

3 Bayonet.

4 Water bottle/canteen.

◄ **SERGEANT, 3RD BATTALION, 60TH RIFLES, 1879** *This fully armed and equipped rifleman in his dark green uniform and black equipment, instead of the usual white for line infantry, is ready for both campaign and battle. His foreign service helmet is tea-stained for active service and he wears a 'belly box' ammunition pouch. The standard canteen is visible on his right hip.*

► **OFFICER, 3RD BATTALION, 60TH RIFLES, 1879** *This well-equipped figure is ready for campaign. Noteworthy are the boots the officer is wearing. His helmet is dyed a sand colour with tea, and his equipment would be either black or brown leather, depending on the officer's tastes. Officers also carried the standard issue sword, which may or may not have been worn in combat.*

Uniform Changes

A major uniform change took place in the British Army in 1855. The coattee was abolished and its place taken by the more handsome and comfortable single-breasted full dress tunic, and its undress equivalent, the single-breasted frock made of serge. The tunic came down to the crotch evenly all round the body and was a handsome and utilitarian uniform. The old shakos were abolished and a new, French-style shako took its place which would remain in use until replaced by the British version of the German Pickelhaube after the Franco-Prussian War.

heavy losses of over 400 Zulu dead while losing only 15 of their own, and earned 11 Victoria Crosses for their steadfast efforts. The defeated and exhausted Zulus retreated.

The climactic battle of the Zulu War was at the Zulu capital, Ulundi, on 4 July 1879, where the fighting power of the *impis* was finally broken by a combination of modern firepower and sensible tactics.

► *On 14 August 1879, following the Battle of Ulundi, chiefs Cetshwayo, Sukani and Umginlana, and other Zulu leaders, surrendered to the British govenor of Natal and Transvaal, Sir Garnet Wolseley.*

Epaulettes were abolished for officers, rank now being shown on the shako, and the tunic was given French-style cuffs. A plainer, shorter shell jacket was still in use, but both it and the two 'versions' of tunic were given lower, more comfortable collars, though they were still of the 'stand-up' type. Trousers would remain dark blue over shoes.

The British invaded Zululand and fielded infantry, artillery and cavalry. The British infantry in South Africa in 1879 generally wore a modified version of its dress uniforms with the usual British infantryman's practice of making it as comfortable as

possible on campaign. Scarlet or red tunic with dark blue trousers was the normal uniform for British line regiments, though Scottish Lowland or Highland regiments might wear trews in the field instead of trousers which bore the pattern of their regimental tartan. The Rifle Brigade wore a dark green uniform, as it had since its inception during the Napoleonic Wars, and its equipment would be black instead of white for the other infantry units. Again, the white foreign service helmet, which was made of cork, would be worn, usually dyed khaki in the field.

There were two types of red coat issued to the British infantryman: the full dress tunic which had seven buttons down the front, was piped in the regimental colour, and had facings also in the regimental colour. The other was the frock, which was less expensive, more comfortable to wear, had only five buttons down the front of the coat and was neither piped nor faced in the regimental colour.

The 24th Foot, later the South Wales Borderers after the 1881 reorganization and the Cardwell reforms, when every regiment was given a title in lieu of their number, was made famous by the two most famous actions in the Zulu

British Infantry Units in Zululand, 1879

Infantry
3rd Foot (2nd Battalion)
13th Foot (1st Battalion)
21st Foot (2nd Battalion, 6 companies)
24th Foot (1st and 2nd Battalions)
57th Foot (8 companies)
58th Foot (6 companies)
60th Foot (3rd Battalion, 7 companies)
80th Foot
88th Foot (6 companies)
90th Foot
91st Foot (8 companies)
94th Foot (6 companies)
99th Foot (8 companies)

Artillery
8 artillery batteries armed with 7- or 9-pounder field guns
1 rocket battery
2 ammunition detachments

Supporting Units
Naval Brigade with artillery
2 engineer companies
Medical detachment
Army Service Corps detachment

War: Isandlwana and Rorke's Drift. However, this was not the only British regular infantry regiment in South Africa during this period even if their experience is the most famous and most well documented.

◀ BANDSMAN, 24TH FOOT, 1879 *Regimental bandsmen generally wore the same as the rest of their regiment with traditional additions to the uniform to make them stand out at parade. In this case, this bandsman from the famous 24th Foot has 'wings' attached to his shoulders. He is off-duty and so also wears the fatigue cap, which is a modified Glengarry cap.*

◀ INFANTRY KIT, C.1879
1 Harness straps for the load-bearing equipment.
2 Waist belt and bayonet frog.
3 White ammunition pouch.
4 Black leather ammunition pouch.

ZULU WAR: BRITISH CAVALRY

There were no British regular cavalry units in South Africa when the Zulu War began. Reinforcements were

▼ OFFICER, 17TH LANCERS, 1879 *This officer is uniformed in undress for campaign. Officers during this period uniformed themselves as comfortably as possible, sometimes wearing civilian pieces of clothing, such as trousers or breeches in the popular corduroy. This also marked them as officers, as the enlisted men would be required to be dressed in more or less correct uniform.*

brought in but the two regular regiments that finally arrived in South Africa were not there in time for the first offensive against the Zulus and missed the battles of Isandlwana and Rorke's Drift.

▼ CAVALRY KIT, C.1879 *1 Pistol holster. 2 Service revolver. 3 Sabre. 4 Lance with pennon, which would either be removed or rolled up on campaign and in combat. 5 Carbine in boot. 6 The Martini-Henry carbine.*

▼ TROOPER, 1ST KING'S DRAGOON GUARDS, 1879 *This regiment, along with the 17th Lancers, was one of two regular cavalry regiments deployed to South Africa after Isandlwana. This officer is fully equipped for field service with the usual replacement of his full dress headgear with the foreign service helmet, in this case dyed with tea to give it a 'khaki' colour to blend in with the terrain, instead of the regulation white. The regimental crest is not worn on the front of the helmet as per regulation, being a standard modification for field service in the bush.*

British cavalry had a tradition of solid mounted service from the time of the War of the Spanish Succession under the great Marlborough. Noted as tough soldiers, usually well mounted, they were not always gifted with competent or experienced leadership. However, a charge by well-mounted British horsemen could still sweep the field.

The British Army adopted the lance after the Napoleonic Wars. There were undoubtedly many reasons for this, not the least of them being the rough handling British infantry and cavalry had undergone at the hands of French and Polish lancers at the Battles of Albuera in 1811, Quatre Bras and Waterloo in 1815. Existing light cavalry regiments, four initially, were converted to lancers and their performance in various colonial theatres of war undoubtedly verified a wise decision.

After the defeat at Isandlwana, two regular cavalry regiments were dispatched to South Africa. These were the 17th Lancers and the 1st King's Dragoon Guards. The 17th Lancers had been part of the famous Light Brigade that had made the almost suicidal charge up the valley at Balaclava during the Crimean War, earning the nickname of 'the death and glory boys'. The regiment's crest is the

▶ TROOPER, 17TH LANCERS, 1879 *The 17th Lancers, 'the death and glory boys', were sent to southern Africa after the disaster at Isandlwana. This enlisted trooper is fully equipped for foreign service, the basic change in his uniform being the use of the foreign service helmet.*

skull and crossbones, also known in the German service as the Death's Head.

Both regiments wore altered dress uniforms that were little modified for active service in the generally hostile climate of Africa. Both regiments wore the foreign service helmet, sometimes white, but usually tea-stained to blend in with the countryside. Overall the lancers' uniform was dark blue with regimental distinctions and they were armed with both sabre

and lance, the lance pennons being either removed or furled on the lance in the field. The dragoon guards wore a scarlet tunic of their branch of service coupled with dark blue trousers. Horse furniture was of the regulation type for the period.

The Zulus were afraid of horses and effective employment of cavalry against them could be a distinct advantage. This was clearly demonstrated at the Battle of Ulundi, when the 17th Lancers attacked the Zulus near the end of the action and inflicted heavy losses among the retreating foe. While it could be difficult to strike at an infantryman, especially if he was prone, with a sword or sabre from horseback, a trooper armed with the regulation lance was at no such disadvantage. The lancers were highly effective in the field and were feared and respected by the Zulus.

Mounted Infantry

Although there were no regular cavalry units in South Africa when the Zulu War began, there were various volunteer mounted units. Lord Chelmsford, the commander of British forces in Zululand who commanded and led the two invasions and gained the victory at Ulundi, had at his disposal two squadrons of mounted British infantry. These units were made up of picked men from the infantry regiments available in South Africa; they were mounted and equipped as cavalry and gave good service during the war. Infantry equipment was changed or modified for mounted use. Most, if not all, of the mounted infantrymen used bandoliers as the Boers did, worn over the shoulder. They were issued corduroy riding breeches as well as leggings and boots, and wore the foreign service helmet.

ZULU WAR: BRITISH ARTILLERY, ENGINEERS AND NAVAL TROOPS

As was their usual practice, the British employed supporting troops on their foreign expeditions to enhance both the numbers on the ground and to increase their combat power. Great Britain was a naval power and not a continental land power, therefore the

▼ **SAPPER, ROYAL ENGINEERS, 1879** *The Royal Corps of Sappers and Miners was established in 1813 during Wellington's Peninsular campaigns because of a lack of suitable and experienced engineer troops. During this period, the engineers were uniformed as the infantry.*

British Army was not as large as other European powers. Inevitably, the employment of naval troops, which would consist of both sailors of the Royal Navy and Royal Marines, as well as auxiliary units of native troops and volunteer units recruited from a colony's inhabitants, were usefully employed and they served alongside units of the Regular Army.

Artillery

The Royal Artillery, horse and field, was excellent and had a long record of worldwide service. Their traditional uniform was dark blue, red being the distinguishing branch colour worn either as facings or the uniform being piped in that colour. The artillerymen, officers and other ranks modified their dress uniforms for field service, maintaining the dark blue colour and the usual smartness, but giving the nod to the exigencies of the hardships encountered in the field. As with the infantry, the undress frock coat would usually be worn instead of the full dress tunic, and it could usually be distinguished from it by having only five buttons down the front while the tunic had seven.

The artillery was equipped with either the 7- or 9-pounder rifled muzzle loader (RML) field piece, although the 9-pounder was preferred. These field pieces were pulled by the standard 16-pounder RML limber. Additionally, some of the artillery units, as well as some of the naval units, were equipped with and employed the 9-pounder Hale's rocket. This was a tube-launched rocket, which could be effective in the field if employed properly. One rocket battery was lost at Isandlwana. Rocket launchers were painted black and the rockets were red. The British Army also employed Gatling guns for the first time on this campaign, and proved that they were effective against massed units.

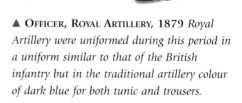

▲ **OFFICER, ROYAL ARTILLERY, 1879** *Royal Artillery were uniformed during this period in a uniform similar to that of the British infantry but in the traditional artillery colour of dark blue for both tunic and trousers.*

Engineers

The Royal Engineers were the other of the 'savant arms', being a technical as well as a military branch of the British Army. The engineer arm had had teething troubles during the

Napoleonic period, but those shortcomings had been made good to a great extent, and by the time of the period of British expansion they were a well-schooled and well-trained branch.

The Royal Engineers wore red, as did the infantry, and their uniforms in South Africa would appear outwardly similar to the infantry. Lieutenant Chard, of Rorke's Drift fame, was an engineer, and was undoubtedly lucky

▼ PRIVATE, ROYAL MARINE LIGHT INFANTRY, (RMLI), 1879 *The full dress uniform of the RMLI was scarlet. In the field, however, they would wear the dark blue undress uniform for both comfort and to save their dress uniforms for better and kindlier times. Weapons and equipment would be much like that of regular infantry.*

to have been at the mission station and thereby missed the disaster at Isandlwana. His services at Rorke's Drift were certainly useful and as he was senior to the commander of B Company, 24th Foot, who were established at the mission station, he assumed overall command of the successful defence.

Again, the frock was usually worn on campaign in place of the more formal and uncomfortable tunic, while the dark blue undress coat and fatigue cap would also be worn. Lieutenant Chard probably wore the scarlet frock coat in action at Rorke's Drift, along with the foreign service helmet, either white or tea-stained.

Naval Troops

As was usual practice for the British on campaign, naval troops were put ashore for land operations if there were naval units in the vicinity. This usually also consisted of detachments of Royal Marines.

Four Royal Navy ships, HMS *Active*, HMS *Tenedos*, HMS *Shah* and HMS *Boadicea*, contributed landing parties, or naval brigades, to the British effort in Zululand. The total strength for all of the naval landing parties was nearly 1,000 all ranks and included detachments of Royal Marine Light Infantry and Royal Marine Artillery.

At this period the Royal Marines was divided into two branches, light infantry and artillery, the first distinguished by scarlet tunics and dark blue breeches with a white foreign service helmet, very similar to regular army infantry regiments, though with Royal Marine distinctions. Marine artillerymen were dressed all in dark blue, much like that of the Royal Artillery, and this was the uniform the Royal Marines would eventually adopt when the two arms were combined.

Both the sailors and Royal Marines wore their regulation uniforms ashore for land service, usually modified or adjusted for comfort during field service. Sailors would add straw hats because of the sun and heat and would also wear leggings

ashore. Both dark blue and white uniforms were worn and the usual small arms were carried. Like their comrades-in-arms in the army, the Royal Marines usually dyed their white foreign service helmets a shade of khaki. Generally speaking, the naval units served along the coast where they could be supported by their ships.

▼ OFFICER, ROYAL NAVY, 1879 *This Royal Navy officer is equipped for field service with the army, and is wearing the regulation navy uniform. The figure is lightly armed and accoutered. Instead of the regulation cap shown here, he might wear a straw hat, as did enlisted sailors, for protection from the hot African sun as well as being a much cooler piece of equipment on land.*

ZULU WAR: BRITISH AUXILIARY TROOPS

In the long series of wars in South Africa, auxiliary units of Europeans and native Africans were formed to support the regular British troops. Some of the units were excellent, and established superb combat records.

▼ TROOPER, FRONTIER LIGHT HORSE, 1879
The uniform of the Frontier Light Horse was both unusual and comfortable. Initially uniformed in black corduroy, this later 'evolved' into a yellowish-brown corduroy tunic with black frogging across the chest, with or without the loops shown on the end of the frogging. The slouch hat was worn by all ranks.

Standard Issue

The uniforms of these units were many and varied, though many preferred to wear some version of a dark blue tunic and trousers or breeches along with a white foreign service helmet, with the unit badge prominently displayed on the front of the helmet and topped off by a metal spike. These units looked similar to British regular units. They were armed and equipped along standard British lines, the mounted units wearing bandoliers to carry their carbine ammunition. Some of the units adopted uniforms of corduroy in colours that blended into the terrain. Black, brown, tan, and some civilian clothing (such as that worn by the Boers) was also evident among the volunteer units, as was the slouch hat that was making its appearance for the first time among troops of a British army in the field.

Although most of the volunteer and auxiliary units that served in South Africa were mounted and equipped either as cavalry or mounted infantry, there were a few infantry units and at least one pioneer (engineer) unit that were issued scarlet tunics.

The mounted units, if well trained and well led, provided good service and were much needed during the first invasion of Zululand as no regular cavalry regiments were available for scouting or screening the invasion columns.

► TROOPER, NATAL CARABINIERS, 1879 *This dashing but practical uniform was quite similar to that of the 6th Dragoon Guards, which was a regular cavalry regiment. The carabiniers were required to furnish their own horses as well as supply the saddle and equipment and other horse furniture. They wore white helmets, complete with spike and badge.*

▲ PRIVATE, MOUNTED INFANTRY, 1879
*Because of the shortage of suitable cavalry,
British commanders from time to time formed
provisional units of mounted infantry. This
'trooper' is equipped and accoutred for
mounted service.*

Native Units

Some native units were also formed for
the invasions and these were led by
white officers. Their effectiveness in the
field and in combat varied. Some
units, such as Wood's Irregulars,
would be 'uniformed' and
armed as native tribesmen
and could look quite
similar to the Zulu
impis, although they

would be armed with a longer spear
than the Zulu *assegai*. They were issued
with army blankets which the men
would wear like a cloak in the field.
Identifying bits of coloured cloth
would be worn either around the head
or upper arm to be able to identify
them in the field or in combat. The
unit was recruited from men of the
Swazi tribe in the Transvaal.

The native members of the Natal
Pioneers were issued with red jackets,
probably the five-button frocks. They
also wore knee-length canvas trousers
and a forage cap in the pillbox style.

The Natal Native Contingent, native
troops officered by Europeans, initially
wore their own dress, again with the
addition of coloured bits of cloth for
identification purposes. The NCOs in
each company were issued with
firearms, but the rest of the units went
to war with spears and the knobkerrie
(an African club).

The officers were sometimes
'uniformed' with blue British Army
patrol jackets and foreign service
helmets, but a variety of civilian
clothing, hastily 'militarized' was quite
often the rule.

Volunteer Units Serving with the British Army in the Zulu War

Auxiliary Units:
- Natal Native Contingent
- Border Guard
- John Dunn's Foot Scouts
- Wood's Irregulars

Natal Volunteer Units:
- Natal Carabineers
- Buffalo Border Guard
- Newcastle Mounted Rifles
- Natal Mounted Police
- Victoria Mounted Rifles
- Stanger Mounted Rifles
- Durban Mounted Rifles
- Natal Hussars
- Alexandra Mounted Rifles
- Natal Hussars
- Alexandra Mounted Rifles
- Isipingo Mounted Rifles

Irregular Cavalry:
- Frontier Light Horse
- Natal Light Horse
- Baker's Horse
- Lonsdale's Horse
- Shepstone's Horse
- Natal Horse
- Carbutt's Border Rangers
- Kaffrarian Riflemen
- Raaff's Transvaal Rangers
- Weatherly's Border Horse
- Transvaal Burgher Force

An interesting unit of native
African soldiers, officered by
Europeans, which was actually
uniformed in European style, was
Shepstone's Horse. A double-breasted
tunic and trousers of cord were usually
worn by the men, with a bush hat
typical of the Boers. Boots were also
issued, but many troops declined to
wear them and rode barefoot.

**◄ TROOPER, DURBAN MOUNTED RIFLES,
1879** *This company-sized mounted unit had
a dark blue uniform similar to the Natal
Carabiniers but with different coloured
facings, and frogging across the front of
the tunic for all ranks, they also had
silver as the button and badge colour
instead of brass.*

ZULU WAR: ZULU WARRIORS

Under kings such as Shaka and Dingane the Zulu nation began to conquer neighbouring tribes with a highly organized, disciplined and tough army that struck fear into its foes. Organized into *impis*, or regiments, the Zulus mustered the largest army black Africa would ever see and engaged the British empire in a war to maintain their independence and wealth.

Battle Dress

While the Zulus would eventually, like most of the Bantu tribes in South Africa, adopt at least partial European dress (and their king, Cetshwayo, would be taken into captivity by the British draped in a damask tablecloth, though he wore the Zulu ring on his head),

► **ZULU, 1879** *This lightly accoutred Zulu carries a long arm in addition to his traditional weapons. Some of the Zulus who attacked Rorke's Drift were so armed and were deployed on the natural terraces that overlooked the mission station. They kept up a lively, if largely inaccurate, fire on the British.*

▼ **ZULU, 1879** *This warrior of a mid-level (regarding experience in combat and seniority) impi, or regiment, carries, in addition to his assegais, a musket taken either from his traditional enemies the Boers or from the British. The Zulus wore no shoes of any type and could cross an incredible amount of ground in a day's march. They were the most formidable, bar none, of any native army in sub-Saharan Africa.*

they fought the British in 1879 in traditional Zulu garb. Zulu military dress was colourful, though sparse, and no footwear was worn, the soles of their bare feet having become hardened by numerous military campaigns. Generally speaking, the Zulus wore 'kilts' of some type around their waist, monkey-tailed kilts being popular, although those made of hide and then decorated with other types of animal tails were also used. Various headdresses could be worn, made of various types of animal hide with the fur still attached and decorated with different types of colourful and full-feather devices.

Sometimes fur hides were used to decorate the calves or worn over the chest as a 'vest'. Distinguished married regiments were ringed, that is they had a ring around their head. Veteran regiments carried an all-white shield, a new one carried dark; as a regiment gained honours and experience, the shield would be changed to white.

Equipment and Tactics

During the signature reign of Shaka, the Zulus began to employ the short, stabbing spear, the *assegai*, instead of the longer throwing spear used by other African nations. The Zulus would close with their enemies and use a combination of shield and short spear to outfight their enemies at close range, much as the Roman legions had done with shield and *gladius* (short, stabbing sword). The tactic proved to be quite deadly and difficult to defeat if the Zulus were allowed to close. The best defences against this tactic were the Boer wagon laager and the British square as employed at Ulundi, where massed long- and medium-range rifle fire decimated the Zulu *impis* in a much larger version of Rorke's Drift.

◀ ZULU KIT, **1879** *1 & 2 The longer, throwing spears that the Zulus replaced with 3 & 4 the shorter* assegai. *5 A knobkerrie, a very effective skull-cracker, still being used by native herdsmen in the 1960s in Kenya.*

▼ ZULU, **1879** *This stalwart Zulu warrior of a veteran* impi *belongs to a 'ringed' regiment and is prepared for battle. He is armed solely with the traditional Zulu weapon, the short* assegai, *designed for stabbing not throwing.*

▼ ZULU, **1879** *This is an example of a man of a senior Zulu regiment in full regalia. The all-white shield designates a senior, veteran regiment whose spears have been 'washed' several times.*

ZULU WAR: BOERS

Faced with fighting their ancient enemy, even at the cost of allying themselves with the hated British, some of the Boers chose to join in the war against the Zulus. They were of the same general appearance as they had been for years, remembering that they were still farmers who owned their own kit and firearms.

Commandos

Boer service with the British was important, and one of the units, commanded by Piet Uys, who was accompanied by his four sons on the campaign, would prove to be invaluable to the British. Fighting against the Zulus in the confused running fight at Hlobane (where the

▼ BOER, 1879 *Corduroy trousers, working shirt, flat-brimmed civilian hat, sturdy shoes, rifle and bandolier could describe any Boer burgher or commando during the period from the First Boer War through to the bitter end in 1901–2. The Boers fought skilfully and hard for the territory they believed to be theirs by right. Strongly religious, they disputed any encroachment on their territory from the British or native Africans.*

Boers did better than the British colonial troops present and were responsible for extricating the colonial troops from a bad situation), Piet Uys was killed in action. His command, the Transvaal Burgher Force, numbered 51 mounted Boers, and these troops, and the Boer volunteers, such as Paul Kruger who accompanied Lord Chelmsford, the British commander in Zululand, were at first generally ignored. Even advice on how to fight the Zulu (such as the tried and tested tactic of putting the wagons in a laager – a circle for defence – at night when they camped) was disregarded. But after Isandlwana and Hlobane, the British were all ears. Independent and hardy, the Boers' knowledge of the terrain and of the Zulu would be invaluable to the British in general and Lord Chelmsford, in particular.

The main Boer unit was still the commando, and uniforms among the troops of any unit would be few and far between. The commandos were noteworthy for not being either uniformly dressed or having any specified uniform prescribed for them.

The top hat had all but disappeared for the Boers who now preferred the lower bush hat that

▼ BOER, 1879 *Some Boers turned out to support the British against the Zulus in 1879, undoubtedly knowing full well that their support would generally be overlooked and that they would have to fight the British again for their existence as a 'free' people. They were not uniformed in any sense and proved to be excellent scouts and reconnaissance units. They were dressed in civilian clothes and armed with their own weapons. They provided their own horses and equipment. The top hat was sometimes worn in the field – even by Boer commanders.*

although many uniform items from the British were used, such as belts, valises and cork pith helmets. Many Boer fighters had also managed to obtain the excellent British firearm, the Martini-Henry rifle and/or carbine. Except for such equipment captured from the enemy the Boers were still dressed in civilian clothes. These had changed, however, from the short coats of the 1830s and 1840s – that were very popular with the Voortrekkers – to the longer coats with skirts were now being worn in the field and at home on the farm. The Transvaal Burgher Force was dressed as they always had been, in civilian clothes, but Piet Uys wore a pith helmet instead of a top or slouch hat.

Weaponry among the Boers had also changed. The percussion cap had been invented and the typical Boer volunteer or commando no longer carried the powder horn. Although many different types of firearms were carried, the Martini-Henry was probably the most popular and would remain so through the 1890s. The Martini-Henry rifles and carbines, as well as the ammunition bandoliers, were British issue and were given to them at the beginning of the campaign.

Field Equipment

Boer field equipment was minimal and basic and easily carried by the mobile troops. Combinations of tents and tarps in the field were common for shelter, and every Boer knew how to prepare biltong, the spiced dried meat that can be seen hanging to dry in period photographs of Boers in the field.

The Boer commandos, while nondescript in their civilian clothes, could appear quite formidable in

groups when mounted. Their horses were tough and well-cared for. The Boers mounted with their assorted rifles slung across their backs that could be brought into action quickly and with little effort. In photographs from the period grim, bearded faces look back at the camera, unsmiling and businesslike, these are men who had fought the Zulu, carved out homes in a very hostile land, and lived and worked hard to settle land. They raised their male children to be able to farm, ride and fight. All of the Boers were expert shots and horsemen, probably learning to ride almost before they could walk, and living in the saddle for much of their waking hours. The horse meant survival, in both peace and war.

▲ **BOER, 1879** *This Boer burgher is again dressed in civilian clothes and demonstrates an interesting piece of equipment the Boers developed for fighting. The vest this man is wearing replaces the ammunition bandolier and is actually more useful for use in mounted warfare as well as on foot. It is easy to wear, holds plenty of ammunition, and is still sometimes used by modern armies to carry grenades for hand-held grenade launchers.*

provided better protection from the sun and was more comfortable to wear, especially mounted in a fast-moving commando. The typical Boer was still clad in his normal civilian attire

▶ **BOER, 1879** *This Boer farmer is armed with his choice of weapons and is dressed 'formally' in civilian clothing. Remove the weapon and bandolier and he would be ready for either church or a social gathering with his neighbours. The leather bandolier was an essential piece of Boer equipment.*

SECOND BOER WAR: BRITISH TROOPS

The Second Boer War became increasingly bitter for both the British and the Boers. Rough new tactical lessons were taught to the British by their Boer enemies.

Khaki

By this time, generally speaking, the field uniform of the British Army was khaki, although certain distinctions from full dress were still worn in the field. For example, Highland units that wore the kilt continued

wearing it in the field, though it now had a khaki 'apron' worn over it in the front. This was maintained at least into World War I, when the Highlanders were nicknamed by their German foes as the 'ladies from hell'.

The British foreign service helmet, which had been worn from before the Indian Mutiny, was gradually replaced

◀ **OFFICER, LANCASHIRE FUSILIERS, 1898** *This well-turned out fusilier officer is ready to lead his troops against the Boer enemy in 1898. The British Army was generally shocked at how well the Boers performed against them, and were equally shocked at the losses they took at the hands of the Boers. This pre-war regulation uniform would change noticeably by the end of the conflict.*

▲ **INFANTRY KIT, C.1898**
1 Full dress infantry spiked helmet.
2 Ammunition pouch.
3 Knapsack.
4 Ammunition pouch.
5 Canteen.

by the slouch hat that was initially worn by Empire troops and such British volunteer units as the Imperial Yeomanry and the City Imperial

▼ **NCO, INFANTRY, 1898** *This NCO is uniformed and equipped according to Queen's regulations for campaign. British units that took the field against the Boers in this last of the Boer Wars would generally appear like this for at least the first year of the war. Hard-earned experience would have the troops modify both their tactics and what they wore in the field.*

◀ **Private, King's Royal Rifle Corps (KRRC), 1898** *The new field uniforms, while still having white equipment along with the new regulation khaki colour for regular infantry, still had the traditional black for rifle regiments. This would also eventually give way to brown infantry equipment for all infantry regiments regardless of designation.*

▶ **Officer, Highland Light Infantry, 1898** *This regiment had the distinction of being the only one in the British Army that was both highland and light infantry. While there is historical argument whether or not the regiment was actually a 'highland' regiment, the unit certainly believed it and traditional trews were worn in the field at the start of the last Boer War.*

usually junior officers, probably inexperienced, possibly under-qualified, inadequately trained and lacking the temperament to work on a staff. There were also no general directives to work from. They wore the uniforms of their regiments and served at the discretion of the commander.

Infantry

In full dress, the British line infantry arm had undergone major changes and improvements since the First Boer War. The coatee had been replaced by the tunic in 1855 and by the time the Cardwell reforms were introduced in 1881 the full dress tunic had been further simplified. Now, instead of the somewhat gaudy French-style cuffs, newly designed cuffs in the pointed Polish style were introduced, again in the facing colour of the regiment. This did not apply to the Guards infantry regiments who still wore the more elaborate French-style cuffs.

The regulation headgear for full dress would now be the spiked helmet. This was inspired by the Prussian-style, and later German-style, helmets on the Continent, with a British-style that was similar to the older foreign service helmet, but with a spike. The helmet was done in dark blue, with white substituted for foreign service, though no longer on campaign or combat, where khaki would be substituted. For undress the red five-button frock was

Volunteers. It was comfortable, broke up the outline of the head, which the foreign service helmet had enhanced, and provided excellent protection from the African sun. Wrap-around puttees, taken from service in India, gradually replaced gaiters in the field even for mounted service, spurs being strapped on to shoes instead of riding boots.

The British Army had no general staff similar to those that were continuing to develop in the European continental armies at this time. Staff officers, therefore, were drawn from the line units serving together under a single command. These men were

preferred, although still with regimental distinctions (the full dress tunic had seven buttons).

Scottish regiments would have additional distinctions to those used by the regulation line infantry, as would fusilier, rifle and some light infantry units.

All Scottish regiments would wear the regulation Scottish doublet in lieu of the tunic and either the kilt, if authorized, or Scottish trews, which would also have the regimental tartan pattern. The kilted regiments would wear the huge, signature feathered bonnet. Pipers of any Scottish unit they were now issued a handsome rifle-style busby, which had a short plume on the front, the plume for officers being taller.

Field grade officers wore boots and spurs when mounted. Those of the Highland regiments would wear trews with boots and spurs when mounted. This would be the full dress uniform until 1914 when the British Army deployed to France as the British Expeditionary Force. The handsome red uniforms would never return to the line infantry regiments as a whole.

For service in South Africa, the dress uniforms and simpler frocks were put away this time and not worn in the field as they had been during the Zulu War and before. Instead, the field service dress of the British infantry was basically the same cut of uniform, though cut fuller for ease of movement, but was entirely in khaki. The exception to khaki would be in the

▲ *Gordon Highlanders standing by their heliographs in the Anglo-Boer War, 1899.*

kilted Highland regiments. They would still wear the kilt in the field, though with a khaki apron in front to break up the outline of colour (which would not work when they were in the prone position and would stand out

◄ **PRIVATE, ARGYLL AND SUTHERLAND HIGHLANDERS, 1898** *Some Highland regiments still wore the kilt in the field, now with an addition of a khaki 'apron' in the front to help with camouflage and concealment in the field. This would continue to be worn through World War I. High, traditional stockings were still worn and here they are shown without gaiters or leggings, showing both the stockings and the shoes.*

► **PRIVATE, GUARDS REGIMENTS, 1898** *The Guards regiments that deployed to South Africa were dressed as regular line infantry units with the exception of the distinctive regimental flashes that were worn on the side of the khaki-covered foreign service helmet. These gradually disappeared from the enlisted men's helmets as they made excellent aiming points for Boer riflemen, but officers tended to keep them longer.*

were undoubtedly kilted. The Highland Light Infantry wore doublet and trews, but also were distinctive in wearing a shako instead of either the spiked helmet or feathered bonnet.

Scottish fusiliers wore the doublet, trews and the smaller fusilier 'bearskin' (which was actually made out of seal skin) while the other fusilier regiments were uniformed in the same way as line infantry regiments.

Lastly, the rifle regiments would be uniformed in dark green with black equipment, instead of the usual white of the other infantry regiments, but

like a sore thumb for the Boer marksmen). They would also wear a cutaway tunic in front that went with the kilt better than the usual khaki tunic would.

For headgear, the foreign service helmet was again worn, this time with a khaki cover, and a unit flash in colour, which identified the unit, would be worn on the side of the

▼ OFFICER, INFANTRY, 1899 *This infantry officer has adopted the enlisted man's equipment for the field and has discarded his foreign service helmet for the popular slouch, or bush, hat. His adoption of enlisted men's equipment and weapons was due to the Boer habit of shooting officers and NCOs first.*

helmet. This splash of colour would make an excellent aiming point for Boer marksmen.

Both styles of tunic had patch pockets on the chest as well as stand-up collars that were similar in size to the full dress tunic and undress frock. The standard issue Slade-Wallace equipment was white for all units except for rifle regiments, which was black. Interestingly, the haversack, which had always been carried at the hip by a strap over the opposite shoulder, was now carried on the back on the equipment harness. Puttees were worn on the calves over shoes, which were brown.

As the war progressed, the foreign service helmet was generally replaced with the slouch hat that was originally worn by Empire troops, especially the Australians. Unit identification in colour on the headgear would gradually disappear, and personal equipment would be modified by the troops, generally becoming simpler

▶ OFFICER, 92ND HIGHLANDERS, 1898 *This Highland officer is wearing the field uniform without a front apron and is smartly attired including a non-regulation sun-shade on his foreign service helmet with its usually khaki cover. This smartness among the uniforms of the British Army in South Africa would disappear as the war wore on and the British became relentless in hunting down the Boer 'bitter-enders'.*

▼ *Boer 'bitter-enders' (Bittereinders), who continued to fight against the British until their independence was established.*

and easier to use. Leather ammunition bandoliers would eventually either augment or supersede the older white equipment, which would eventually either be blackened or replaced. Tunics would disappear for many units in the field and a typical infantryman might be seen in civilian corduroy trousers, grey shirt with the sleeves rolled up, a floppy bush hat, brown leather equipment of either a waist belt for ammunition and bayonet or a bandolier over one shoulder, or both. Puttees would disappear and trousers would be worn loose over shoes. The difference between how the British infantry looked at the start and end of the war was striking.

Cardwell Reforms of 1881

In 1881 the British infantry of the line, including the light infantry and Highland regiments, were reorganized into the so-called County Regiments, where each regiment was amalgamated and renamed. Their original numbers, though retained for tradition and *esprit de corps*, were now relegated to 'second place' to the new name of the

▲ *Colonel Baden Powell (seated, centre) and officers of the Protectorate Regiment in camp at the Mafeking siege of 1900.*

amalgamated regiments. Because of the Cardwell reforms, and the reorganization that was the result, the British line from a total of 109 regiments were reduced to 65 infantry regiments, each of 2 battalions. The first 25 line regiments were directly converted to their now official names and new second battalions were formed for them. They were not amalgamated with a higher numbered regiment. This was also the situation with the 60th Foot, the once-named 'Royal Americans', which was now known as the King's Royal Rifle Corps.

Cavalry

The full-dress appearance of the British mounted arm at the beginning of the Boer War had changed dramatically since the British had first come to South Africa. The cavalry arm now consisted of the Household Cavalry (three regiments) in either scarlet or dark blue and wearing cuirasses for full

◀ PRIVATE, MOUNTED INFANTRY, 1900 *This mounted infantryman is equipped as cavalry and has not yet 'converted' to the bush, or slouch, hat. Mounted infantry units were effective in countering the mounted and far-ranging Boer commandos and for line of communication security duties. They were mobile, disciplined and hard-hitting troops.*

mounted dress. Dragoon guards, dragoons, hussars and lancers made up the remainder of the cavalry and their handsome uniforms made an outstanding appearance on parade

▼ TROOPER, 12TH LANCERS, 1900 *This is more or less regulation dress. The added sunshade was worn depending on the unit and personal choice. Note that the cavalrymen did not wear boots, but shoes and puttees, the latter being adopted after service in India. The spurs were worn over shoes.*

▶ STAFF OFFICER, 1900
This is a typical staff officer in regulation dress with the now-popular Wolsely helmet instead of the older, less functional foreign service helmet. This officer appears as he would in garrison without his usual equipment of Sam Browne belt and sidearms, which would include his sword.

and for formal full dress wear. They consisted of dark blue tunics with – for the hussars – lace and busbies for headgear, for the dragoon guards and dragoons – standard heavy

cavalry tunics with either brass or silver dragoon-style helmets (with the exception of tall bearskins for the 2nd Dragoons, the Royal Scots Greys); and for the lancers – tunics with coloured plastrons on the chest in the regimental colour. Lancer tunics would either be dark blue or scarlet (for the 16th Lancers) and topped by the now smaller and more utilitarian czapka.

infantry had. Slouch hats appeared, unit flashes had disappeared, and lances and swords had been superseded, all of the imperial horsemen having resorted to pistol and carbine and being issued or finding

▼ **OFFICER, CITY IMPERIAL VOLUNTEERS, 1900**
This volunteer unit was one of the first units, along with the Imperial Yeomanry, a mounted unit, to be deployed to South Africa. They were smartly uniformed in khaki dress and field uniforms and all ranks wore the slouch hat turned up on one side. Conditions in the field and on campaign led to a decline in the initial smartness of the unit's uniforms, but the unit performed well under adverse conditions, as did the Imperial Yeomanry.

▲ **OFFICER, INFANTRY, 1899** *This infantry officer has adopted the enlisted man's equipment and kit for the field and has also discarded his foreign service helment for the now-popular slouch, or bush, hat. He has adopted enlisted men's equipment and weapons, protection against the Boer tactic of targetting officers and NCOs first.*

However, in the field the cavalry wore the khaki uniform as the infantry did, in the same style and with puttees with spurs over shoes. The usual foreign service helmet topped off the ensemble. By the end of the war, these proud rough riders had simplified their uniforms and equipment as the

▲ **INFANTRY KIT, 1900**
*1 The normal leather belt and 'suspenders' for an officer's field equipment. The pistol with holster, cartridge pouch and sword frog are shown. It was usually in brown leather.
2 The initial regulation load-bearing equipment for an enlisted infantryman. The bayonet and cartridge pouch are carried on the belt and the suspenders support the knapsack, blanket roll and other ancillary equipment. Canteen and haversack would complete the field equipment. This would later evolve into webbing equipment made of cotton and other materials, and bandoliers of brown leather would be worn over the shoulder and across the body.*

▲ *Three of the valuable native scouts working with the British during the Second Boer War.*

bandoliers to carry their ammunition, sometimes modifying them to fit extra rounds around the necks of their horses. Cavalry officers carried shoulder holsters, wore civilian clothing, and sported white shirts with bow ties at times, over which they would sometimes wear a civilian-style corduroy coat.

Mounted Infantry

There were never enough cavalry regiments to go round for all the necessary missions on campaign. As the British had done before in the series of wars in Africa, the problem of a lack of regular cavalry was solved by temporarily establishing provisional units of mounted infantry, the men being drawn from the infantry regiments of the command.

These ad hoc units proved to be quite useful on campaign and as they became used to working with one another, and used to their animals, they would become excellent

units in the field. By the time of the Boer War, the mounted infantryman was making a decisive contribution to the war. They wore the uniforms of their parent regiment suitably modified for mounted service. They moved and fought the way the Boer commandos did. They were highly

▼ NATIVE SCOUT, 1900 *While the war in South Africa was proclaimed by both sides as being a 'white man's war', black auxiliaries were used by both sides. This well-equipped native scout employed by the British was an effective addition to any cavalry or mounted infantry unit, knowing the land and the languages of at least some of the native peoples in South Africa.*

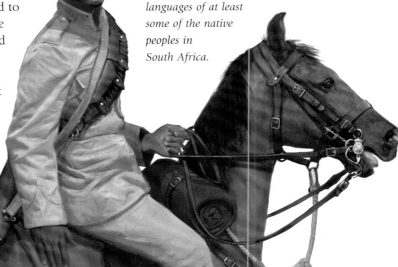

mobile troops who could respond much more quickly to a fluid situation than regular infantry and were more flexible than cavalry when fighting the Boer in the bush or on the veldt.

Volunteer Units

Militia and volunteer units had existed in Great Britain and were used as a recruiting ground for the Regular Army since the Napoleonic period. For the first time, however, entire volunteer units were deployed to fight in South Africa. Two of the units that went to fight the Boers were the City Imperial Volunteers and the Imperial Yeomanry.

The City Imperial Volunteers was a London regiment raised for service in South Africa. They were not regular troops, but they established an excellent reputation in the field and fought well and skilfully against the

▶ **TROOPER, 5TH LANCERS, 1900** *British cavalrymen fighting the Mahdists in the Sudan uniformed and equipped in this manner did well. Fighting against the Boers in South Africa was a different proposition and the British Army had to modify dress, equipment and tactics to be successful.*

Boers. Their uniform, in khaki, is quite modern in appearance, and the slouch hat, which was part of their originally issued uniform, became the norm in South Africa among the combat troops.

The Imperial Yeomanry was a cavalry unit that was employed as mounted infantry and did good service. Uniformed in khaki like the City Imperial Volunteers, they too chose to wear the bush hat as part of their regulation uniform.

Artillery

The artillery arm, both field and horse artillery, underwent the same uniform changes as the rest of the British army, starting with the adoption of the tunic in 1855. By the time of this last Boer war, the field artillery was dressed like the infantry, but in dark blue. The helmets were the same, but in

place of the spike was a ball which demonstrated a difference in the troops' appearance. The Royal Marine Artillery used the same device and it was adopted by the entire corps when the distinction between the Royal Marine Artillery and the Royal Marine Light Infantry was abolished in 1922.

The Royal Horse Artillery was uniformed as the hussar arm but they wore the short shell jackets and carried

equipment because they were mounted. The main colour of the equipment was brown leather, which eventually changed to cotton webbing.

▼ CAVALRY KIT, 1902 *1 The 1890-pattern cavalry sword. 2 Scabbard. 3 Lee-Enfield magazine carbine. 4 Regulation saddle – the 1890-pattern Universal Arch saddle. 5 Chain shoulder scales, which were eventually phased out in the field.*

Boots, except for those worn by staff officers and some other mounted troops, would be switched for shoes with spurs, and leggings or puttees.

► TROOPER, 17TH LANCERS, 1900 *The slouch hat, still with the regimental badge, has replaced the helmet and the lance has been discarded. The trooper is equipped as a cavalryman or mounted infantryman. Puttees, shoes and spurs are worn in the field instead of boots and spurs for home service.*

the hussar tunics and if they were not with their gun teams, it would be difficult to tell them apart at a distance. However, once in the field on campaign, the same reversion to all khaki took place for both field and horse artillery. Basic equipment for the artilleryman and infantryman was similar, but the cavalryman's

▲ TRUMPETER, CAVALRY, 1900 *This regulation trumpeter, carrying both bugle and trumpet, shows what the fully equipped British cavalryman carried into the field early in the war. Comparing him to the 17th Lancer trooper one can see how streamlined the uniform and equipment became based on combat experience as to how the army worked to overcome the problems of fighting the Boers.*

SECOND BOER WAR: BOERS

The Boers were a formidable enemy and now had the support of a state structure, something which reinforced their traditional abilities.

Two Enemies

With the coming of the second, decisive, and final Boer War, the British were facing both an old and a new enemy; old in the sense that the Boers were still the tough, independent fighting men that had fought Briton and Zulu with equal enthusiasm and skill for decades; new in the sense that there were now regular units of Boers, depending on which Boer state was involved.

State Troops

This time, in addition to the Boer commandos that had been encountered before by the British, the Boers also fielded uniformed regular troops from the Transvaal and the Orange Free State. The Transvaal Staatsartillerie was a regular unit that took the field in a mixture of uniforms, and civilian clothing was also conspicuous among them. Service dress would be used on campaign and could be khaki, sometimes white, while the greatcoats, at least for the officers, would be dark blue. A formal version of the bush hat was part of the uniform, a hat that became a symbol to those in the field on both sides during the war. Some of the artillerymen wore the regulation blue uniform on campaign along with those who wore the khaki field dress.

As had been typical for all Boer troops during the wars in southern Africa, Boer units, regular and commando alike, were accompanied by African *agyterryer*, African servants, who many times were also armed and equipped as the Boers were.

The Commandos

Boer commandos were still very mobile, and their rifle fire was deadly, singly or in groups.

◀ CORPORAL, TRANSVAAL STAATSARTILLERIE, 1898 *This is a regular unit of Boers from the Transvaal in service dress, which would be undress in normal times except for his civilian trousers, undoubtedly in the usual corduroy. Some Boer units were uniformed when the war began, as were some of the commandos, but the realities of warfare against the British would force most of them to resort to civilian dress or in taking uniforms and equipment from British dead.*

▲ AFRICAN AUXILIARY (*AGYTERRYER*), 1900 *Even though the Boers fought against the native Africans for years, they still used them as support troops when fighting against the British. This African is clothed and equipped as any Boer soldier, and would have fought against the British for his Boer 'comrades'. Though he and his fellow auxiliaries performed essential military and logistic support services for the Boers, they would never be treated as equals.*

The Boers were able to fight on the veldt against larger numbers of British troops and win, but were also capable of attacking in skirmish order in highly disciplined assaults. They were even able, technically and with sufficient manpower and artillery, to conduct sieges and pound the besieged British forces with accurate artillery fire which the British could not match in the initial stages of the war. To counter the excellent Boer artillery, the British had to take converted 4.7-inch naval guns ashore for use as heavy artillery.

While the Boers still wore civilian clothes in the field, they had become much more uniform in their choices of coats and breeches or trousers.

Equipment, much of it taken from the British, as were many of their long arms, is seen in period photographs with men who look just as determined as their antecedents had been, but much neater and military-like than the trekkers who had fought the British with muzzle-loading single shot weapons and shotguns. Martini-Henrys, Mausers and other more modern weapons appear in the photographs of the commandos, and under such commanders as Jan Smuts (who would later fight for the British in World War I). Strict discipline was applied to the natural fighting ability of the Boers, making them even more formidable oponents.

Foreign Volunteers

Imperial Germany supported the Boers during the war, and some German volunteers were present in South Africa fighting the British. They would wear either khaki or civilian attire in the field. The excellent German Mauser rifle would be imported by the Boers, sent as support from Germany. Other foreign volunteers included an American unit, the Chicago Irish-American Corps, which numbered 58 all ranks, and served as ambulance drivers. They wore a khaki uniform similar to that worn by the US Army, and at first they wore a red cross armband.

With the British gaining the upper hand in the latter years of the conflict, more Boers would either surrender or go home; some even fought for the British. Those that didn't, and still fought against their hated foes, would be termed 'bitter-enders' and could lead a hand-to-mouth existence, always

on the jump from British patrols who were hunting them down. They resupplied themselves from ambushed British troops, taking weapons, ammunition, clothing and boots from enemy dead and kept on the bounce, sometimes one step ahead of their pursuers, sometimes cornered and fighting for their life out in some far-off corner of the veldt.

▼ GUNNER, TRANSVAAL STAATSARTILLERIE, 1900 *This is the dress uniform tunic of this artillery unit, which also included machine gun troops. The tunic was based on an Austrian pattern and the officers, like their British counterparts, sometimes wore a braided 'patrol' jacket which was tunic-like in design and cut. The regular forces fielded by the Boers were small and were generally only artillery and police units.*

◄ BOER COMMANDO, 1899 *Arms and equipment for the Commando units, including artillery, was supplied to the Boers by Germany during the war and there was general support of the Boers by Imperial Germany against the British, whom the Germans hoped to supplant as the world's leading naval power. This well-dressed commando would degenerate to the usual civilian clothes and captured equipment and dress as the war progressed.*

TROOPS OF THE EMPIRE

The British, realizing that this war against the Boers was threatening their holdings in southern Africa and that a defeat by the Boers would have drastic consequences throughout their empire, reached out and brought in troops from their overseas empire. These were, in the main, Canadian and Australian regiments.

Indian Regiments

Unfortunately, no troops from India would be deployed to South Africa because the impression that the British wanted to convey to the outside

▲ *By 1900 British troops in South Africa all looked very similar, regardless of which part of the empire they came from.*

world was that no 'native' troops were being employed. This was somewhat hypocritical as native Africans were employed by Boer and British sides as scouts, usually armed and dressed as European troops. Native Africans were also employed as spies by both sides and were harshy treated and usually executed if caught.

◄ TROOPER, NATAL CARABINIERS, 1899
The Natal Carabiniers were equipped as mounted infantry and had traded their old dark blue uniforms in for the prevalent khaki. The leather equipment, however, was of a different style than the British used and the 'boots' worn for mounted duty were quite different from puttees and shoes.

▶ PRIVATE, ROYAL CANADIAN
REGIMENT, 1899 *Alongside the regular British units and the territorials, Canadian and Australian troops were employed in South Africa. All performed good service and were generally uniformed as their British comrades. This infantryman from one of Canada's regular infantry regiments would eventually discard the helmet and other items for the slouch hat, as the British infantry did.*

Canadian and Australian Troops

This deployment of colonial troops outside their native countries was largely unprecedented in the modern era. In recent years, colonial troops had only been employed for the defence of their particular native land in conjunction with British troops at times, but not always.

The Canadians could field many units when they were needed at home, for example during the War of 1812 against the United States. Canadian regular units gained an outstanding reputation

fighting against the Americans; that reputation stayed with them and was both earned and well-deserved.

During the Canadian North-west Rebellion in 1885 both infantry and cavalry units were raised and employed in suppressing the rebellion of the Metis, native French Canadians who wished to be independent of Canadian rule. The Canadians quickly raised volunteer militia units and despatched them, along with a few regulars, across the huge expanse of Canada, covering up to 4,828 km (3,000 miles), to re-establish order. This was the first time the Canadians had undertaken a military expedition without the assistance of the British.

Canadian Voyageurs were employed by the British in the 1884–85 Nile Expedition to move the British Army from Egypt into the Sudan. These troops were uniformed after their own model with grey trousers and smock, blue shirts and either foreign service helmets or a form of bush hat. The officers were more smartly uniformed in khaki tunics on the British model, brown breeches, dark blue puttees and foreign service helmets. The Voyageurs served well and established a reputation that would again be employed in South Africa.

Canadians and Australians fought alongside English, Scottish, Welsh and Irish

▶ TROOPER, RIMINGTON SCOUTS, 1900 *This unit was a local outfit that wore bush hats with a distinctive leopard skin band around the base of the hat. They had a reputation for quiet efficiency and were steadily successful working in the bush hunting down Boer commandos. Their nickname was 'Rimington's Tigers'. It should be noted that all mounted infantry and cavalry units used a 'bucket' to 'house' their carbines or rifles.*

regiments and established excellent reputations. The Canadians and Australians fielded impressive units, though none of them could be considered 'regular' units on the British model. Raised, equipped and trained in the 'colonies,' these units were excellent and performed good service wherever they were employed during the war. The units from the empire did not wear their full dress in South Africa and

were deployed dressed in the ubiquitous khaki worn by British troops. In the field, it became almost impossible to physically distinguish English, Scottish, Irish and Welsh troops from the Australians and Canadians, especially in the latter two years of the war, as uniforms had been simplified, generally by the troops themselves. The accents might be different, however, but all those serving were considered to be British, and the uniforms were basically identical, though regimental badges, buttons and other identifying items would tell a different story.

WARS IN THE COLONIAL EMPIRES

The conquest of overseas colonies by the major European powers, and later the United States, led to a need to establish law and order in areas that often had little or none to begin with. Constabulary forces were usually raised to augment the military presence, and were trained to keep the peace. For major operations complete native units were recruited and were usually officered, at least initially, by Europeans or Americans as the case may be. Many of these units served their new masters faithfully for years, giving excellent service and fighting for their overlords in far-flung actions of empire, sometimes against their own people. When colonies were eventually granted independence, these units formed the nucleus of the armies of these new nations, and they proudly and jealously guarded their hard-won traditions in their new role.

▲ *The Boxer Rebellion in China was put down by a coalition of European powers. In the British contingent were troops from the empire, including this unit of Bengali soldiers.*

◀ *The charge of the 2nd Dragoon Guards (Queen's Bays, so-called because of the colour of their horses) at Lucknow during the Indian Mutiny.*

COLONIAL EXPANSION

In 1815, with Napoleon finally defeated and sent into exile in the south Atlantic, the nations of Europe – utterly exhausted by 23 years of uninterrupted warfare – were ready for peace. However, ambition for further gain was seldom lacking in the Great Powers of Europe.

The 100 years from 1815 to the start of World War I in 1914 was a period of great colonial expansion not only for Great Britain, which already possessed a sizeable overseas empire, but for other European powers as well. France, shorn of her colonies during the Revolutionary and Napoleonic period (1792–1815) set out to re-establish a colonial empire and ventured into northern Africa and the Far East. Three new colonial powers emerged during the late 19th century, namely Germany, Japan and the United States. All three

came to the game late, but all three attained the status as both colonial powers and world powers, two of them being maritime nations (Japan and the United States) with the last, Germany, which grew in strength because of three successful wars of unification, attempting to become a dominant land and naval power.

India

The Indian continent had been the stage for wars between the British and the French for two centuries before the French were finally forced out by 1815. The British continued to expand their interests in India through the offices of the British East India Company and British Regulars fought side by side with the company's regiments of native and European troops until the end of the Indian Mutiny. Thereafter, governance of India passed to the British crown and that control also extended to the company's troops. From then on until India was granted independence in 1947, famous Indian

▲ *These native officers and non-commissioned officers are serving members of the British 2nd Cavalry Regiment, Punjab Frontier Force.*

regiments served alongside their British comrades in some of the most famous campaigns of the day. They did not, however, serve in South Africa during the Boer Wars as the Indian units were specifically prohibited.

North Africa

The northern countries of Africa became French territory when Algeria and Morocco were overrun from the 1830s onward.

The Far East

Germany moved into Africa and Asia and took possession of many islands and island groups in the Pacific, which were to be lost to the Japanese in World War I and would be made famous by bloody battles between Japan and the United States in World War II. The Japanese also colonized Taiwan, Korea and parts of China. Japan also became a world power, especially a seapower after her major victory over Russia in the Russo-Japanese War of 1904–5. Japan, a feudal nation until the Mejei Restoration in 1868, had quickly modernized and had a well-trained and equipped army and an outstanding blue-water navy by late in the century.

▼ *A group of British officers and native troops during the Indian Mutiny. The officer seated in foreign service helmet is William Hodson, commander of Hodson's Horse.*

Major Colonial Campaigns of the British Army, 1837–1901*

Campaign	Location	Year(s)	Campaign	Location	Year(s)
First Afghan War	Afghanistan	1839–42	Basuto War	South Africa	1868
Opium War	China	1839–42	Third Maori War	New Zealand	1868–70
Sind Campaign	India	1843	Second Ashanti War	Africa	1873–74
Gwalior Campaign	India	1843	Kaffir War	South Africa	1877–78
First Maori War	New Zealand	1843–48	Second Afghan War	Afghanistan	1878–80
Mahratta Campaign	India	1844–45	Zulu War	South Africa	1879
First Sikh War	India	1845–46	First Anglo-Boer War	South Africa	1880–81
Kaffir War	South Africa	1846–47	Campaign in Egypt	Egypt	1882
Second Sikh War	India	1848–49	Gordon Relief Expedition	Sudan	1884–85
Afridi Expedition	Africa	1849–50	Third Burma War	Burma	1885–87
First Basuto War	South Africa	1851–52	First Matabele War	Africa	1893
Second Burma War	Burma	1852–53	Third Ashanti War	Africa	1893–94
Persian War	Persia	1856–57	Second Matabele War	Africa	1895–96
Indian Mutiny	India	1857–59	Jameson's Raid	South Africa	1895–96
Maori Insurrection	New Zealand	1860–61	Fourth Ashanti War	Africa	1895–96
First Ashanti War	Africa	1863–64	Reconquest of the Sudan	Sudan	1896–98
Second Maori War	New Zealnad	1863–66	Second Anglo-Boer War	South Africa	1899–02
Abyssinian War	East Africa	1867–68	Boxer Rebellion	China	1900

*There were over 200 British campaigns, expeditions, rebellions or interventions during the Victorian period (1837–1901)

During the Boxer Rebellion in China in 1900, Japan's troops served alongside those of the European Great Powers and the United States in quelling the rebellion.

The Americas

A French attempt to establish an empire in Mexico, headed by an Austrian archduke, was defeated by a rebellion of the Mexican people. This revolt was eventually supported by the American assertion of the Monroe Doctrine, backed up by an army on the border of the United States and Mexico at the end of the American Civil War.

The United States also fought a series of wars with American Indian tribes west of the Mississippi River from the end of the Civil War until 1890, when the last of the hostile tribes was subdued. These wars were fought over a huge area which now makes up half of the United States and while the combats were small by European standards they were vicious. The United States fought these wars with a small, expert Regular Army that was made up of Civil War veterans.

▶ *A stylized painting of what became known as 'Custer's Last Stand,' 25 June 1876.*

Bitter Campaigns

Colonial wars were fought against varied peoples with different traditions and ways of fighting, and many were wars to the death for an entire way of life. Some indigenous peoples assimilated into the new way of things; others bided their time to gain their independence. It was a different type of warfare, guerrilla-style in fashion, and, what is often ignored in the study of this period, it changed the way in which the Great Powers would wage war. This was reflected in their changes in weapons and uniforms, and the tactics employed on the ground.

THE INDIAN MUTINY: BRITISH TROOPS

The uprising of the Bengal Army, native Indian troops who had a long tradition of honourable service with the British, was both a shock and a bloody interlude the British did not need in the aftermath of the Crimean War.

The mutiny of the sepoys of the Indian Army marked the passing of the British East India Company, commonly known as 'John Company', as the actual ruler of British India to the British government at home.

There were multiple causes of the Mutiny, but it was ignited by the rumour that the new Enfield rifles that were going to be issued to the Bengal Army had cartridges that were coated with cow and pig grease or fat. The cartridges had to have the ends bitten off in order to properly load the rifles; this was abhorrent to the sepoys, as it was against their religion, both Hindu and Muslim, to handle or eat beef or pork.

In January 1857 came the rumour of the infamous cartridges from Dum Dum. The next month the 19th Bengal Native Infantry mutinied at Barrackpur and there were also outbreaks of vandalism and arson at Ambala. The Mutiny soon began in earnest. European officers were found and slaughtered by their own native sepoys, with whom many had served through war and peace for years. European civilians were not spared either. Women and children were butchered in their quarters, on the parade ground or street, and there was little mercy for anyone in the first days of the rebellion.

Confusion and inaction among senior British officers made things worse, and what action was done immediately to secure posts, depots and magazines was performed by quick-witted and alarmed junior officers who, on their own initiative, realized what the situation was and that immediate action was necessary to avoid a much more catastrophic situation. When the situation was finally understood by those in command, mutinies that might have been avoided were also

◀ OFFICER, 2ND PUNJAB CAVALRY, 1857 *This imposing officer is dressed in a combination of European and native dress, as was typical of British officers serving with irregular native troops.*

▲ PRIVATE, KING'S ROYAL RIFLE CORPS, 1857 *This is a very simplified dress for this famous formation, which was descended from the famous Rifle Brigade of the Napoleonic Wars. The short shell-type jacket, loose trousers and the cap with sunshade are typical of uniform 'changes' that were unofficial but practical while serving in India.*

breaking out, and a limited initial rebellion by a few units spread across the Bengal Army like a forest fire. Outside assistance from regular British Army units was deemed a necessity.

Relief Expeditions

Help would come from diverse sources. Native units under intrepid commanders such as John Nicholson would soon be on the march to fight this unexpected enemy. Veteran commanders would take the field, such as Sir Colin Campbell and Sir Henry Havelock, who would fight with what forces were available against any rebel unit or 'army' that they encountered. In the early days of the mutiny, as British units were organized to take the field, the British field commanders had a polyglot force to command in different sectors. Cries for help came from Cawnpore and Lucknow, as well as Delhi, and there were not enough available troops to put out all of the fires at once.

However, the relieving expeditions were organized as troops arrived and as soon as practicable troops were put into the field, even to the point of having volunteer civilians assembled into hasty provisional units, some of them quite small. With relief expeditions on the march, battles were fought against the insurgents where they were found, and generally speaking, British commands were successful. The largest problem the British encountered was a lack of troops and units to get the mission accomplished swiftly. Even so, sieges were mounted, assaults on fortified places launched, and the insurgents met defeat after defeat. Sometimes the British arrived too late to relieve besieged garrisons, as at Cawnpore, but eventually the revolt was defeated, and the rebels killed, taken or dispersed.

Troop Shortage

More troops were sent to India to quell the mutiny than had been sent to the Crimea a few years before. It was a herculean effort on the part of the British, and the sepoys who remained loyal were remembered by their British comrades in the years ahead. There was, however, no mercy for those who had betrayed their oaths of service and while British retaliation was not as brutal as the acts of murder by the mutineers, it did demonstrate that mutiny would not be tolerated.

The British military effort in quelling the Mutiny was hamstrung from the first because of many factors. There were not many European troops available for immediate service against the mutineers and insurgents. There was also a surplus of officers from native units that had mutinied. The troops were short of everything from personal kit to weapons, ammunition, artillery and especially transport.

▶ TROOPER, 9TH LANCERS, **1857** *This lancer is in modified dress for campaign and combat. The sunshade has been added to his fatigue cap, though he is still wearing the regulation blue uniform modified for field service. Others might wear an all-white uniform in the field in the same cut and style, as well as dyeing the white tropical uniform with tea to present a khaki appearance.*

Further, campaigning in India was brutal, something the British had learned through hard experience. The area to be covered was huge, and the climate was harsh. In addition, disease was a great enemy to both troops and civilians, and the protection of European civilians was another great factor in the coming campaigns. The cost of suppressing the Mutiny was great both in lives and treasure, but the will to continue to the bitter end was never in doubt.

The fighting itself was generally of the 'neither accept nor grant' quarter variety. Small numbers of British regulars usually defeated larger numbers of sepoys and insurgents.

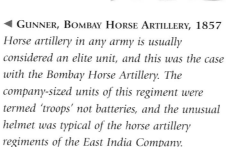

◀ **GUNNER, BOMBAY HORSE ARTILLERY, 1857** *Horse artillery in any army is usually considered an elite unit, and this was the case with the Bombay Horse Artillery. The company-sized units of this regiment were termed 'troops' not batteries, and the unusual helmet was typical of the horse artillery regiments of the East India Company.*

▲ **RISSALDAR, HODSON'S HORSE, 1857** *This cavalryman is typical of the irregular regiments raised by British officers that would later become regular regiments in the Indian Army. Like his British officers, he wears a combination of European and native dress. The beard and turban are typical of the Sikhs who largely made up this unit.*

There was no senior leadership on the mutineer side of the struggle supplied by the rebelling sepoys. While there were native officers in sepoy units, none of them was senior and none commanded the regiments. This lack of experience was a definite liability on the military side of the equation. No native officer had ever handled any unit higher than a regiment at best, and they were therefore completely at a loss in

commanding large numbers of troops, and this became increasingly problematic as the mutineers' ranks were swollen by insurgents who were enthusiastically violent and brutal, but lacking any military training whatsoever. Try as they might, the high quality of the sepoys in small units was increasingly diluted as the fighting progressed. That, coupled with the continued entrance into the theatre of operations of well-trained and

▲ TROOPER, 14TH LIGHT DRAGOONS, 1857
This trooper has modified his dress to his comfort on campaign in the Indian subcontinent. He is fully equipped for field service. Instead of the regulation headgear, he has chosen to wear a native-style turban.

competently led British units, put the mutineers and insurgents at an increasing disadvantage militarily, and no amount of fanatical native leadership could compensate for the lack of trained and competent higher-level commanders.

While the mutineers had a definite support base among the native population, they had immense logistical problems, which grew worse as the mutiny progressed. As British numbers grew, as well as the supporting arms of artillery and

transport, the overall British situation improved. The mutineers still had an advantage in numbers, but experience diminished exponentially, along with the ability to sustain the numbers of armed personnel in the field. As the British organized and assumed the offensive, insurgent successes diminished, and besieged garrisons were relieved with great loss of life among the insurgent forces. Insurgent casualties became ruinous and after the eventual success of British arms, British vengeance for mutiny and murder took over. Order was eventually restored with great loss of life to those who had dared mutiny against lawful authority and the quality of British mercy was indeed strained to the limit.

What was damaged almost irretrievably was the trust between native soldier and British officer. There was a tradition of long service and hardships shared between native sepoy and British officer, and these ties were broken in the Mutiny. Old units that had mutinied were disbanded and new units recruited to take their place.

British Troops

While the dress uniform of a British general officer was an ornate form of the red tunic and dark blue trousers (usually topped by a plumed feathered headdress) common to the rest of the army, on campaign British generals and commanders generally wore what they wanted. Usually a dark blue frock coat was favoured, but this could change in hot climates such as India. John Nicholson wore khaki with riding boots, the jacket being frogged and loose to be more comfortable. His hat was a type of British-style kepi with a 'havelock' attached to the rear to keep the sun off his neck.

Both Havelock and Campbell, hard men in a hard army, were generally dressed in dark blue; Havelock wore a long frock coat while Campbell preferred a shorter jacket. Both general officer's uniforms would be termed as undress. Everyone in India would make sure that they were wearing headgear that would protect the wearer from the sun.

The Highlanders strove to preserve their distinctive uniforms, even in India. Officers would wear a feathered bonnet, although many opted for trews in the regimental pattern in place of the kilt. The appearance of khaki jackets was the harbinger of uniform changes to come in the British Army. From this period on, uniforms would change from the finery of formal European warfare to the reality of field service against modern weapons.

▼ SOWAR, 2ND PUNJAB CAVALRY, 1857
This Sikh is another of the irregular Punjab regiments. The famous Sam Browne belt and accoutrements originated in this regiment, named after a junior officer who, after losing an arm in combat, devised a belt and harness system so that he could alternately draw his sword and pistol.

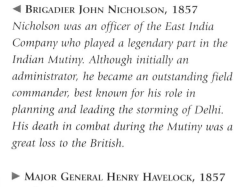

◀ **BRIGADIER JOHN NICHOLSON, 1857**
Nicholson was an officer of the East India Company who played a legendary part in the Indian Mutiny. Although initially an administrator, he became an outstanding field commander, best known for his role in planning and leading the storming of Delhi. His death in combat during the Mutiny was a great loss to the British.

▶ **MAJOR GENERAL HENRY HAVELOCK, 1857**
Tough, devout, and an outstanding combat officer, Major General Havelock performed excellent service, dying of dysentery before the end of the Mutiny. His was the command that finally reached the garrison at Cawnpore, unfortunately too late to save the women and children, who were slaughtered in the brutal massacre.

Regulations

Changes to British uniform regulations came in 1855 and tunics were now being worn by the infantry (initially double-breasted but soon changed to single-breasted), cavalry and foot artillery. The infantry, heavy cavalry, general officers and staff officers, as well as the Royal Engineers, all wore red as the basic colour for the uniform, the exception among the infantry being the Rifle Brigade, which still wore dark green (sometimes known as 'rifle green') uniforms. The rest of the cavalry arm as well as the artillery arm wore dark blue. The Medical Service, the Military Train and the Ordnance personnel also wore dark blue. During this period, infantry bands wore white,

◀ **LIEUTENANT GENERAL SIR COLIN CAMPBELL, 1857** *Son of a Scottish carpenter, Campbell was an outstanding soldier who was present as a junior officer at the Siege of San Sebastian in Spain during the Napoleonic Wars. He commanded the Highland Brigade during the Crimean War, and was one of the driving forces that suppressed the Mutiny in India. A self-made man, Campbell was one of the best general officers Britain ever produced.*

with the exception of drummers who wore red, as did buglers, and all this looked colourful on parade. Pipers in the Highland regiments wore green tunics. There was no change in trousers or riding breeches, with the exception of the infantry who now wore dark blue. White uniforms were authorized in hot weather.

Significant Actions of the Indian Mutiny

Action	Date	Year	Outcome
Mutinies at Meerut & Delhi	10–11 May	1857	British on the defensive
Mutiny at Lucknow	30 May		Lucknow besieged
Mutinies in Rohilkand	31 May		British on the defensive
Mutiny at Cawnpore	5 June		Garrison besieged
Battle of Badli-ke-Serai	8 June		British victory
Siege of Delhi begins	15 June		British besieged
Massacre at Jhansi	8 June		Rebel victory
Cawnpore surrenders	25 June		Garrison massacred
Battle of Chinhut	30 June		British defeat
Mutinies in Punjab, Malwa, Ganges Valley, Agra	1 July		British on defensive
Cawnpore	15 July		Civilian massacre in Cawnpore
First Battle of Cawnpore	16 July		British victory
Battle of Unao	25 July		British victory
Relief of Mhow	2 August		British victory
Battle of Bithur	16 August		British victory
Oudh in rebellion	16 August		British on defensive
Capture of Delhi	20 September		British advance on Lucknow
First relief of Lucknow	25 September		Garrison reinforced
Agra relieved	10 October		British victory
Revolt in Kotah	15 October		British on defensive
Second relief of Lucknow	17 November		Lucknow evacuated
Lucknow evacuated	27 November		British setback
Second Battle of Cawnpore	26–28 November		British defeat
Third Battle of Cawnpore	6 December		British victory
Fategarh captured	6 January	1858	British victory
Capture of Lucknow	21 March		British victory
Capture of Kotah	29 March		British victory
Battle of the Betwa	1 April		British victory
Jhansi captured	5 April		British victory
Battle of Bareilly	5 May		British victory
Battle of Kunch	7 May		British victory
Kalpi captured	23 May		British victory
Battle of Kotah-ki-Serai	17 June		British victory; Rani killed
Gwalior captured	20 June		British victory
Tantia Tope captured	7 April	1859	British victory
Tantia Tope executed	18 April		Mutiny suppressed

The usual headgear for infantry was now the shako, in the French style, which was slanted forward in the rear at an angle (the same style worn by the United States Army at this time; the British Army would be affected by Continental military styles up to the outbreak of World War I as can be seen by the adoption of the British form of the German Pickelhaube sometime after the defeat of France by Prussia in 1871). Heavy cavalry headgear would not change, but the light cavalry adopted the French-style shako for mounted troops, while smaller busbies would be adopted by hussars, and czapkas by lancers. The Royal Artillery and Royal Engineers would both adopt busbies of the same size and pattern, though they would differ in particulars such as busby bags, plumes and cords. Highland regiments would differ even from each other. Those men that wore the kilt would continue to wear the feathered bonnet, while two of the non-kilted regiments (the 71st and 74th, who later amalgamated to form the 1st and 2nd battalions of the

▼ OFFICER, 2ND PUNJAB CAVALRY, 1857 *This imposing officer is dressed in a combination of European and native dress, as was typical of British officers serving with irregular native troops. Troops from the Punjab played a great part in the suppression of the Mutiny, and they followed their European and native officers with loyalty and dedication.*

Highland Light Infantry) wore the infantry shako. The other non-kilted regiment, the 72nd, continued to wear the feathered bonnet. All three of the non-kilted regiments wore tartan trews.

Undress

In undress uniforms the new regulations changed very little, and these uniforms would be worn in the field, usually with modifications based on the local conditions. Glengarry caps now came into vogue in the Highland regiments, though some continued to wear the older Kilmarnock bonnet. Blue frock coats were worn by officers of all ranks, and cavalrymen wore the plainer, shorter shell jacket (sometimes

referred to as the stable jacket). Again, Highland regiments were different to the rest of the line infantry, shell jackets being scarlet for officers and NCOs, while those for the enlisted men were white. After 1856 regiments stationed in India would be issued a red frock coat made out of either kersey or serge and this garment would have fewer embellishments than the dress red coat and fewer buttons (eventually going from nine on the dress coat to five on the frock). This coat was cut looser than the dress coat making it more comfortable for campaign and service wear. Generally speaking, soldiers' equipment was the same as it was in the Crimea.

In the field in India there were many modifications. Coats were dyed khaki, generally a very light tan (and these would be in different shades even within the same unit depending on who was doing the work). White, and sometimes grey, uniforms were worn in the field and the undress caps, often with some type of sun protection attached to them, were favourites on campaign, especially for troops with unpopular or cumbersome headgear. Troops belonging to the East India

Company would also greatly modify their uniforms and it should be noted that these units had different uniform regulations than those regiments belonging to the British Army.

Native Troops

As well as the European regiments that were part of the army of the East India Company, there were also native sepoys from the Bengal Army that stayed loyal because of traditions of service with 'John Company' over the years and probably to recover their regimental honour lost because of the Mutiny. These native regiments usually fought well against the mutineers and rebels.

◀ SEPOY, 4TH PUNJAB INFANTRY, 1857
This Pathan infantryman is simply uniformed in khaki tunic and trousers, topped by the turban. He is simply armed and equipped, the leather equipment being in black or brown leather. Units from the Punjab had no love for the mutineers and fought savagely for their British officers. They were excellent troops and without their gallant and timely service the Mutiny might not have been suppressed.

▶ PRIVATE, 95TH FOOT, 1857 *After the Napoleonic Wars, number '95' was assigned to a regular line regiment and 'taken away' from the 95th Rifles who were permanently assigned the name 'Rifle Brigade'. This sometimes causes confusion to historians, but this infantryman is not a rifleman, but a member of a line regiment whose uniform has been suitably modified for field service in India. On campaign, especially the long, gruelling ones during the Mutiny, the troops would become ragged and scruffy in everyday campaign dress.*

◀ **PRIVATE, RIFLE BRIGADE, 1857** *This rifleman, part of a provisional 'Camel Corps' formed during the Mutiny, wears a grey field uniform topped by a near-regulation foreign service helmet. The usual and prized dark green rifle uniform was undoubtedly very hot and uncomfortable, and would be replaced by this more suitable uniform in the field. The usual black leather equipment is worn.*

Other units arrived, mostly irregular regiments such as Probyn's and Hodson's cavalry units, which would later be put on the regular establishment for distinguished service during the Mutiny. They generally wore native dress and their officers either wore a type of European uniform or a combination of native and European dress. These units were loyal to their commanders and some of the excess officers who had been left unemployed because their units had mutinied joined these units.

The Gurkhas were Nepalese who enlisted for service in the British Army. They wore rifle-green uniforms and the Gurkhas were, and still are, considered elite units. They performed excellent service in the Indian Mutiny and have always had the reputation of loyal and reliable troops. There are still Gurkha units in the British Army and they are not considered to be mercenaries.

East India Company
There were regiments of Europeans in the employ of the East India Company during the period, and

▶ **PRIVATE, 92ND (GORDON) HIGHLANDERS, 1857** *This imposing infantryman, complete with kilt, sporran and large feathered bonnet, is also wearing the white drill tunic which was much more suited to the Indian climate than the traditional red. The 'field expedient' sunshade worn under the bonnet would protect the wearer from the unforgiving rays of the sun. Other Highland regiments that served in the Mutiny, such as the 79th, might wear either grey or light blue 'smocks' instead of the regulation red doublet, or the white drill tunic shown here.*

these regiments usually fought well against the mutineers and rebels.

The East India Company army was composed of both native and European units. The European units' uniforms were based on those of the British Army with some unique features, such as the helmets of the Bengal and Bombay horse artillery units. The native units, with British officers, wore native dress modified to conform to conventional European styles, but retaining enough native features to accommodate the Indian culture.

The Bengal Horse Artillery in particular distinguished itself during the Mutiny. Its uniform was a handsome one of dark blue tunic and trousers and they wore a magnificent helmet in the Grecian style with a long horsehair plume.

New units, some recently raised in other parts of India specifically to combat the Mutiny, arrived to support the meagre British forces on hand. The famous Corps of Guides, composed of five cavalry regiments and ten infantry battalions, arrived from the Punjab. This corps was recruited from peoples on the subcontinent, such as the Sikhs, who had no love for the Hindus of the Bengal Army.

THE INDIAN MUTINY: REBEL SEPOYS

Both Hindus and Muslims took part in the rebellion; the Muslims were told their Enfield cartridges had been greased with pig fat, which their religion forbade them to eat, and the Hindus were told cow fat was used, which was just as horrible, if not worse, as the cow is sacred to Hindus.

▼ REBEL SOWAR, 1857 *This former regular cavalryman of the Bengal Army has reverted to native dress with the exception of his equipment and arms. Mutineers were joined by non-army Indians, and by the time the Mutiny was suppressed, there would be little or no difference between them.*

The term 'sepoy' is usually used to denote any Indian native troops, but it is only proper for infantry regiments; the equivalent term for cavalry units was 'sowar'. All were uniformed as closely to British style as practicable, and organization and distinctions also followed the British system.

Mutineers

The two regiments usually credited with starting the Mutiny were the 11th Native Bengal Infantry and the 3rd Bengal Light Cavalry in Meerut in May 1857. The mutineers who fought the British during the Mutiny did so initially in the uniforms of their old regiments. Insurgents who joined them later in the Mutiny wore native clothing and armed themselves as best they could from what was available. Generally speaking, sepoy units were uniformed in the European manner. The Bengal cavalry regiments were uniformed in French grey, which was a colour akin to sky blue or a bluish grey. Sepoys would often adapt the native *dhoti* in lieu of European-style trousers.

With the exception of three infantry regiments, parts of three others, three irregular cavalry regiments, three Gurkha regiments, elements of three Sikh regiments, some other irregulars, and parts of two artillery units, the entire native Bengal Army mutinied. The Madras Army remained loyal as did all but two regiments of the Bombay Army. While these units did aid in suppressing the Mutiny, along with other units raised in other areas, they were not instantly available, which put units in Bengal in a bad way. The rebellion was centred in the cities, and the rural population

▲ SOWAR, 3RD BENGAL LIGHT CAVALRY, 1857 *This was the regiment that began the Mutiny in Meerut on 10 May. Eighty-five of them had been jailed for refusing to use the cartridges for the new Enfield rifles. Fellow troopers broke their comrades out of jail, along with other criminals incarcerated there. This act of defiance began the bloody chain of events.*

largely did not either support or take part in the revolt, but as rebellion spread through India, native insurgents who had not been part of the army joined in the Mutiny.

Leadership

The four principal leaders during the mutiny were Nana Sahib, Bahadur Shah, the Rani of Jhansi, and Tantia Tope. Nana Sahib was infamous for being part of the Cawnpore slaughter, and due to his advanced age was more of a figurehead than a real leader. Bahadur Shah, another octogenarian at 82 was the King of Delhi, 'the last of the Moghul Emperors'. He was proclaimed the Emperor of India by the mutineers and surrendered to the British when the Mutiny was all but over. The Rani of Jhansi was killed in action at the Battle of Kotah-ki-Serai in June 1858. She was described as a handsome woman who, like the Nana

Sahib and Bahadur Shah, was literally forced to support, and become a figurehead of, the revolt. Bahadur Shah's 'general', Tantia Tope, was run down and captured in April 1859 and was tried and executed.

▼ REBEL SEPOY, 1857 *The rebels began the Mutiny in their regulation uniforms. Without resupply, and under native commanders who were more fanatical than practical, most of the mutineers gradually reverted to native clothing, which many of them probably preferred now that they had rebelled against the British.*

The Indian rebels, sepoys and insurgents, while posing a definite threat to the British presence in India, never had a proficient senior leadership that could mount an equal military force to face the British and loyal Indian troops, nor could they furnish a substitute for either the East India Company leadership, as inept as that could be from time to time, or for the British government. The native forces continued their internecine struggles for power while the Mutiny was in progress and were never united in a common cause to defeat the British. If they had, and if the Mutiny was better planned and led, they might have been able to throw off what they considered the British yoke. As it was, they caused considerable trouble for the British and in the end managed to get rid of 'John Company' as administrators of the subcontinent. It would take until 1947 to win independence from Great Britain.

EGYPT AND SUDAN: BRITISH TROOPS

Of all the colonial expeditions the British Army mounted and the colonial wars they fought in the 19th century none were more important than those fought in Egypt and the Sudan.

Time of Change

The Egyptian campaign of 1882, which ended with the British victory at the Battle of Tel-el-Kebir, was one of the last campaigns in which the British force wore the traditional red tunics into combat.

The British involvement in Egypt was sparked by a revolt of Egyptian Army officers against their nominal overlords the Turks, represented by the Khedives in Egypt.

The Egyptian Army had traditionally been officered by Turco-Circassians, the enlisted men being lower-class Egyptian peasants. However, by the 1860s Egyptians were being commissioned and, growing tired of their overlords who were proving themselves incompetent to the detriment of the native Egyptians, they finally revolted. This alarmed the British, who were committed to support the Khedives mainly because of access to the Suez Canal, which was a strategic lifeline of the British empire. A fleet and army were dispatched to Egypt, and the country invaded and the Egyptian revolt suppressed.

However, this opened the door to support Egypt in the Sudan, which led to the disastrous Gordon Relief Expedition and a series of wars with the fanatical Mahdists in the Sudan.

Generals and Staff

The British commander in the Egyptian expedition of 1882 was Sir Garnet Wolseley, whose stamp on the British Army lasted long after his retirement. He was one of the outstanding British commanders in history. The conqueror of the Sudan was Sir Herbert Kitchener, whose influence on the British Army rivalled that of Wolseley.

British general officers, though having prescribed uniforms, generally wore what they wished on campaign. Wolseley undoubtedly dressed for comfort, but Kitchener was a stickler for regulations and that included dress. Kitchener was a hard man, and was not as popular as Wolseley or Lord Roberts, but his

◀ **GENERAL STEWART, 1884** *Brigadier General Sir Herbert Stewart is comfortably uniformed for foreign service in the Sudan in grey tunic, khaki riding breeches and riding boots. He is wearing his medal ribbons in the field. This handsome uniform is typical for the British Army of the period and was both practical and reasonably comfortable.*

▶ **GENERAL GARNET WOLSELY, 1873** *This eminent knight of the realm became the Victorian ideal of a 'modern major general' and was an officer of long and distinguished service who would set the tone for the British Army for decades. The phrase he inspired of 'all Sir Garnett' was a euphemism for everything being as it should be.*

contributions to the British Army and empire were just as great. He remains one of the great commanders in British military history.

After his victory in the Sudan, Kitchener commanded the British in the last of the Boer Wars and at the beginning of World War I he was

▼ GENERAL KITCHENER, 1898 *General Sir Herbert Kitchener was held in high esteem during the period of Queen Victoria's colonial wars. He commanded in the Sudan in 1898 and he is dressed here in the new khaki service dress that was made regulation two years before in 1896. It again is a handsome and practical uniform, suited to the hot climate.*

named Secretary of State for War, a position for which he was most qualified. He raised the volunteer army of over 3 million that replaced the pre-war Regular Army and Territorials that were nearly destroyed in the initial battles of the war and were known affectionately as 'Kitchener's Mob'. In 1915, en route to Russia, the ship he was travelling on, HMS *Hampshire*, struck a German mine off the coast of the Orkneys. Kitchener and his staff were lost, his body never recovered.

Infantry

Uniform for the infantry remained red, though the tunics were different for each type of wear, with officers and NCOs in scarlet with regimental distinctions, including button arrangement for the Guards regiments. Cuffs and collars would be in the regimental colour, with blue for the Guards and Royal regiments, white for English and Welsh regiments, green for Irish, and yellow for Scottish. Rifle units were dressed in green with the same pattern tunic and black facings. Scottish regiments, including those that did not wear the kilt, wore the doublet instead of the tunic. All had seven brass buttons down the front of the tunic and the doublet.

Line infantry and rifle regiments wore the British version of the Prussian spiked helmet (the Pickelhaube). Later, the rifle regiments would change to a type of busby. The Guards regiments wore the bearskin and fusilier regiments wore a smaller bearskin with a brass grenade device on the front. The Highland Light Infantry wore a low French-style shako along with the Scottish doublet and trews in the regimental plaid. Other Highland regiments wore the kilt and bonnet.

▶ PRIVATE, 5TH GURKHAS, 1878 *The Gurkha battalions of the British Army were, and are, exclusively Nepalese. They were awarded the green uniforms and black leather equipment of rifle regiments, denoting elite status. The cloth would be dyed so dark as to look almost black, and would then fade to green.*

For field service, red tunic and dark blue trousers were still worn in the 1880s, and a foreign service helmet, usually white or sometimes dyed a khaki colour with tea, was worn. The foreign service helmet for full dress on overseas stations was worn white with spike and the regimental badge on the front of the helmet. White personal field equipment was worn, except for the rifle regiments who wore black equipment, that of the Slade-Wallace system. Gaiters or leggings were worn at the ankle to gather up the trousers above the shoes. Later, the infantry changed to a field uniform of khaki, although the Highland regiments still wore the kilt, though with a khaki 'apron' added in front.

◀ **PRIVATE, 42ND FOOT (BLACK WATCH), 1882** *The famous Black Watch (or Royal Highland Regiment) was deployed to Egypt in 1882 wearing their regulation scarlet doublets, along with kilt and sporran, the only modification being the white foreign service helmet. Originally formed to police the Highlands after the last Jacobite rebellion in 1745, the Black Watch wear the government tartan and are the only Highland regiment to wear the red tunic, all other Highland regiments wearing white.*

traditional hussar jacket with rows of regimental braid across the chest as well as a fur busby with the busby bag in the regimental colour. The lancers wore both the traditional Polish-style czapka as well as the lancer tunic with a coloured plastron on the front of the jacket.

On campaign, until the army adopted khaki service dress between the first and second Egyptian expeditions, cavalry would wear the foreign service helmet.

The 21st Lancers was a new lancer regiment in 1898. They had previously been the 21st Hussars and were converted to lancers in 1897. Originally raised in India as the 3rd Bengal European Light Cavalry in 1858, they had been converted to hussars in 1861. After distinguishing themselves at Omdurman, they were given the honorific title of Empress of India's Lancers, keeping their regimental number. In 1922 they were amalgamated with the 17th Lancers of Balaclava, of the charge of the Light Brigade fame, and the new regiment was known as the 17th/21st Lancers. Their field dress was khaki service dress, but their full dress lancer uniform was spectacular. Wearing the usual lancer tunic, the plastron on the front of the tunic was French grey, as was the top of the lancer cap, the czapka (of Polish origin and much

Cavalry

In the 1880s British cavalry consisted of both light and heavy cavalry. The heavy cavalry, which included the three regiments of Household Cavalry (two regiments of Life Guards and one of Horse Guards) wore the cuirass and steel helmet in full dress. The Dragoon Guards wore the standard red heavy cavalry tunic with dark blue trousers and steel dragoon helmet. The dragoon regiments wore essentially the same uniform, though their helmets were steel instead of brass as in the Dragoon Guards. The only exception to the

general rule was the 6th Dragoon Guards whose tunics were dark blue and matched the trousers. The 2nd Dragoons, also known as the Scots Greys, wore the bearskin instead of the steel dragoon helmet and, as their title suggests, the entire regiment rode grey horses.

The light cavalry, the hussars and lancers, were both in a uniform inspired by continental styles and tradition for their arms of service. The hussars wore the

▶ *The Black Watch at the Battle of Tel-el-Kebir on 13 September 1882.*

◄ **OFFICER, QUEEN'S OWN CORPS OF GUIDES, 1879** *This distinguished regiment was a native outfit with British officers who wore this handsome uniform in undress. This junior subaltern wears a modified Sam Browne belt. The shoulder belt that carries his cartridge box is not attached to the waist belt. The foreign service helmet with spike was a peculiarity of the Guides' officers.*

▼ **TROOPER, 21ST LANCERS, 1898** *The 21st Lancers had recently been converted from a hussar regiment and their first action as a lancer regiment was at the Battle of Omdurman during the Sudan expedition. This trooper is fully equipped for campaign. His lance pennant would either be furled or removed for combat. Note the local sunshade used for his horse, and also the feedbag attached to the rear of the saddle. His sword and carbine are both attached to the saddle and not to his person as in previous periods.*

bags and cords and that uniform can still be seen today in the King's Troop, Royal Horse Artillery.

The Royal Marines were divided into two branches during this period; the Royal Marine Light Infantry – which was dressed and accoutred as line infantry – and the Royal Marine Artillery, who were uniformed similarly to the field artillery arm of the Royal Artillery. They served afloat on the Royal Navy's capital ships or ashore as need be.

copied by other European lancer units during and after the Napoleonic Wars). The plume of the czapka was white. When amalgamated with the 17th Lancers, however, the uniform colours of the 17th were kept, and the old regiment lost its distinctive facing colour.

Artillery and Marines

The Royal Artillery wore dark blue as it always had, the field artillery wearing an almost identical uniform to the infantry. The Royal Horse Artillery was dressed in hussar style, complete with busby,

EGYPT AND SUDAN: MAHDI TROOPS

The Sudan became part of Egypt after being conquered by Muhammad Ali Pasha al-Mas'ud ibn Agha, who administered the territory as a provincial colony. Britain was drawn into conflict by her interests in Egypt.

By the 1880s the Sudan was more than ready to revolt against the Egypt of the Khedives. The revolt was largely religious in nature, led by Mohammed Ahmad, a Danaqla Arab from Dongala Province in northern Sudan. A fanatic Muslim, he called himself the Mahdi ('the proclaimed one'), a disciple of the prophet Mohammed. His campaign began among the poorer classes of Arabs, where the promise of

paradise to all who opposed the hated oppressors from Egypt had wide appeal. As support grew he proclaimed holy war (*jihad*) against Egypt, and anyone else who opposed him, and set out on a campaign of conquest.

The Mahdi's Advance

The number of followers grew, and Ahmad established his base in the western Kordofan Province and captured the provincial capital, El Obeid. He and his 'army' also surprised and defeated an Egyptian field force sent to suppress the revolt under the British commander William Hicks, known as Hicks Pasha. Hicks's force was totally destroyed, which alarmed the British who now had a full revolt in the Sudan on their hands. Reluctant to send in British troops, they dispatched the famous, enigmatic and very religious general Charles 'Chinese' Gordon to suppress the revolt and save the Sudanese capital of Khartoum. Khartoum was a strategic city, at the junction of the Blue and White Nile. The Mahdi's forces attacked the city in overwhelming numbers, slaughtered the Egyptian garrison, killed Gordon and raised his severed head on a spear for all to see. The British had dispatched a relief force to

◄ **MAHDIST, 1898** *The Mahdists were religious fanatics and were formidable in combat. They were well organized and usually well led and were generally indifferent to casualties in the heat of battle.*

▼ **MAHDIST, 1898**
The Mahdists were a formidable fighting force and quite well organized. Arranged in three 'divisions' known as rayaa *(flags), they were distinguished by the colour of their flags: black, red or green.*

help Gordon and relieve Khartoum, but they were too late and fell back after Gordon was killed.

The Mahdi died six months later, but his place was taken by the Khalifa Abdullah. He and his followers attempted to establish an Islamic state in the Sudan, and Abdullah consolidated the gains made by the Mahdi. Tribal divisions were dealt with by the call of co-religionists of the movement, and an invasion of Egypt was attempted in 1888 but defeated.

▼ **MAHDIST AMIR, 1898** *An amir was a Mahdist commander and they were normally seen mounted in order to lead their troops more effectively. The multi-coloured jibbeh, the long tunic, would be more elaborate for an amir than it would for the rank and file troops, though the purpose of this 'uniform' would be the same as that of European armies – that of identification in combat. Sometimes red turbans would be worn, which would indicate household or guard troops.*

Mahdist Warriors

The Mahdists were tough, inured to the hardships of a very harsh environment, and fanatical in their beliefs. Early successes made them believe themselves invincible on the battlefield. The Mahdi prescribed a uniform for his troops; basically the native clothing of the poor Sudanese peasant – a white tunic called the *jibbeh*, trousers, sandals, a skull cap, white turban, and a sash-like garment of woven straw. The followers of the Mahdi were called the Ansar, translated as 'helpers', and the coloured patches – initially used to repair torn clothing on the *jibbeh* – proclaimed their allegiance. Later, different tribes would wear different coloured patches to distinguish themselves.

Their weapons included single-shot long arms; Remingtons taken from the Egyptians, British Martini-Henrys, and some Italian and French weapons. Spears and swords were also used, and many, if not most, of the Mahdists also wore daggers strapped to the left arm. The Mahdists also had artillery, mostly brass mountain guns, and field guns they had captured from the Egyptians.

THE BOXER REBELLION: ALLIED TROOPS

By 1900 China was occupied by most of the European powers, at Chinese expense in treasure and territory. A backlash against such conquest by stealth was inevitable.

China in 1900

The wishes of the Chinese imperial government were being largely ignored, as the Europeans sought more concessions in order to gain more wealth for their respective empires. The occupation of Chinese ports and the maintenance of troops in

Peking, were deeply resented, and militant groups of Chinese, such as the Righteous Harmony Society Movement, were formed, dedicated to fighting the foreign administrators.

In the summer of 1900 this resentment exploded into conflict with the allied powers. The militants were now known as the 'Boxers', and at the beginning of June they destroyed the Peking racecourse. The allies realized that a little over 400 troops might not be enough to protect the legations, and a request was sent to Admiral Seymour to send reinforcements to Peking. In reaction Admiral Seymour began to march on Peking. The Boxers took Tientsin on 15 June and Seymour's column was forced to retreat.

The Chinese government declared war on the allies on 21 June, and the Boxers marched on Peking. Under the command of the British minister to China, Claude Maxwell MacDonald, the legation staff and security personnel defended the Peking compound with one old muzzle-loaded cannon, and held until they were relieved by the allied expeditionary force from Tientsin.

Allied Expeditions

The allied response to the Boxer emergency was unprecedented up to that time, as the eight Great Powers all sent contingents of troops to China.

◄ TROOPER, 16TH BENGAL LANCERS, 1900
In overall appearance, the Indian cavalry regiments maintained their general uniform characteristics of full dress in the new khaki field and service uniforms. These were both smart and functional.

► OFFICER, ROYAL WELCH FUSILIERS, 1900
This is how a well-turned-out British infantry officer would be attired on campaign. Khaki was by now standard issue field service uniform for the British Army, and officer accoutrements, including the Sam Browne belt, made for a handsome effect.

British Troops

The Royal Welch Fusiliers, one of the units to be sent to China, were an immensely distinguished regiment and wore a khaki service dress very similar to that of the Americans. The British Sam Browne belt worn on this campaign has since lasted for dress occasions in both the British Army and the United States Marine Corps.

The lancers of the 16th Bengal Cavalry also wore the popular khaki (originally an Irdu word meaning 'dust' or 'dust coloured'),

which is generally modelled on the regiment's dress uniform but much looser in cut for active service.

The Royal Marines, who fought beside their American Marine 'cousins' in Peking, mostly wore an order of dress still

▼ ARTILLERY OFFICER, UNITED STATES ARMY, 1900 *This new khaki uniform was prescribed for the US Army at the turn of the century but was slow to be utilized outside the continental United States. The branch colour (red for artillery, yellow for cavalry, and sky blue for infantry) was noticeable against the colour of the uniform and the overall contrast was effective in the field.*

known as 'work order'. It was, and is, practical, comfortable and suited to the adverse circumstances the troops in Peking found themselves in. The Slade-Wallace personal equipment would be stained a light brown colour instead of being kept white.

American Troops

The United States Army had converted to the new khaki uniform, which was cooler than the old blue uniform for field service. As the summers in China are brutally hot, this was fortunate. While the uniform itself somewhat resembled the British model, the headgear was a uniquely

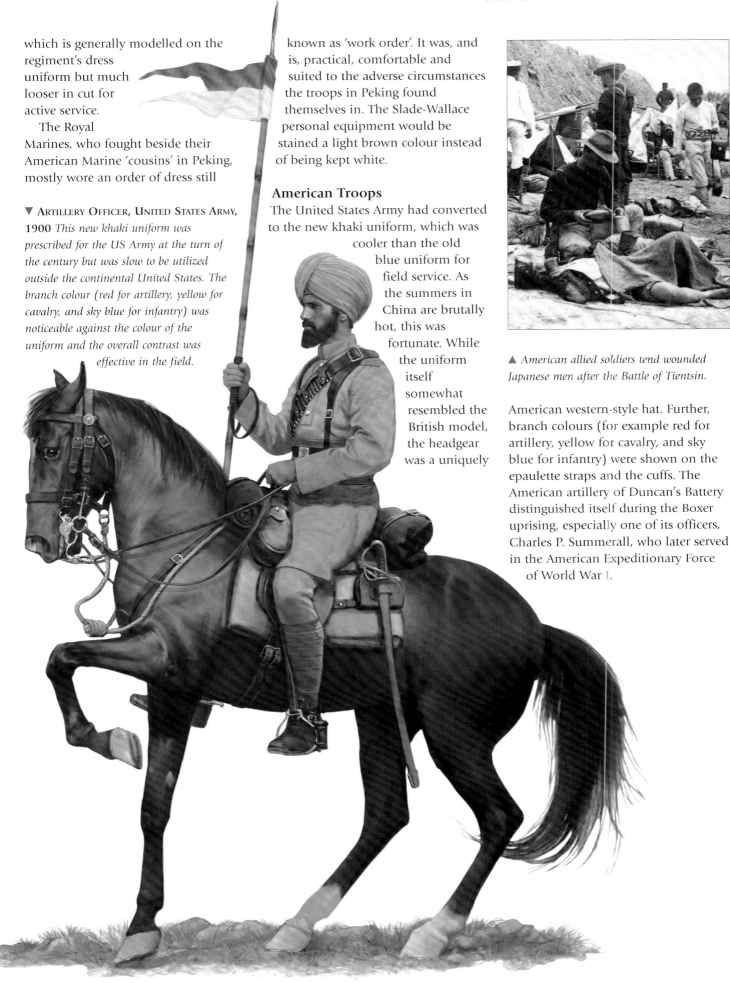

▲ *American allied soldiers tend wounded Japanese men after the Battle of Tientsin.*

American western-style hat. Further, branch colours (for example red for artillery, yellow for cavalry, and sky blue for infantry) were shown on the epaulette straps and the cuffs. The American artillery of Duncan's Battery distinguished itself during the Boxer uprising, especially one of its officers, Charles P. Summerall, who later served in the American Expeditionary Force of World War I.

The United States Marine Corps also gained fame and martial reputation on the international level for its distinguished service in the Boxer uprising. A detachment of Marines served in the legation siege for '55 Days in Peking' and there were more Marines in the expeditionary force that came to the legations' relief.

Marine service dress during the period was practical, comfortable and adaptable to campaign conditions. The dark blue shirt, light blue trousers and the khaki campaign hat were typical of the period. The 56-man Marine detachment that served in Peking was taken from the Marine detachments aboard the battleship USS *Oregon* and the cruiser USS *Newark*.

▲ PRIVATE, ROYAL MARINE LIGHT INFANTRY, 1900 *The Royal Marines were besieged in the Peking legations during the 55-day siege by the Boxers, later supported by the Chinese Imperial Army. This is a handsome and practical uniform, similar to that of the United States Marine Corps.*

▶ PRIVATE, UNITED STATES MARINE CORPS, 1900 *This is how the Marines who defended the allied legations in Peking in the summer of 1900 would have looked. The uniform is distinctly American in design, and the campaign hat, with the Marine Corps emblem of eagle, globe and anchor, was proudly displayed by this die-hard organization.*

French

The French *marin* was a visible figure during the siege. He was not a marine, but a sailor serving as infantry. (The French word *marin* means sailor and not 'marine' as usually mistranslated in English.) These naval infantry would probably wear white gaiters, and could be dressed in either a comfortable white uniform or in dark blue. During the siege, they probably could have been seen in any combination of the uniform. Instead of the beret, also in white or dark blue (which would have the ship's name on the ribbons in gold lettering, and a red pompon), straw hats might be worn. His equipment would be of black leather and his rifle was the infantryman's famous Lebel.

Germans

The German East Asian Brigade did not serve in the legation siege in Peking, but was formed hurriedly in Germany for service in China. The hat was quite distinctive and the uniform would be a light grey, though for tropical service the troops were issued a khaki uniform with tropical helmet. The brigade consisted of infantry, Jägers and cavalry, and they arrived in China on 21 September 1900.

The German 3rd Seebataillon also saw action against the Chinese. Stationed in Tsingtao, the field uniform was a khaki tunic over khaki trousers wtih a German-style foreign service helmet.

In full dress these German infantrymen wore medium-blue tunics and trousers with white cuffs and shoulder straps. The khaki tunic also had white shoulder straps, but the cuffs were khaki.

Others

The Russians fielded sailors, infantry and Cossack units. Seamen and infantry generally dressed the same in the field with a summer service tunic (the *kittel*) in white, a pullover tunic that was both functional and comfortable. The usual dark green trousers were worn as well as a white, peakless fatigue cap. Cossacks wore the long traditional coat, overtrousers and cavalry boots, topped by the fur cap. Russian sailors wore the usual naval dark blue trousers and blouse and the sailor cap with a ribbon at the rear. Underneath the blouse the sailors wore a red-striped shirt, which was normal outerwear in the heat.

The Japanese generally wore a dark blue tunic and dark blue trousers with a dark blue peaked cap. White or khaki would be worn in summer or hot weather. Regimental and branch distinctions would be visible as different coloured bands to the peaked cap and on the collar. On the cavalry tunic, coloured lace, such as on a hussar tunic, would be worn.

International Contingents in China

Nation	Infantry	Cavalry	Artillery	Service Troops
Great Britain	18 Regts	4 Regts	1 Btry +1 Bn	2 Pioneer Regts 3 Cos sappers and miners
United States	10 Regts	4 Regts	2 Regts	Signal, medical and engineer detachments
France	6 Bns	2 Btries	1 Regt	
Germany	4 Regts	1 Regt	1 Regt	
	1 Naval Bn	1 Btry	1 Commando	
Austro-Hungary	1 Bn			
Italy	1 Bn (Sep)	1 Btry		MG section, engineers
	1 Regt			
Russia	12 Regts	7 Regts	14 Btries	
	12 Bns (Sep)			
Japan	8 Regts	2 Regts	2 Regts	

The Italian contingent consisted of the famous light infantry, the Bersaglieri. They wore a dark blue tunic and trousers, black leather equipment and a white foreign service helmet with the usual cock feathers on the right side, a regimental distinction.

The Austro-Hungarian seamen wore a white summer uniform with a wide naval collar that hung down the back to the shoulders. This collar was light blue with a double row of thin white stripes along the edge. The usual naval cap was worn together with black leather equipment.

◀ PRIVATE, FRENCH NAVAL INFANTRY, 1900
This naval uniform is both smart and practical and is akin to the naval uniforms of the other European powers and the US Navy. This is the summer version of the French naval uniform; the winter version would be in dark blue. The method of wearing the cartridge pouch is interesting, along with the Gallic red tuft on the headgear.

▶ PRIVATE, GERMAN EAST ASIAN BRIGADE, 1900 *This German unit was raised to serve in China and in the relief of the Peking legations. The bush hat with its turned-up brim was worn by other troops of the period, such as the Australians and some of the British units, and was probably copied somewhat from the hats worn by the Boers in South Africa, to whom the Imperial German government gave support in their war against the British.*

THE BOXER REBELLION: CHINESE FORCES

The ruling Qing dynasty of China fielded regular troops, which were were supported by the civilian Boxer rebels.

Infantry

The Chinese infantryman deployed in the campaign were often regulars, and troops of this type were committed by their empress to support the Boxers against the allies. Uniforms might have been westernized to an extent, but certain native Chinese elements still remained quite prominent. Most men would wear the traditional long pigtail common in China during this period, and the ancient 'chest plate' contrasted sharply with the rest of the uniform. Many Chinese troops were raised by different military commanders in China in the 1890s with the permission of the empress, which would later lead to difficulties after the defeat of the Boxer insurrection. Rifles were of various kinds; some troops used rifles of Austrian manufacture.

Cavalry

Chinese cavalry were usually irregulars from either Mongolia or western China. The only Chinese regular cavalry were not engaged in the fighting. Curiously, the Chinese were chronically short of regular cavalry as an arm. Troopers were not in any prescribed uniform and would be dressed as they were in civilian life. Hats were made of animal skin and the rest of their clothing would show local influences. Along with more modern weapons, they would still carry a composite bow, and cavalry would be mounted on the tough Asiatic horse.

Boxer Rebels

The Boxers wore civilian dress and identified themselves by wearing something red on their persons. It could be a sash, armband or turban. If a turban was not worn, then the

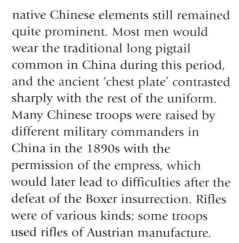

◀ **BOXER, 1900** *The Boxers were civilians who formed an anti-western organization that resorted to violence to rid China of the 'foreign devils'. They were ferocious in combat, reckless of their own lives and anxious to kill as many Europeans as possible by any means. Most Boxers were not equipped with modern firearms and employed old Chinese-type pole arms, such as this pitchfork, which were effective in close-quarter fighting and left hideous wounds.*

▲ **BOXER, 1900** *Sometimes the Boxers would decorate their clothing with red-coloured Chinese characters. The weapon carried is a they old-style Chinese halberd. The Boxers carried what was available and generally spurned the modern, western weapons.*

ubiquitous conical straw 'coolie hat' was worn. The Boxers did not use western weapons generally, as they were avowed to drive the foreigners from China. They carried the peculiar Chinese halberd, which was at least frightening, or swords and spears. Sometimes they also carried wicker shields which were of no help against modern weapons. Typically, Boxer losses were very high against western firepower.

After the Uprising

China suffered very heavily at the hands of the Europeans after the rebellion was suppressed and foreign troops occupied the country. After the rebellion was put down, the only significant change in the relationship between China and the European powers was that China became much weaker than she already had been and her enemies became stronger. There

was no strong, central leader on a national level that could rally the Chinese to become interested in and take charge of their own destiny. This was in large part the fault of the Chinese administration, which invited foreign political intervention in the late 19th century, leading to further

foreign involvement and a disastrous 14-year war that caused much suffering to the Chinese population. This would lead to further revolutions in the country and eventually the rise of the communists under Mao Tse Tung, who succeeded in taking over the country in 1949 after defeating the Nationalists under Chiang Kai Chek. Before that eventuality, however, the Chinese underwent Japanese occupation and dreadful depredations in the long war that lasted from 1931–45.

◀ CHINESE IRREGULAR CAVALRYMAN, 1900
This border stalwart had not changed much in appearance since the days of Genghis Khan and was still considered something of a mercenary during the waning days of the Chinese empire. The clothing and equipment are typical of the nomadic light cavalry of the steppes, as is the armament.

THE FRENCH IN MEXICO

During the 1860s the French, now under the rule of the Emperor Napoleon III, attempted to establish an empire in Mexico under the Hapsburg Archduke Maximilian.

With the United States racked by civil war, the French invaded Mexico without fear of American intervention, and formed an army of native Mexicans 'loyal' to the new regime, backed by regular French troops and volunteer units from Europe, especially from Austria and Hungary, but also with units from Belgium, the Ottoman empire and Egypt. Undoubtedly the most reliable units were French.

With the Civil War over and the United States once again 'united', the American government turned its attention to Mexico, and assembled a 50,000-strong army under the Civil War veteran commander General Phillip Sheridan on the United States–Mexican border. The French had little choice but to evacuate the country, especially with trouble brewing in Europe.

Anti-guerrilla Units

During the 'ill-fated' Mexican adventure the French organized a contra-guerrilla unit to respond to attacks from resistant fighters. The unit, noted for its indiscipline and viciousness, was organized in two mounted squadrons, four infantry companies and a two-gun artillery detachment. Designed for rapid movement, the infantry were at times mounted on mules for speed. The men were colourfully uniformed in a combination of red jackets and white pantaloons, and the Mexican sombrero was the favourite headgear. Jackets were heavily braided and the infantry were uniformed in semi-zouave style, with red fezzes and a red zouave jacket and shirt. Ammunition was carried in a belly box.

► TROOPER, CHASSEURS D'AFRIQUE, MEXICO, 1863
The Chasseurs d'Afrique was one of the units that came out of the French conquest and occupation of Algeria. There were three regiments of Chasseurs d'Afrique, and the units sent to Mexico were uniformed as prescribed in regulations. These troops were used to hard service and were ideal units to send to Mexico. They were withdrawn from Mexico in increments through 1866 and 1867.

with additions for personal preference and comfort, such as the usual Mexican sombrero as protection against the elements. One of the Legion's enduring traditions comes out of the Mexican adventure. One of its infantry companies, under Captain Danjou, was trapped by Mexican insurgents. Summoned to surrender, the tough survivors refused, fixed bayonets, and charged into the mass of Mexicans. Captain Danjou was killed in the action, but his wooden hand was recovered and is preserved as one of the relics of the Legion.

Other Troops

The Chasseurs d'Afrique were 'imported' from North Africa and were a crack cavalry unit. Uniformed in light blue or 'French grey' jackets and wide red trousers, they were mounted on tough Arabian horses and were veterans of campaigning in North Africa. Seven squadrons were sent with the French expeditionary corps (three from the 1st Regiment, and two each from the 2nd and 3rd regiments) and they performed good service throughout the relatively short stay of the French in Mexico.

There were also French Imperial Guard units sent to Mexico and they furnished units of artillery and train troops. Artillery and train troops were all uniformed in basic dark blue, and their jackets resembled hussar uniforms. Either the colpack or kepi was worn along with trousers with leather fashioned like boot tops at the bottom. Enlisted men sometimes wore simple jackets of dark blue, dark blue trousers with red stripes and white gaiters over shoes. The Mexican wide-

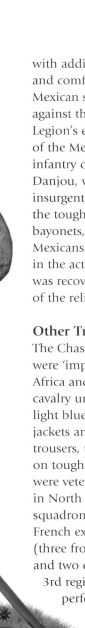

▲ OFFICER, CONTRA-GUERILLAS, MEXICO, 1865 *The French contra-guerilla units were reasonably effective, but too many were indifferently trained and disciplined. The uniforms could be somewhat fantastic, as pictured here, with this officer looking like a cross between a Turkish potentate and a dashing cavalier from some bygone age.*

The Foreign Legion

The French Foreign Legion in Mexico eventually grew to six eight-company infantry battalions, two cavalry squadrons, 'several' artillery batteries of both field and pack or mule, with an engineer company and a train company. The Legion generally wore its regulation uniform on field service,

▼ LEGIONNAIRE, FRENCH FOREIGN LEGION, MEXICO, 1864 *The French Foreign Legion was an ideal organization to serve in Mexico to support the puppet regime of the Emperor Maximilian. This uniform, with the exception of the sombrero, was typical of Legion units of the period.*

THE SPANISH–AMERICAN WAR

The Spanish–American War was the result of tension between the United States and Spain over the Spanish occupation of Cuba, and it erupted on 15 February 1898 when the battleship, the USS *Maine*, blew up in Havana.

The American campaign in Cuba was fraught with problems, from antiquated weapons to disease and logistics. Even so, Cuba was finally taken, as were Puerto Rico and the Philippines. All told, this was an unnecessary war brought on by politicians and journalists who wanted to see Spain shorn of her remaining colonies. One result was to make the United States, in a somewhat limited way, a colonial power and to thrust the nation, ready or not, on to the world stage as a 'world power'. This was exploited by Theodore Roosevelt, a combat veteran of the war with Spain, when he became president. The war also led to a vicious, bloody counter-insurgency in the Philippines.

American Troops

The US Army had a strength of only 28,183 at the start of the war, so volunteer units had to be mobilized to augment those regulars who could be spared. Some units had to be kept in the west to keep a wary eye on further Indian troubles (the last uprising had been in 1890), so the amount of regular units and individual regulars to cadre new units was limited.

The typical field dress for the period, whether regular or volunteer, was usually a dark blue shirt over sky-blue trousers, khaki leggings over shoes and the Montana round hat. Some units, such as the 10th Cavalry, were issued khaki trousers instead of the usual sky blue, but many units went into the tropics in the older blue uniforms. Khaki had not taken hold as yet as the usual fatigue or field dress for the US Army, and the mixture of dark blue blouse and khaki trousers and leggings demonstrates a uniform in transition.

The 10th Cavalry, one of the two black cavalry regiments in the US Army, was a battle- and campaign-tested veteran outfit that was sent to Cuba where it distinguished itself at San Juan Hill and got little credit for it. One of the regiment's junior officers was 1st Lieutenant John J. Pershing, who would rise to be the commanding general of the American Expeditionary Force in World War I. He obtained his nickname, Black Jack, because of his service in the 10th Cavalry, of whom he was justly proud.

The United States Marine Corps wore two uniforms in the war with Spain. The first was like the army's, dark blue tunic over sky-blue trousers and khaki leggings over shoes, though in Marine Corps style. Sometimes, white trousers were substituted for the sky-blue ones. Later, a khaki tunic and trousers, again with khaki leggings over shoes, with the Marine Corps campaign hat, was worn with brown leather or webbing equipment.

Spanish and Cuban Troops

In 1898 Spain held the remnant of a once-powerful empire. Spanish colonies now consisted primarily of Cuba, Puerto Rico and the Philippines.

◀ **PRIVATE, 10TH PENNSYLVANIA INFANTRY, 1898** *This is a typical American infantryman in Cuba during the Spanish–American War. This is essentially the same uniform worn in the American west against the Plains Indians and little was done to adapt to the realities of the Cuban climate or countryside. This regiment was one of the last American infantry units to carry their colours in combat.*

▼ **INFANTRY KIT, 1898** *1 Canteen cup. 2 Canteen and cover. 3 Pistol holster. 4 Cartridge belt. 5 Haversack.*

The Spanish wore a practical and comfortable uniform for service in the tropics. They wore a tropical uniform of white and blue striped ticking with slouch hats. Sometimes straw hats were worn. The officers wore a similar uniform, though it was more neatly tailored than that of the enlisted men.

▼ **BANDMASTER, UNITED STATES NAVY, 1897**
This unusual and sharp uniform is uncharacteristic of the US Navy and would at first glance appear to be a Marine Corps uniform. In undress bandsmen would wear the kepi as a fatigue cap and the overcoat was a caped, dark blue overall with scarlet lining that matched their full dress uniforms.

▲ **OFFICER, UNITED STATES MARINE CORPS, 1898** *This is the undress uniform of the US Marine Corps at the beginning of the Spanish–American War. Undoubtedly it was worn initially in combat, though the fatigue cap probably was not, the slouch hat being substituted. As the short war progressed, a more practical khaki uniform was adopted with the usual Marine Corps distinctions.*

Sometimes a foreign service helmet much like the British version was used. The officers wore a uniform cap known as a Leopoldina. These troops acquitted themselves very well in the battles in Cuba, but their efforts were wasted by their demoralized superiors.

▲ **GUNNER, 4TH MOUNTED ARTILLERY REGIMENT, 1898** *Spain was ahead of the US in weapons and equipment for their troops, for instance being issued ammunition that employed smokeless powder, along with modern artillery. Their uniforms tended to reflect this trend and they were issued clothing and equipment that was suited for service, as shown, in the heat and humidity of Cuba.*

The Cubans who fought for the Americans, and who were quite often militarily worthless, wore parts of American uniforms if they could get them, civilian clothing, a mixture of both, or a uniform that they developed themselves in either light tan or khaki.

NORTH AMERICAN INDIAN WARS

When the Americans won their independence in 1783, a chain of events began between the Americans and the Indian nations that would continue in violent confrontations until 1890. As US expansion moved west across the Mississippi, beginning with the Lewis and Clark expedition of 1805, Indian tribes were met that were quite different from the woodland Indians that the Americans had previously been most familiar with. The Plains Indians of the west were excellent fighters, and tough opponents.

Post-Civil War American Troops

After the Civil War it was decided to maintain six black regiments in the post-war United States Army. Two of them, the 9th and 10th Cavalry, were formed and sent west to help stabilize and settle the frontier. They proved themselves to be some of the best units in the service and were sent to fight some of the toughest opponents of the War, the Apaches. The 10th Cavalry had full dress uniforms, modelled in the Prussian style.

The 7th US Cavalry Regiment is famous for its defeat at the Battle of the Little Bighorn in June of 1876. Led by the flamboyant and reckless George Armstrong Custer, the battalion was wiped out to a man. The regiment had full dress uniforms but, in the field, the usual campaign uniform was worn. Their guidon was the same as used during the Civil War.

Uniforms 'evolved' for the US Army during the period, but the overall look of 1865 was generally the same as it would be in Mexico in 1898. The new khaki uniforms were being introduced, but they were far from universal.

Many of the uniforms worn, especially by the officers, had an almost British look to them, such as the pillbox cap and a braided frock coat, though the US version was not as long as the British one. Buckskin jackets were worn, as were buffalo coats in the bitter winters, and the sabre was usually dispensed with, all ranks being armed with at least one revolver and some type of carbine. One item of

◄ **NCO, 10TH UNITED STATES CAVALRY REGIMENT, 1890** *The 10th Cavalry's service against the Indians in the south-west was long, hard, dedicated and distinguished. The first black graduate of the Military Academy at West Point, Henry O. Flipper, was assigned to the regiment and later became a renowned engineer in the western United States.*

▲ **GUIDON BEARER, 7TH UNITED STATES CAVALRY, 1876** *The 7th Cavalry, commanded by Lieutenant Colonel George A. Custer met disaster and defeat at the Little Big Horn against the massed warriors of the Sioux and Cheyenne nations.*

clothing did change after the Civil War and that was the overcoat of sky blue. Outwardly it appeared to be the same, but the lining of the cape was changed to the branch colours for artillery, infantry and cavalry: red, sky blue and yellow, respectively.

Plains Indians

This major cultural division included such tribes as the Sioux, Cheyenne, Blackfoot, Commanche, Arapaho, Crow, Kiowa Apache, as well as the Gros Ventre and Assiniboin in Canada, all of whom frequently engaged in deadly intertribal warfare.

The other major culture groups west of the Mississippi included the Plateau Indians, located generally between the Rocky Mountains to the east and California, Oregon and Washington to the west, ranging again into Canada to the north with the southern border being the great south-western deserts. Tribes in this area included the Shoshoni, Nez

Perce and Utes. The South-west Indians were another major cultural group, being various tribal groups of Apaches, some of the most dangerous and implacable foes the United States Army ever fought. The Apache also hunted and raided into northern Mexico. The last group was the California Indians, the most dangerous and independent of the tribes being the Modoc.

The Indians never organized into a single entity or nation, though at times fought in collaboration such as when the Sioux and Cheyenne massed against Custer in 1876. They were not a numerous people, but were warlike, fought for their tribe, for their concept of honour, for prestige, and generally for their way of life. The original native dress of the various tribes slowly evolved, with exposure to the Americans and Mexicans, to using combinations of native and other clothing types. Trousers and shirts were not unknown among the Apache, though there was a distinctive Apache flavour to the overall appearance of the people. The original weapons of the American western Indian were definitely influenced and augmented by firearms, such as rifles and pistols, many of them of more modern manufacture than those carried by the US Army, and the Indians frequently outgunned their adversaries in combat.

◀ APACHE WARRIOR, 1880 *The Apache were superb warriors and guerilla fighters. Comfortable fighting their enemy both mounted and on foot, they maintained military superiority to both the Americans and Mexicans for years. They were finally defeated by American troops who adopted their fighting methods and employed Apache scouts.*

▶ CHEYENNE WARRIOR, 1876 *This is the typical dress of a Cheyenne who took part in Custer's defeat in 1876. Feather bonnets were popular among the Sioux and Cheyenne. The Cheyenne who defeated Custer were better armed than the American troopers and inflicted heavy losses on cavalrymen who dismounted to fight on foot.*

Tribal Variations

Most of the American Indian tribes adopted some form of American dress combining it with their native dress, but were able to clothe themselves from natural resources and the abundant wildlife of their environment until, that is, they were overwhelmed by the American forces.

Different tribes attached feathers, beads and other decorative additions to their clothing. Plains Indians used paint to prepare for battle, and warriors would be identified by symbol and colour combinations applied to their faces and bodies, as well as to the hides of their mounts.

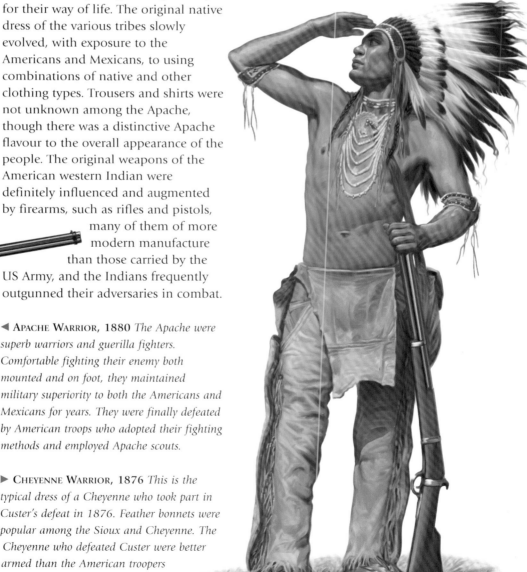

COLONIAL TROOPS

European expansion into East Asia, Africa, India and the Americas prompted the raising, equipping and training of native troops, usually led by European officers, to fight for the European nations that now held suzerainty over their lands. Many of these units became the 'jewel in the crown' of the British forces, including the Bengal Lancers (a ubiquitous, and generally

incorrect term, as many Indian cavalry units were neither lancers nor from Bengal), the African 'Askaris,' the Nepalese Gurkhas, and the Spahis, Turcos and Zouaves from North Africa, all of whom became world famous troops who fought for their colonial masters skilfully and devotedly on battlefields that were far from their native homelands.

Loyal Service

The colonial troops of the Great Powers fought superbly for their foreign overlords during World War I. Many, fortunately, never saw the grim Western Front and the hideous trench warfare, but some eventually did. Regiments of Senegalese and Indochinese (later Vietnamese) served long, well and gallantly in a war not of their making.

British Indian Units

There is one word that describes the lancer units of the British Indian Army: ubiquitous. Lancer regiments were common and they were uniformed in various colours and shades, although the general style of the uniform was similar if not exactly alike. The headdress, a combination of turban (*lungi*) and a pointed cap (*kullah*), was in regimental colours for each unit, as was the sash or cummerbund. The tunic was either termed a *alkalak* or *kurtha*. The British

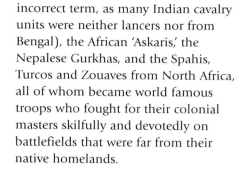

◀ **TROOPER, NEW SOUTH WALES LANCER, 1886** *This Australian trooper is smartly uniformed in traditional lancer uniform, including a coloured plastron (the piece of cloth on the front of the tunic), with the exception of the bush hat, which came to be identified with Australian units. The colour of the uniform and equipment is in concert with the trend in the British Army of changing uniform colour from the old full dress to a practical service dress which would blend in with the countryside.*

▲ **OFFICER, 1ST SKINNER'S HORSE (DUKE OF YORK'S OWN LANCERS), 1886** *Raised in 1803 this unit was originally an irregular unit that was 'regularized' by good and faithful service. At first the uniform was a mustard colour but this would evolve into an overall yellow kurtka, or tunic, with the regimental particulars as shown. In 1922 this unit was amalgamated with the 3rd Skinner's Horse and retitled 1st Duke of York's Own Skinner's Horse. When India won independence in 1947 this unit became part of the Indian Army and left British service.*

officers of Indian cavalry regiments wore a more European-style uniform, although in the regiment's colours, but many, if not all, wore native regimental dress as well. These are some of the most colourful units in military history and they were deadly with the lance. Such units included the 19th Bengal Cavalry and 1st Skinner's Horse, both famous and distinguished regiments.

Sikhs served the British after being defeated by them, and distinguished themselves against the rebels in the Indian Mutiny. Tough, self-reliant and highly religious, the Sikhs were some of the best troops produced on the Indian subcontinent. Their religion forbade the cutting of hair or beard, so beards were rolled up when in uniform and the hair was hidden under the turban.

The 27th Light Cavalry wore a very handsome uniform in French grey. This had formerly been a lancer regiment but had been converted to a 'normal' light cavalry regiment during its long service. Both regiments remained in the service of India when it gained its independence in 1947. The Ludhiana Sikhs became the 11th Sikh Regiment and the 27th Light Cavalry had its regimental number changed to '16'.

Such lancers, many from one of the excellent native Indian cavalry regiments that served the British in India for decades, wore the typical British lancer uniform of the period but were distinguished by the colours used for the tunics and

turbans. The design was mostly drawn from the native dress of India and the result was that he British Indian Army that guarded and protected the Indian subcontinent was one of the most colourful armies of the period.

From the time of the first European incursions on to the Indian subcontinent the different European countries enlisted native Indians to fight for them, and with the exception of the

bloody Indian Mutiny against the British East India Company in 1857, Indians served the British long and loyally. After the country won independence from Britain it was partitioned into the two nations of India and Pakistan, the one predominantly Hindu and Sikh, the other Muslim. The Indian troops were similarly divided in 1947, depriving Great Britain of some of the most famous units to serve the British.

▶ **Sowar, 19th Bengal Cavalry, 1888**
The overall regimental colour for this unit was dark blue with regimental distinctions as shown. As with the other Bengal Cavalry regiments, the 19th was formed after the Indian Mutiny and served loyally and with distinction until 1947, when it was transferred into the Indian Army and departed British service. British officers who were assigned to the regiment were issued with both the regimental uniform with all the native Indian accoutrements and one that was more European in cut and nature.

◄ SEPOY, 15TH LUDHIANA SIKHS, 1888
This unit was a distinguished infantry unit. They wore a steel ring on the turban which was originally employed as a missile weapon. It would be thrown like a discus and its outside would be sharpened to an edge. This unit later transferred to Indian service as the 2nd Battalion of the 11th Sikh Regiment.

► OFFICER, 27TH LIGHT CAVALRY, 1888 *This was a Madras regiment and the colour of the kurtka, or long tunic, reflected its origins. British officers in the regiment wore a lancer uniform in the regimental colour.*

patterned after troops of the British Army, though the trend to khaki, especially during and after the Boer War, was both necessary and apparent. There were differences in the khaki field service and dress uniforms, including regimental distinctions, such as plastrons in the regimental colours for lancer regiments. Personal equipment was usually of brown leather on the British pattern, except for rifle regiments which followed the British tradition and issued theirs in black leather.

Canadian uniforms, while following the British pattern, were sometimes unique, and both practical and comfortable. The Canadian regular army was small and was usually reinforced by newly raised militia, or militia units of long-standing. There were two Guards units in Canada. The infantry, namely the Governor General's Regiment of Foot Guards, was uniformed in the same way as the Guards infantry regiments in Great Britain. The look was almost identical to the Coldstream Guards, except that the red plume on the bearskin was worn on the opposite side. The Governor General's Horse Guards were uniformed in the dragoon or dragoon guards manner, but in dark blue with white facings and piping. Regiments of rifles, fusiliers and other infantry units were dressed as their British counterparts in full dress, but the field dress, before they went completely into khaki, was a combination of dark blue patrol jackets, corduroy trousers in a

Other Colonial Units

The British formed excellent units in their colonies of Canada, Australia (which started as a penal colony) and New Zealand. Canadians and Australians served in South Africa. Uniform colours for Australian uniforms were usually khaki, brown or grey. The bush hat was a typical Australian uniform accessory and became very prevalent during the last Boer War among troops of Great Britain and the empire. It was also worn during World War I in the desert campaigns. The cut and style of the uniforms of British empire troops during the period was very much

khaki colour and khaki undress frocks with regulation dark blue breeches and boots, such as those worn by the Regiment of Canadian Artillery.

American Colonial Units

As the United States came into the colonial game somewhat late, few colonial units, compared to their European counterparts, were formed, the most famous being the Philippine Constabulary and the Philippine Scouts. The efficient Philippine Constabulary was one of the units created and organized by the United States to administer its new possession of the Philippine Islands. Officered by the US Army, its service was difficult at the best of times and sometimes unpopular with the native population. First formed in 1901 with the motto of 'Outnumbered, always; outfought, never!' it gave good service and was originally uniformed in a slate-grey uniform with red piping and rank distinctions, but in an American-style uniform. In reality, they wore what they could get hold of and were armed in the same fashion. The first field uniform was very much like the American field uniform for infantry units in the Spanish–American War. It had a dark blue shirt, some shade of grey for trousers,

light khaki canvas leggings and a type of broad-brimmed hat, sometimes made out of straw.

The uniform situation improved after 1907 and the Constabulary was issued brown and khaki uniforms of American cut with tan and khaki personal equipment; this was now of cotton webbing, which was replacing the black or brown leather equipment that was worn previously. British-style puttees were worn over shoes. Some of the enlisted men who were recruited from the 'pagan' tribes in the Philippine 'back country', however, wore native dress from the waist down. The ubiquitous US-style campaign hat was adopted, but with the handsome service dress – which consisted of khaki tunic with high collar and khaki trousers with shoes – a British-style foreign service helmet was worn.

During the American interventions in Central America and the Caribbean in the 1920s, constabulary units were also raised. These had a cadre of, and were officered by, United States Marines. These were effective and were employed in establishing law and order in the interior of these small nations.

French Troops

The famous Spahis in North Africa were formed from the native population by the French in 1834. They were recruited from various local tribesmen and were officered by the French. Their colourful but practical uniforms for service in North Africa remained essentially the same from 1834 to 1939. The assigned French officers wore their usual regulation uniforms but many used the Arab *burnouse* (or *haik*) as a cloak against the elements and, no doubt, for its dashing appearance.

◄ **NCO PHILIPPINE CONSTABULARY, 1901**
This constabulary was the oldest of the four service commands of the Armed Forces of the Philippines. They performed good service in policing the islands. The unit later changed to a uniform more in line with the Philippine Scouts and the American Army.

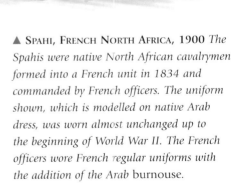

▲ **SPAHI, FRENCH NORTH AFRICA, 1900** *The Spahis were native North African cavalrymen formed into a French unit in 1834 and commanded by French officers. The uniform shown, which is modelled on native Arab dress, was worn almost unchanged up to the beginning of World War II. The French officers wore French regular uniforms with the addition of the Arab burnouse.*

The famous zouaves of the 19th century were formed in North Africa and took their version of dress from there. The Algerian Turcos also wore a version of zouave dress, though their short jackets were sky blue with yellow trim and their wide trousers were white instead of the zouaves' red.

GLOSSARY

Aiguillette: A braided cord hanging from left or right shoulder, to denote special or elite status. It can also denote an award to the unit for valor.

Attila: A simplified type of dolman, with five or six rows of lace across the chest, popular with some European cavalry in the mid-19th century.

Baldric: A large and rather ornate shoulder belt worn by a drum major.

Bandolier: An ammunition belt, usually of leather, which was worn over the shoulder and across the body.

Battalion: two or more companies of infantry or artillery or other arm, such as engineers, that are permanently assigned together.

Battery: (1) an artillery emplacement of any number of guns on a battlefield or for a siege; (2) the term coming into common use *c.*1830 for a company-sized artillery unit.

Bayonet: A bladed weapon, either triangular or flat like a sword, that is attached to a long-arm, allowing the rifle or musket to remain a lethal weapon if unloaded.

Bearskin: A tall fur cap worn by units such as the fusilier regiments of the British Army, to denote elite status.

Belly box: A cartridge box worn on a

▼ *The seige of Lucknow, 1857, during the Indian Mutiny.*

waist belt on the front of the body instead of hanging on the right hip by a shoulder strap. Initially for use by mounted troops.

Beshmet: A traditional kaftan-type garment worn by the Cossacks.

Bicorne: A round hat with two sides folded up symmetrically. Usually worn by officers after the Napoleonic Wars.

Braid: Coloured cord that was used to highlight uniforms along the seams, along the collar and cuffs, and down the front of the tunic.

Brigade: A higher-level formation of two or more regiments, found most normally in the infantry and cavalry. In many armies they were becoming permanent formations.

Busby: British term for a colpack, a bearskin cap, flat on the top, worn by hussar and horse artillery units.

Burnous: A long cloak of coarse wool with a hood, usually white, worn by Berbers and Arabs of North Africa.

Bush hat: A hat turned up on one side, popular in Australia and South Africa.

Carbine: A light firearm, shorter than a musket, carried by cavalrymen.

Cartouche: A cartridge pouch for cavalry and horse artillery officers, usually worn on a shoulder strap.

Cartridge: The combination of the projectile and propellant charge for a round of ammunition.

Chasseur: French for 'hunter'; the equivalent term was 'Jäger', usually denoting an elite light infantryman.

Chevron: Stripes on the sleeves of the uniform coat to denote either rank or length of service.

Chinscales: Metal plates, mounted on a leather chinstrap, to secure headgear.

Coattee: A close-fitting jacket that finished at the waist in front, with short coattails at the rear.

Cockade: A piece of coloured cloth on the hat to indicate nationality.

Colpack: *see* 'Busby'.

Colour: An infantry regimental flag, used to identify the regiment and as a rallying point on the battlefield.

▲ *Union Army camp, Slocum, Washington DC, during the American Civil War.*

Commando: A Boer mounted organization that varied in strength.

Corsican hat: A form of military headgear with one side of the brim extended and turned up.

Company: This was the basic unit organization from which all others in an army were built. Strength varied, but was usually between 100–200 men.

Corps: (1) any military organization that was homogenous in an organizational sense, with the same training and purpose, i.e. the United States Marine Corps; (2) a permanent operational organization consisting of all the combat arms (infantry, artillery and cavalry) that ranked just below that of a field army, which would be composed of a number of corps.

Cossack: Tough frontiersmen who fought for the czar of Russia.

Czapka: The traditional Polish military headgear adopted by lancer units of combatants in the Napoleonic era.

Division: A higher level, tactical unit composed of two or more brigades of either infantry or cavalry.

Dolman: A waist-length, tight-fitting jacket worn by hussars, heavily decorated with lace and buttons.

Epaulette: Shoulder straps with or without fringe on the ends that denoted either elite status or rank.

Facings: The lapels, collar and cuffs of a uniform coat, usually in a different colour to the coat.

Forage cap: A soft-topped, cheap cap, worn by soldiers when off parade.

Frock coat: A single- or double-breasted, mid-thigh length coat.

Frog: An attachment to a waist belt used to carry a sword, bayonet or hatchet, or a combination of two.

Frogging: The lace across the chest of hussar dolmans and pelisses.

Fusilier: Originally a term for soldiers carrying lighter muskets than regular infantry. Later, these became elite units, as in the British Army. In the French Army, it denoted the non-elite troops in a line infantry regiment.

Gaiters: Cloth coverings of the lower legs designed to keep the stockings clean and pebbles out of the shoes.

Glengarry: A soft cloth cap, shaped like a tent, worn by British regiments.

Grenadier: Elite troops trained to carry and throw hand grenades in the 17th century. They eventually became companies, battalions and regiments of elite troops.

Guidons: Small flags used by dismounted units for alignment in formation and combat. Swallow-tailed standards in mounted units were also termed guidons.

Hardee hat: Black felt dress hat, brim turned up on one side, issued to US troops, except horse artillery, in 1858.

Haversack: A light canvas or cloth pack, worn on a bandolier to carry food and personal items.

Horse furniture: Saddle, portmanteau, shabraque, harness and saddle bags.

Hummel bonnet: Also known as the Kilmarnock bonnet, worn by Scottish Highland regiments.

Hussar: Light cavalrymen whose uniform was inspired by Hungarian horsemen of the 17th century.

Jäger: German word for 'hunter', light infantryman, usually armed with rifle and dressed in green; considered elite.

Janissary: Taken from the Turkish word 'Yeniçen', meaning 'new soldier'; elite troops who fought for the sultan.

Kepi: A small, peaked, practical forage cap, originally French, which became popular during the US Civil War.

Kilmarnock hat: *see* Hummel bonnet

Kurtka: A traditional, short-skirted tunic worn by lancers.

Kutsma: A low, Astrakhan hat, with coloured bag and eagle's feather, worn by Austrian hussars from about 1862.

Lancer: A cavalryman who carried a lance.

Limber: The two-wheeled vehicle to which a field artillery piece would be attached for movement.

Marines: Naval troops, usually infantrymen, assigned aboard ship.

Overalls: Trousers worn on top of expensive parade breeches to protect them. Also known as coveralls.

Pelisse: Fur-lined and trimmed outer jacket of the hussar, usually worn over the left shoulder.

Percussion cap pouch: A small leather pouch, usually worn on the waist belt, to hold percussion caps which were used to ignite the musket charge.

Pickelhaube: German word meaning 'spiked hood', a term describing the Prussian-style spiked helmet.

Picket duty: Outpost duty; sentries deployed to the front of a unit on campaign, responsible for giving warning of enemy approach.

Plastron: The coloured portion of the front of the lancer tunic, usually in the regimental colour.

Pontonnier: Soldiers who were responsible for building pontoon bridges. In European armies these troops were usually artillerymen.

Portmanteau: Saddle bag or valise, attached to the rear of the saddle.

Puggaree: The cloth wrapping around the foreign service helmet, sometimes in the regimental colour.

Puttee: A strip of cloth, wound around the ankle and calf to protect the lower leg. These replaced gaiters and originated in India.

Regiment: A military organization of a number of companies belonging to one unit, or a unit of two or more battalions or squadrons.

Regimental lace: Braid of a colour and design peculiar to a regiment.

Sabretache: A highly decorated pouch, attached to the left side of a cavalryman's waist belt and used in lieu of pockets in the tight breeches.

Sapper: Troops equipped and trained to dig field defences and siege works. 'Sapeur' in French means a combat engineer. Also known as pioneers.

Sepoy: The generic term for the Indian troops who fought for the British. In actuality, 'sepoy' meant an Indian enlisted man in the infantry, and 'sowar' was the equivalent term for the Indian enlisted man in a cavalry unit.

Shabraque: An ornate and decorative saddlecloth, derived from the Turkish word 'tschprak'.

Shako: A tall, cylindrical stiff cap with a peak, generally out of use by the second half of the 19th century.

Shell jacket: A waist-length, single-breasted, close-fitting coat.

Shoulder wing: Short, ornamented strips of cloth, worn at the tops of the sleeves to indicate elite company status or that of a musician or bandsman. Also referred to as 'wings'.

Swallows' nest: *see* Shoulder wing.

Trefoil: An ornamental shoulder knot with an outer end like a clover leaf.

Tirailleur: French for 'sharpshooter'. it also denoted a specialized type of light infantry.

Tunic: The successor to the frock coat, of the same basic design but shorter and more practical. Tunics were almost, if not all, single-breasted.

Turnback: The skirts of a coat, turned back to show the lining.

Ulan: German term for a lancer.

Voltigeur: Elite French light infantry employed with cavalry as light troops.

Zouave: French colonial infantry units, first raised in Algeria in 1831 from members of the Zwawa Berber tribe. Their costume was adopted by many units in the American Civil War.

▼ *Artillery driver's saddle of the Hanoverian Guards during the German War of Unification.*

INDEX

▲ *Helmets of the Prussian Infantry, 1848, Hanover (left), and Oldenburg (right).*

▼ *Helmets of the Prussian Infantry, 1848,*
Saxony (left), and Wurttemburg (right).

▲ *The colours of the 28th North Carolina Infantry Regiment, American Civil War.*

▼ *A 3-inch ordnance rifle 1861–65, used during the American Civil War.*

▼ *Epaulette of a major of the Russian 20th
Infantry Division (left), cap plate of an officer
of the Russian 22nd Infantry (right).*

▶ *A Confederate trooper of the 12th Virginia Cavalry from the American Civil War, 1862.*

Author Acknowledgements

The study of uniforms, sometimes termed uniformology, is an inexact science. Trying to pin down what a certain unit wore in a certain place during a specific period can be a frustrating experience. What a soldier was supposed to wear, and what he actually did could be, and usually was, two different things altogether. During my own active service as a Marine in South-west Asia in 1990–91 most of us wore what was available and what could be traded with neighbouring US Army units. After a few weeks in the Saudi Arabian desert the word 'uniform' generally did not apply.

The scope of this volume is very wide; a survey work of the 19th century, and while not a definitive work, it gives an excellent viewpoint of the development of western military uniform during the wars covered. Having the opportunity to work with Digby Smith again is a treat for me and his vast knowledge of the uniforms of the various German states is encyclopedic. His work in this volume is expert, and he continues to be a model of inspiration for me as a military history author. Joanne Rippin has once again proved herself an editor par excellence. Her patience, skill and irreproachable taste are unequalled. This is her book as much as it is anyone else's. She has also tolerated my scribblings, moods and ignorance of deadlines with grace and aplomb, and deftly wields the iron hand in the velvet glove. She has my deepest thanks and admiration, and I count her as a good friend. Without her these uniform books would never see the light of day.

The artists who have supplied the superb artworks for this book are extraordinary gentlemen, who not only had to decipher the complex briefs from the authors, but also had the difficult task of making their work look like soldiers – something not every artist is able to do.

I cannot write of anything without thinking of my late friend, Colonel John Elting, who continues to inspire what I do with pen and paper and who I believe is always by my side. He was a good friend, mentor and teacher, and his passing still leaves a void. Last, but certainly not least, great thanks go to my two biggest supporters, my lovely, and very patient, wife Daisy and my son Michael. They have endured the writing of four volumes with grace and have continued to encourage me in my journey through military history. They are the best of companions.

Unfortunately, I have never found any history book without error. Any contained in this volume are mine alone.

Kevin F. Kiley, MMH, FINS, FMS

Picture Acknowledgements

Figure illustrations by: Simon Smith, Tom Croft, Matt Vince, Jim Mitchell, Carlo Molinari, Nick Spender, Rob McCaig and Sailesh Thakrar.

The Publishers would also like the thank the following agencies for the use of their images. Bridgeman Art Library: pp2, 6, 8t & bl, 9 all, 10 all, 11tl&r, 12 all, 13 all, 14 all, 15 all, 16 all, 17 all, 18, 19, 20 all, 21 all, 22 all, 23 all, 35t, 48t, 51t, 52t, 59, 60 all, 70, 92, 96, 97, 98 all, 99t&br, 108t, 118t, 124t & br, 127b, 129tr, 134, 135, 136 all, 137 all, 138tr, 143t, 149tr, 151tr & br, 156t, 157t, 169tr, 171tr, 174, 175, 176 all, 177 all, 181t, 230b. AKG Images: pp 7, 8br, 11b, 58, 188b, 215, 216 all, 217, 235t, 250 all, Art Archive: 99 bl, 202tr, 203br, 204tr, 207tl, 212t, 214, Eon Images pp111t. Kevin K. Kiley: p165t.